09954

The Postwar Novel in Canada

Narrative Patterns and Reader Response

Bibliothèque de la *Revue Canadienne de Littérature Comparée*, vol. 8
Library of the *Canadian Review of Comparative Literature*, vol. 8

DIRECTEUR/EDITOR: M. V. Dimić, Alberta

SECRÉTAIRE DE RÉDACTION/EDITORIAL SECRETARY: E. D. Blodgett, Alberta

1   E. J. H. Greene. *Menander to Marivaux: The History of a Comic Structure*. Edmonton: University of Alberta Press, 1977. Pp. 201

2,3   M. V. Dimić and E. Kushner, with J. Ferraté and R. Struc, eds. *Proceedings of the VIIth Congress of the ICLA/Actes du VIIe Congrès de l'AILC* [Montréal-Ottawa, 1973]. Budapest: Akadémiai Kiadó; Stuttgart: Kunst und Wissen, 1979. Pp. 562 and 728

4   Mario J. Valdés and Owen J. Miller, eds. *Interpretation of Narrative*. Toronto: University of Toronto Press, 1978. Pp. 202

5   Linda Hutcheon. *Narcissistic Narrative: The Metafictional Paradox*. Waterloo, Ontario: Wilfrid Laurier University Press, 1980. Pp. xii + 168

6   Nina Kolesnikoff. *Bruno Jasieński: His Evolution from Futurism to Socialist Realism*. Waterloo, Ontario: Wilfrid Laurier University Press, 1982. Pp. x + 148

7   Christie V. McDonald. *The Dialogue of Writing: Essays in Eighteenth-Century French Literature*. Waterloo, Ontario: Wilfrid Laurier University Press, 1984. Pp. xviii + 109

8   Rosmarin Heidenreich. *The Postwar Novel in Canada: Narrative Patterns and Reader Response*. Waterloo, Ontario: Wilfrid Laurier University Press, 1989. Pp. xvi + 197.

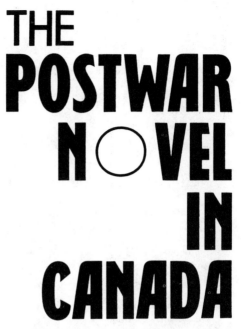

THE
POSTWAR
N○VEL
IN
CANADA

Narrative Patterns
and
Reader Response

**ROSMARIN
HEIDENREICH**
Foreword by
Linda Hutcheon

Wilfrid Laurier University Press

Canadian Cataloguing in Publication Data

Heidenreich, Rosmarin Elfriede
  The postwar novel in Canada

Bibliography: p.
Includes index.
ISBN 0-88920-980-4

1. Canadian fiction — 20th century — History and
criticism.   I. Title.

PS8187.H44 1989   C813'.54'09   C88-095229-6
PR9192.5.H44 1989

WILFRID LAURIER UNIVERSITY PRESS
Waterloo, Ontario, Canada   N2L 3C5

89 90 91 92 4 3 2 1

Cover design by *Vijen Vijendren*

Printed in Canada

For
Stephanie and Philip

Contents

Acknowledgments

Much of the argument in this study is derived from work that I had done in connection with my doctoral thesis at the University of Toronto. For this reason I should like to express once again my thanks to Owen J. Miller, David M. Hayne and Claude T. Bissell, who guided me in that enterprise. I also extend my warmest thanks to Mario J. Valdés for the interest and encouragement with which he supported my previous work and more particularly the undertaking of writing this book. I should further like to thank Wolfgang Iser for his advice and encouragement, and also for his willingness to discuss with me various aspects of his theory as I have applied it to Canadian and Quebec writing. The responsibility for any inaccuracies in the representation of his ideas as I have applied them rests of course with me. Linda Hutcheon's work on parody proved extraordinarily helpful in my analysis of the more recent novels. To her I offer my affectionate thanks not only for writing the foreword to the present volume, but also for the many other ways in which she has supported my work. I am also indebted to Milan V. Dimić and E. D. Blodgett of the *Canadian Review of Comparative Literature* for their helpful suggestions regarding the manuscript.

Parts of this book were written abroad, and for their logistical help in procuring articles and texts which were then unavailable to me I thank my friends Caroline Bayard, Annie Brisset and Irini Papatheodorou, all of whom also acted as sympathetic sounding boards as the manuscript progressed.

To Brigitte Fenez-Grégoire and Donata Thibault I express my thanks for their help in typing the manuscript, and to Madeleine Samuda for helping me track down some elusive articles. In connection with my work on this manuscript I also wish to acknowledge a grant from St. Boniface College.

Parts of some chapters of this volume have appeared in print elsewhere, and appear here with the permission of the various editors:

ix

Chapter Four is an expansion of my article entitled "Aspects of Indeterminacy in Hubert Aquin's *Trou de mémoire*," published in *Gaining Ground. European Critics on Canadian Literature*, Reingard M. Nischik and Robert Kroetsch, eds., Edmonton: NeWest Press, 1985. Chapter Five is a revised version of an article which appeared in *Leaflets of a Surfacing Response*, Jürgen Martini, ed., University of Bremen Press, 1980 under the title "A. M. Klein's *Second Scroll* and Joyce's *Ulysses*: some allusive relationships." Chapter Six is a revised and expanded version of the article "Hubert Aquin's *Prochain épisode*. An exercise in the hermeneutics of reading," *Revue de l'Université d'Ottawa* (Spring 1987).

This book has been published with the help of a grant from the Canadian Federation for the Humanities, using funds provided by the Social Sciences and Humanities Council of Canada.

Acknowledgment is hereby made for kind permission to reprint excerpts from the following copyrighted material:

Fifth Business, 1970, and *The Manticore*, 1972, by Robertson Davies, reprinted by permission of Macmillan of Canada, A Division of Canada Publishing Corporation, and Curtis Brown, Ltd.

Beautiful Losers, 1966, by Leonard Cohen, reprinted by permission of Viking Penguin Inc. and Watkins/Loomis Agency, Inc.

The Edible Woman, 1969, by Margaret Atwood, used by permission of the Canadian Publishers, McClelland and Stewart, Toronto.

The Second Scroll, 1951, by A. M. Klein, used by permission of the Canadian Publishers, McClelland and Stewart, Toronto.

L'Hiver de force, 1973, by Rejean Ducharme, reprinted by permission of Editions Gallimard, Paris.

Poussière sur le ville, 1953, by André Langevin, reprinted by permission of Le Cercle du Livre de France Limitée; *Prochaine episode*, 1965, and *Trou de memoire*, 1968, by Hubert Aquin, reprinted by permission of Le Cercle du Livre de France Limitée.

Un Saison dans la vie d'Emmanuel, 1966, by Marie-Claire Blais, reprinted by permission of Editions Grasset, Paris, and Sogides Ltée, Montreal.

Foreword

With *The Postwar Novel in Canada: Narrative Patterns and Reader Response* something new has appeared in Canadian criticism. To my knowledge, this is the first extended application of the insights and analytic tools of Iserian reader-response criticism to Canadian literature. That it is time for such an approach is clear from the current debates in critical theory. This study responds to a double call: first, that of the fiction itself, which is here convincingly presented as becoming increasingly aware of its own potential interpretive strategies, and second, that of the critical community, which for the last decade has been involved in a serious self-examination. Hans Robert Jauss's 1967 "provocation" to literary scholarship to move beyond the formalist paradigm has been echoing through the academic establishment: both Anglo-American New Criticism and French structuralism have been submitted to radical critiques. One form of that challenge has been what is generally called reader-response criticism, a focus on the role of the reading interpreter of the text and of the text's means of engaging the reader in a process of meaning-making. With the work of Gerald Prince, Stanley Fish, Jane P. Tompkins, and many others, formalism and pragmatics have worked together to condition our awareness of the process of signification engaged in by a reader facing a text. To this, the important work on the actual act of reading by Wolfgang Iser has added another level of theorization and analysis, a level that forms the basis of this present study.

In offering a portrait of the narratological trends in Canadian fiction since the war, Rosmarin Heidenreich brings a point of view to Canadian criticism that is thrice rare and thrice welcome. First of all, this is a genuinely comparative work that is always careful not to efface the very real literary, linguistic, socio-cultural, and historical differences both between Quebec and English Canada and between these and the rest of the French- and English-speaking world. Second, this study is neither nationalist nor internationalist, neither particularist nor universalist, neither provincial nor cosmopolitan. It goes beyond such distinctions in its concern for both the specificity of context (Québécois and English Canadian) and the broader cultural (e.g. post-modernism) and socio-historical (e.g. postcolonial) situation in which these texts are both written and read. The search for narrative and hermeneutic models here is conducted within a theoretical framework that presents models as "carriers of meaning" within particular cultures. The search is for generic narrative paradigms which still allow for the articulation of distinctive features of Canadian and Québécois experience.

The third welcome perspective of this study is its focus on the generic, on the Canadian novel's development as a form since 1945, presented (cautiously and wisely) as an evolutionary line of change and illustrated by means of a corpus of admittedly extreme examples of what are seen as representative trends. The focus here is clearly on the changes in interpretive strategies deployed by texts, but we are never allowed to lose sight of the ideological and social context of the reading as well as writing process. The narratological features are revealed to be inextricably linked to ideological positions and this linking is effected through the reader.

The first stage outlined here is that of the novel of the 1940s and 1950s, where seemingly conservative modes of narrative still flourish—conservative even in comparison with earlier British, French, or American fiction. In her study of what she calls the "structural anachronisms" of *Two Solitudes, The Mountain and the Valley, Swamp Angel*, and the Québécois novel of social realism, Rosmarin Heidenreich investigates the consequences of the *absence* of narrative ambiguities, of any challenges to traditional novelistic point of view, and of any radical complication of character presentation that readers might have come to expect from fiction written after that of Joyce, Woolf, Proust, or Faulkner. She ties this to a cultural need to define identity in those years, a need which created a kind of "programmatic function" for fiction. This was what she sees as a quasi-didactic function of consensus-seeking: the texts seek to invoke in their readers a consensus about values and identity by using certain communicatory strategies which invoke a set of norms (social, literary). Using Iser's theories of perspectival structures and norm repertoires, she shows how these schematic strategies function in specific texts.

In the sixties, with novels like Atwood's *The Edible Woman* and Blais' *Une Saison dans la vie d'Emmanuel*, she sees a move away from this programmatic structure towards an increasing problematizing of social norms, on the one hand, and towards an interest in the psychology of the individual subject, on the other. With the focus on subjectivity and the technical means of presenting it in narrative come different demands upon the reader. Less controlled, the reading process has to deal with fragmentation of perspective and multiplicity of possible interpretations. Choices made at this level determine the reader's interpretation, not only of character or plot, but of the social norms activated by the texts (respectively, those of consumer capitalism and of familial, religious, and economic power structures within the social system). These texts tend to invoke but then undercut the reader's moral, ideological, socio-cultural, and literary norm repertoires, but they also investigate the interrelations among these categories of norms. This can be seen as a response to the earlier novels, for irony here contests the function and intent of the norms invoked in the more traditional realist works.

The subsequent examination of three novels by Davies, Langevin, and Ducharme shows how some texts move to play even more self-consciously with the reader's familiarity with literary and social norms. Conventions are both inscribed and deformed, and the reader is expected to recognize both acts. Each text instigates this process differently, however; their common communicatory strategies do not deny their individuality of response. What these novels also do is foreshadow the rather more radical contestation that follows in the seventies and eighties: the problematizing of memory as both a personal/subjective and also a national/political issue (later explored by Timothy Findley's *Famous Last Words* and Margaret Atwood's *The Handmaid's Tale*) or the overdetermination of narrative and plot motivation and the confusion of teleology and causality seen here in *Fifth Business* (and later complicated even further in the ironies of *Beautiful Losers*).

In more recent fiction, increasing activity is demanded of the reader to make sense (literally) on the levels of plot, characterization, point of view and even just language. Here Rosmarin Heidenreich uses Iser's theories of indeterminacy to study the challenges to the reader's usual concepts of both reality (social or psychological) and fiction brought about by some novels' mixing of the historical and documentary with the self-reflexively literary. Realism here is less social or psychological than material and hermeneutic; this is the realm of the "obsession with the reader" and with the text he or she reads. Narrative time, space, perspective are radically problematized and the result is an upsetting of most norms the reader might find invoked. Much is expected of readers of this kind of novel: in Klein's *Second Scroll* and Aquin's *Prochain Episode*, for example, they must recognize both the intertextual references and their ironic deformation and destabilization. Intertextuality here is not just narcissistic self-reference or inconsequential play: through the reader, it is made into the vehicle for serious social and political critique.

If we were to translate this evolution into more traditional literary historical terms, we would see, in the three-stage progression, a rough analogy with the familiar lines of change from realism to modernism and then postmodernism, on the one hand, and from thematic to formalist to reader-response criticism, on the other. While it seems true that different literary forms provoke or demand different critical approaches, what this study does is to bring the insights of postmodern and reception theories to bear on a range of earlier as well as contemporary texts. The novels of the forties and fifties are viewed through realist concern for social context, but always as mediated by the readers' role. Here the readers follow; they follow the omniscient narration and its evoked norms (which are assumed to be common and shared—or are intended to be so by the end of the novel). The modernist problematizing of art's relation to the world is investigated through the readers' means of dealing with increasing textual self-consciousness about the autonomy and self-sufficiency of the art object. Modernism's psychological realism is studied less through its formal properties of expression (ambiguity, fragmentation) than through the interaction of these properties with the readers' awareness of the process of interpretation in which they are engaged.

The postmodern problematizing of subjectivity and of narrative form in such a way as to reveal the potential political linking of radical form to liberational politics (Québécois, feminist, etc.) posits the active involvement of the reader in the act of—not only interpreting—but of creating the text's meaning. The move from realist to postmodernist, through modernism, is a move from product to process. It suggests the need for a break from both thematic and formalist critical perspectives in order to investigate the role of the reader as both hermeneutic and ideological subject. It is one of the significant merits of this study that it goes beyond traditional reader-response criticism in its insistence on the implications of the relationship of discourse to power.

While offering a literary historical evolution, this study does so by means of very meticulous, detailed analyses of the relations engaged between text and reader. The modified use of Iserian theories offers new and often exciting insights into particular texts, as well as a new perspective on the genre as a whole. For example, there are impressive, extended studies of parodic intertextuality in *Beautiful Losers* (Joyce and Goethe join in) and *Prochain Épisode* (Balzac and Büchner are added), along with a careful teasing out of the elaborate communicatory strategies in *Fifth Business* and *L'Hiver de force*. This is a rare book, one that offers individual textual interpretations, a historical overview, and new tools of analysis derived from reader-response theory. In short, it is a most valuable addition to a field which has much need of such work: comparative Canadian criticism.

Linda Hutcheon
University of Toronto

— La différence entre ce que je sais et ce que je dirai, qu'en
faites-vous?
— *Elle représente la part du livre à faire par le lecteur. Elle existe*
toujours.

Marguerite Duras, *L'Amante anglaise*

Introduction

This book is a study of the narrative structures that appear in Canadian[1] novels since 1945. While the number of formalistic analyses of individual works of Canadian fiction has increased in the past decade, a systematization of the narrative patterns observed has yet to be undertaken. As a sort of inventory of the communicatory strategies occurring in the modern Canadian novel, this study may provide a point of departure in obtaining an overview of the genre as it has recently developed in Canada, stimulating comparative studies involving literatures of other countries.

The invocation of literary models involved in comparative analysis is of course a part of any serious critical investigation, and it goes well beyond the identification of individual author influence. The recognition of models and paradigms is indispensable in establishing the cultural context that allows the significance of literature to emerge as a carrier of meaning in the culture producing it. Comparisons do not diminish the "uniqueness" of the Canadian experience as expressed in its literature; rather they allow its distinctive features to become visible, as they are thrown into relief against the background of past and contemporary writing of other literatures.

My study proceeds from established historical and contemporary premises concerning the novel as genre. The resulting generic approach stands in contrast to a large segment of Canadian criticism which sees the Canadian situation—historical, political, geographical and climatic—as a point of departure for the critical analysis of Canadian literary works.[2]

The critical problems involved in adopting the latter, inevitably thematic, approach have become increasingly evident. The base of the thematic approach is an implied consensus concerning the nature of

Reference notes for the Introduction are found on p. 8.

the "Canadian experience" which remains, ultimately, an unverified construct. Aesthetically, the thematic perspective has proved increasingly unsatisfactory since it tends to focus on the historical or psychosociological genesis of the text, rather than on the text itself and its effects.

Furthermore, with its hypothesis of thematic specificity, the latter type of criticism assumes that fiction is still viewed as representing a given extra-textual reality. But this position has revealed itself inadequate in describing the effects of an increasing number of Canadian works. For in Canadian fiction since 1945, there appears to be a marked trend away from the representation of a social reality which characterized many pre-war novels towards an exploration of the human consciousness in all its irrationality, subjectivity, ambiguity and fragmentation. As in other literatures, the experience of contemporary Canadian fiction increasingly involves the shifting of the reader's attention from traditional constituent elements (plot, character, setting) to the narrative act itself, the structuring principle of which is no longer directly given but which it is the reader's task to discover.

Another significant point of difference between the thematic approach and the approach taken in this study is of a more theoretical nature. The thematic studies tend to view the identification of the reader with the central figures of a text as consisting largely in the specific Canadian reality shared by text and reader.

Following Hans Robert Jauss's typology of reader identification,[3] I take the position that although there may be identification with Canadian theme or setting on the part of Canadian readers (or a sense of the "exotic" on the part of non-Canadian ones), such responses are pre-critical and superseded by the recognition of the deformation of all extra-textual reality, including Canadian elements, in the work of art. Such "naïve" identification may be taken into account in an attempt to describe the mechanisms which govern the personal experience of an empirical reader in the reception of the text, but it does not constitute its main communicatory strategy unless we are dealing with works which belong, by definition, to a didactic genre, for example the *roman de moeurs*.

A further hypothesis underlying thematic criticism is the notion that the role of fiction is to be viewed differently in a developing culture than in a traditionally established one. In an established culture, the literature is taken to reflect an already pre-existing collective national identity, while in a developing culture the literature itself is seen to contribute to the creation of such an identity.

The notion that Canadian literature differs from other contemporary literatures because of Canada's unique situation has various implications. Thus for instance the occurrence in Canadian literature of patterns long almost obsolete in other contemporary literatures has been explained by introducing the view that a literature in its development tends to follow patterns of older, established literatures. Northrop Frye sees the role of the Canadian epic in such a phylogenetic context. But analogies as striking as those identified by Frye (between Pratt's epics and Old English poetry)[4] can hardly be recognized in Canadian fiction. Other studies, including some which also insist on the "differentness" of Canadian fiction, have ignored the phylogenetic theory entirely and have followed a purely socio-historical line of argument, as in Ben-Zion Shek's attempt to explain the late appearance of social realism in the Quebec novel.[5]

The present study denies this "differentness" of Canadian literature on both theoretical and pragmatic grounds. The theoretical objection, already touched upon, consists in the fact that in a work of fiction, or at least what is termed "serious" fiction, the extra-textual reality is always alienated and transformed; it serves as a point of departure for that which is to be communicated, but it never constitutes the object of communication itself.

The pragmatic objection consists in that unlike the situation in developing tribal cultures, Canadian writers have always had access to the thought systems of their respective parent cultures and to the larger context of western civilization. In creating literary works, Canadian writers have invoked patterns and traditions which were as familiar to them as to their contemporaries writing in England, France, Germany, or the United States. Like their contemporaries in these countries, they have explored the reality familiar to them, but in communicating the discoveries resulting from these explorations they have invoked the equally familiar system of literary conventions determining the whole of western literature.

Although thematic criticism has often provided relevant and valid interpretations of the Canadian reality as reflected in its literature, it is inevitably reductive in that it does not adequately take into account the ways in which the fictional reality is communicated. In focusing upon the communicatory strategies themselves, the present study attempts to present an alternative way of viewing the fiction which has recently emerged in Canada. It does not claim to be the only valid one, nor do the analyses of individual works claim to be exhaustive interpretations.

The novels analyzed cover a period of about three decades, and it is tempting to see them as reflecting a historical development. In the forties and fifties the omniscient narrator and perspectival structures unambiguously indicating the norms the reader was to affirm or negate predominated; this type of novel seems to have been followed by one with a non-omniscient narrator/hero who demonstrated problematic aspects of norms and values determining a fictional reality very much like the reader's own. In the more recent novels, a narrative structure can be observed in which the norms underlying human perception and cognition themselves are called into question. Finally, we note the appearance, particularly since the late sixties, of a number of highly complex auto-referential novels.

While the novels analyzed do seem to indicate the development of a historical trend, its formulation is only partially valid.

This situation is not peculiar to the development of the novel in Canada and Quebec. Rather it may be seen to reflect on the one hand the tendency of "experimental" novelists in all western literatures to explore the communicatory possibilities of the genre, that is, to react to the patterns established by their predecessors by violating or parodying them. On the other hand, as any bestseller list indicates, the primarily social thematic persists, often in highly traditional forms. In connection with the present study, it seems more accurate to refer to different types of novels that have appeared in Canada over a given period of time, than to describe as a historical development a series of features which in any case refer only to a particular segment of novelistic literature.

Nevertheless it cannot be denied that the "classics" of any given epoch in western fiction in most cases represented the violation of a particular narrative tradition, and that these works, when they first appeared, were eminently "experimental." Their experimental nature was recognizable, however, only against the background of the established cultural consensus constituting the national literature (and its place among other western literatures). True, Canada forms part of the cultural consensus of western literature, but since its own literary history is relatively recent, it has in the past done so largely through its European and American parent cultures.

On the basis of the texts analyzed in this study, Canadian fiction seems to have been able to assert an "identity" recognizably Canadian in two ways. The first has been to use traditional narrative patterns derived from the "parent" literature to communicate the nature of the Canadian "experience," or the geographical, social, historical, climatic, and ethnic particularities of the Canadian situation. This alternative can be recognized, for instance, in Hugh MacLennan's *Two Solitudes*, but it is also reflected in much more recent novels. That the problem of a recognizable Canadian identity reflects an attitude still to be found in Canadian letters may be explained by the fact that in English Canada, ethnic and regional diversity and American cultural predominance have led to a cultural plurality. A number of Canadian writers and critics perceive cultural plurality to demonstrate the lack of a Canadian cultural identity, reflecting a society lacking an established cultural consensus.

The other way in which Canadian or *québécois* "identity" has been asserted in fiction has been to allude to its own narrative and cultural tradition. Since the "parent" culture forms part of that tradition, the latter type of novel signals that the broader socio-cultural repertoire of western literature, of which the "parent" literature forms a part, has been incorporated by the emerging one, and that there exists a sufficient consensus in the emerging culture concerning the nature of its own cultural identity to let allusions to itself become recognizable.

Only in the past two decades has the *québécois* novel shown the tendency to refer to the *artistic* repertoire of Quebec (rather than to its social and political reality) as to a manifestation of a recognizable cultural identity. One reason may be the implicit equation in Quebec of the artistic *avant-garde* with generally emancipatory movements.

Among the Canadian novels that allude to English Canada's own narrative and cultural tradition are Leonard Cohen's *Beautiful Losers*, Robert Kroetsch's *The Studhorse Man*, and Margaret Atwood's *Surfacing*. The emergence of the type of cultural consensus that can be observed in the Quebec novels, however, does not seem imminent. The plurality of artistic alternatives manifested in recent Canadian novels written in English indicates a strongly individualistic trend, which may in part be a reflection of English Canada's ethnic and regional diversity and its consequent cultural plurality. Postwar English-Canadian fiction is thus to some degree characterized by its concern with the achievement of a cultural consensus and the creation of a national identity, while in recent *québécois* fiction the social and political-cultural situation in Quebec undoubtedly is of strong thematic interest.

It is a sign of the maturing of both literatures that various developments in the genre of the novel itself have begun to play an increasingly important role in communicating the respective national realities and their individual manifestations. Since World War II, Canadian narrative has been moving from social realism towards novel forms that are concerned with perceptual processes, the aesthetic alienation of reality, and the creative act, in other words towards the auto-referential, "narcissistic," parodic forms characteristic of what has come to be identified as postmodernist writing.

That Canadian fiction would take such a direction was, of course, predictable, given the evolution of the genre in other literatures. What makes the emergence of postmodernism in Canadian writing particularly significant is the way it is interpreted in the socio-political context of Canadian reality, that of Quebec on one hand, and that of the rest of Canada on the other.

In any literature, postmodernist writing, whether or not the term is used as a synonym for literary avant-gardism, signals an emancipation from traditional literary norms and conventions whose social and aesthetic effect no longer corresponds to the reader's (and the writer's) contemporary reality. In the Canadian context, the emergence of post-modernist writing represents an emancipation in a broader sense, namely emancipation from the parent literatures. Speaking of parody, Linda Hutcheon has pointed out that traditional forms cannot be aesthetically violated or transcended unless they have been thoroughly mastered or incorporated.[6] Such violation implies, then, that the works in question are willing to be measured against the very models from whose conventions they deviate. In this sense of emancipation from "parent" models, there is a common ground between postmodernist writing in Quebec and that of the rest of Canada.

In Quebec, however, the emancipatory function of postmodernist writing takes on a highly ideological dimension. The equation of the revolutionary separatist movement of the sixties with the artistic *avant-garde* in general and postmodernist writing in particular gave rise to a perception of the latter as being part of a generally emancipatory movement. In its ideological intention and subsequent interpretation, the postmodernist writing of Quebec is by and large closer to that of postmodernist Latin-American literature than to most contemporary Canadian writing outside Quebec. This becomes clear when one considers the revolutionary models alluded to in the novels of Hubert Aquin and Jacques Godbout, and the surrealistic parodying of social realism in the earlier works of Marie-Claire Blais and the later ones of Michel Tremblay, calling to mind novels by writers such as Jorge Luis Borges, Gabriel García Márquez, Carlos Fuentes.

From a socio-critical perspective, the relatively recent divergence of literary trends in Quebec from those developing in the rest of Canada, and their striking resemblance to those emerging in Latin-American fiction, implies that the respective literatures are reflecting social, cultural and aesthetic perceptions more profoundly different than most Canadians would care to admit. The common themes, the common problematic, and—dare one speak the word—the common identity invoked in so much of the critical writing that has come out of English Canada have been revealed, in the last few decades at least, to be a projection of the will to Canadian unity, at least in the cultural sense, while tacit acknowledgment of the existence of separate literary canons testifies to the fact that such a cultural unity remains an artificial construct. (Consider the literary histories, surveys, and genre studies that have appeared in Canada—Frye's "Haunted by Lack of Ghosts,"[7] Atwood's *Survival*, Falardeau's *Notre Société et son roman*,[8] Marcotte's *Une Littérature qui se fait*[9] are only a few examples—that deal exclusively with English- or French-Canadian writing. Works like Margot Northey's *The Haunted Wilderness*[10] and Ronald Sutherland's comparative studies—and the term "comparative" is revealing in this context—continue to be relatively rare.)

To examine contemporary Canadian novels from the global perspective of the narrative strategies used in them precludes the thematic, regional, and ethnic categorization that has so far played such an important role in both text canonization and the demonstration of cultural unity. While the intention of this study is not to revise the existing canon (nor to undermine Canadian unity), it may contribute a perspective on Canadian writing that permits a clearer understanding of the conditions that have governed the canon formation in both cultures/literatures. A canon is the product of a critical evaluative process. Like the process of making literature itself, it must constantly violate its own existing norms if the resulting canon is to be a carrier of meaning in and beyond the culture that produces it.

Much of the theoretical framework underlying my analysis is derived from the reader-reception models developed by the so-called new hermeneutics school at Constance (Wolfgang Iser, Hans Robert Jauss).[11] Iser's typology of perspectival arrangements proved particularly useful in the Canadian context as a point of departure in the discussion of novels of the forties and fifties. His conception of indeterminacy as "structured blanks" stands at the centre of much of the analysis, particularly of the more recent novels.

The Iserian model applied in the present study is to some extent reflected in its organization. In the three parts broadly indicating what are posited to constitute three central categories—perspectival structures and norm repertoires, relationships between social and literary norm repertoires, and aspects of indeterminacy—there is a progression from more general aspects to the more particular, and from the discussion of traditional and easily accessible narrative forms to more demanding ones.

Since my intention is to illustrate the range and breadth of communicatory patterns occurring in postwar Canadian fiction and to formulate the emergence of certain trends, the selection of the novels analyzed was undertaken according to principles which, inevitably, at times conflicted. On the one hand, I tried to select novels which seemed to me to be the most extreme with regard to their narrative structure, either in conforming to certain literary traditions or in modifying or breaking with them. Another consideration was to balance, at least to some extent, the representation of English-Canadian and *québécois* novels. The balance is nevertheless not symmetrical; to seek such symmetry in a study of this type would risk doing violence to the subject, since certain patterns which seem to predominate in one literature cannot be found in the other.

Other criteria for the selection of novels presented were critical acknowledgment and presumed familiarity. "Critical acknowledgment" does not necessarily refer to positive evaluation, but to the fact that the novels in question have had a certain impact on English-Canadian and *québécois* letters and can be seen as part of the respective literary canons.

Reference Notes to Introduction

1 The use of the terms *Canadian, Québécois, English-Canadian, French-Canadian* is contextually determined throughout this study. Hence my use of "Canadian" here refers to texts written in French as well as those written in English.

2 In addition to Northrop Frye's famous "Conclusion" to the *Literary History of Canada*, Vol. 3 (Toronto: University of Toronto Press, 1965), pp. 318-32, the following are among the best-known Canadian studies that take a thematic approach: Margaret Atwood, *Survival: A Thematic Guide to Canadian Literature* (Toronto: Anansi, 1972); Ronald Sutherland, *Second Image: Comparative Studies in Quebec/Canadian Literature* (Toronto: New Press, 1971); John Moss, *Patterns of Isolation in English-Canadian Fiction* (Toronto: McClelland and Stewart, 1974); by the same author, *Sex and Violence in the Canadian Novel: The Ancestral Present* (Toronto: McClelland and Stewart, 1979).

3 Hans Robert Jauss, "Negativität and Identifikation: Versuch zur Theorie der ästhetischen Erfahrung," in *Positionen der Negativität: Poetik und Hermeneutik VI* (München: Wilhelm Fink Verlag, 1975), pp. 263-339.

4 Northrop Frye, "The Narrative Tradition in English-Canadian Poetry" and "Silence in the Sea," both in *The Bush Garden* (Toronto: Anansi, 1971).

5 Ben-Zion Shek, *Social Realism in the French-Canadian Novel* (Montreal: Harvest House, 1977).

6 Linda Hutcheon, "Parody Without Ridicule: Observations on Modern Literary Parody," in *Canadian Review of Comparative Literature*, 5, no. 2 (Spring 1978), p. 208.

7 Northrop Frye, "Haunted by Lack of Ghosts," in David Staines, ed., *The Canadian Imagination* (Cambridge, Mass.: Harvard University Press, 1977), pp. 29-45.

8 Jean-Charles Falardeau, *Notre Société et son roman* (Montreal: HMH, 1976).

9 Gilles Marcotte, *Une Littérature qui se fait* (Montreal: HMH, 1968).

10 Margot Northey, *The Haunted Wilderness: The Gothic and Grotesque in Canadian Fiction* (Toronto: The University of Toronto Press, 1976).

11 For the purpose of this study, the most important works of these two authors are:
Wolfgang Iser, *Die Appellstruktur der Texte* (Konstanz: Universitätsverlag, 1970); *The Implied Reader: Patterns of Communication in Prose Fiction from Bunyan to Beckett* (Baltimore: Johns Hopkins University Press, 1974); *The Act of Reading: A Theory of Aesthetic Response* (Baltimore: Johns Hopkins University Press, 1978).
Hans Robert Jauss, "Negativität und Identifikation: Versuch zur Theorie der ästhetischen Erfahrung," in *Positionien der Negativität: Poetik und Hermeneutik VI* (München: Wilhelm Fink Verlag, 1975), pp. 263-339; *Toward an Aesthetic of Reception*, trans. by Timothy Bahti (Minneapolis: University of Minnesota Press, 1982).

Part I

Perspectival Structures and Norm Repertoires

The generic context

Traditionally, point of view in the novel referred mainly to the interpretive significance of the narrative perspective. The explicit or implicit evaluation of characters and events was seen as a function of the narrative perspective, even when the narrative voice ostensibly withheld judgment, did not intrude, or formulated a position contrary to that which the reader was to be induced to take.[1]

Where the point of view of a novel is to be situated—in the narrative perspective, in the perspective of one or more characters of a novel, or in the views known to be held by the authors themselves—has been the subject of critical and theoretical inquiry since Henry James.[2] Well into the present century, the normative definition of the narrative perspective was to produce as completely as possible an illusion of reality,[3] which was seen to be effected in proportion to the "unobtrusiveness" of the role of the narrator, a view culminating in the latter's theoretical abolition.

This theoretical demand was not easily fulfilled in applied criticism, in part because it was rarely met by novelists. Wolfgang Kayser's contention that "the death of the narrator would mark the death of the novel"[4] has proven itself prophetic, though not in the sense that he intended: with the modern novel's increasing preoccupation with its own modes of communication, the narrator—what is more, the "intruding" narrator—has enjoyed a renaissance which is due pre-

Reference notes for Part I and Chapter One are found on pp. 38-40.

cisely to the fact that the narrator's role eminently lends itself to drawing the reader's attention to the fictionality of the text.

This re-emergence of "intruding" narrators, though their contemporary function may differ from that of the dramatized narrator of the eighteenth century, has changed the critical focus in defining the role of the narrative perspective. The issue is no longer whether or not a narrator should create or break an illusion of reality. In critical terms, the narrator's role is once more seen as a matter of mediating (often ironically) between the empirical reality of author and reader and the fictional reality of the text. The points of tangency between the role of the narrative perspective in mediating between two different kinds of reality, and its function in indicating to the reader the position to be taken with regard to the norms to which the novel's figures and events allude, stand in the foreground of the discussion of perspective in the present study.

The term "narrative perspective" as it is used here requires closer definition. It is, first of all, to be distinguished from the "narrator's perspective" in the sense of narrative voice, and also from the perspectives of those characters in whom the reader tends to see the most valid views presented in the novel. It is seen in this study as a composite perspective, made up not only by the cumulative perspectives represented in the text but also by those communicatory features which instruct readers as to how they are to view the individual perspectives, characters and events of the novel. The "narrative perspective" may thus be seen as corresponding to the point of view or "standpoint," to use W. Iser's term, to be taken by the implied reader, and can therefore never be identical to the "narrative voice," though the narrative perspective and the views expressed by the narrative voice may sometimes be seen to coincide. (This is frequently the case in didactic novels.)

The individual perspectives in the novel represent a selection of norms illustrated by the hero or heroine and/or the narrator, and the secondary characters.[5] The interrelationships among these multiple perspectives, including the perspectives implied in the plot, represent connections to be made by the reader, and so act as a set of instructions as to how the reader is to perceive and evaluate the norms in question.

If throughout the history of the novel the selection of norms represented has changed, so have the narrative strategies through which they are communicated. As Iser points out, in the eighteenth century the point of view from which the events of a novel were witnessed or experienced was seen to coincide with the norms and values embodied by the hero, though not necessarily with the hero's behaviour.[6] Although the narrator critically evaluated the behaviour of the hero, the interaction of the perspectival views represented by the various figures indicated that certain elements of the norm repertoire itself—as designated by the narrator and/or the hero—were to be negated by the reader. These elements were inevitably those with which the hero came into conflict in the practical experience of day-to-day life, so that while the reader might recognize deficiencies in the primary characters and in the views they actually expressed, the norms which they represented, through their behaviour, for example, were nevertheless those suggested as valid by the narrative perspective itself.

In the nineteenth century the diminishing authority of the narrator resulted in a relativization of the validity of the various perspectival views presented in a novel, even when the normative authority seemed to be merely transferred to the central figure perspective, as, for instance, in many of the Victorian novels. Elsewhere, the convention of narrative authority itself was being challenged, most notably by Dostoievsky and Flaubert.

In the present century, the non-dramatization of the narrator, the increasing occurrence of interior monologue, and the representation of stream of consciousness, have had a far-reaching consequence. The implied fictional reality of the novel remains withheld from the reader, because the consciousness of the character perceiving it represents the only available perspective at any given time, and thus inevitably deforms this reality. A series of perspectival views may be available, in sequence, but they are rarely intended to add up to a whole in the realistic sense. Furthermore, their "normative hierarchy," to use Iser's expression, has been for the most part dissolved. The reader must decide the validity of one view as compared to another on the basis of the total structural features of the novel.

A number of these structural features are related to the notion of perspective in its broadest sense. This involves not only the way in which the implied reality of the world of the novel is deformed by the consciousness perceiving it, but also the ways in which perspectives are arranged to communicate the norms which the various perspectival views may be seen to represent. The reader's tendency to perceive one view as more or less valid than another, however, is determined not only by the predominance of a particular perspective (for instance, that of the hero) and the norms it represents, but also by what is traditionally called characterization. The vagueness of the term in a systematic context requires its closer definition. In this study, the *types* of characters by whom the events are witnessed or experienced are distinguished from the *structures of consciousness* through which the reality of the world of the novel is apprehended. *Type* designates those features which determine the possibility of reader identification with the way characters act and interact with their environment. Such features include the affirmation or negation of social, cultural and aesthetic norms, for example, but also the ways in which a character's attitude towards a given norm is communicated. *Structure of consciousness* refers to the way in which characters subjectively experience themselves, their environment, and their interaction with it. Increasingly in the modern novel the text presents the subjective deformation of an "objective" reality unavailable to the reader, resulting in the reader's attempt to determine the nature of this "objective" reality in order to be able to perceive the ways in which it is deformed in the consciousness of the character. The communicatory intention of the text then lies not so much in the presentation of the type or even consciousness of the character in question, but in making readers aware of the principles and mechanisms causing the distortion and so increasing their awareness of their own perceptual processes.

The social norm repertoires of Quebec and English Canada

Assuming that a literature may be defined as the expression of an epochal culture—in the sense of the social norms and values generally accepted in a given historical period—and the simultaneous exposure of its deficiencies, and that a literary work always represents a reaction to a given situation, it becomes clear that the selection of the norms represented in English-Canadian and *québécois* novels is determined not only by the different attitudes and values prevailing in the two societies, but also by two highly dissimilar historical backgrounds, including those furnished by literary models. The diverging norm repertoires of Quebec and English Canada are almost too much of a commonplace to mention. The one is seen to be determined by the influence of the Roman Catholic church, its role in maintaining a rurally oriented society and traditional family patterns, the other by a materialistic, success-oriented and increasingly urban industrial society.

The problem with this distinction is not the crudeness of the oversimplification with which it is presented here (for the *québécois* novel this normative system is well-documented in a number of studies, such as Max Dorsinville's *Caliban without Prospero*,[7] Ben-Zion Shek's *Social Realism in the French-Canadian Novel*, and Jean-Charles Falardeau's *Notre Société et son roman*), but the fact that it no longer applies. If the heroes of *québécois* novels no longer come from a large family, no longer demonstrate their emancipation from the village *curé*, and generally cease to invoke the pressures of a parochial society, it is for the obvious reason that it is superfluous to negate norms that are already invalid. If, on the other hand, the heroes of English-Canadian novels return, literally or in their memories, to the place of their childhood or ancestry, abandon the city for a rural idyll, and attempt to salvage some remnant of a mythical identity, all in a quest for meaning transcending their materialistic, anonymous urban existence, one can motivate their actions and attitudes by invoking the opposite pole of the same assumption, namely that it is superfluous to affirm a norm if it is not in some way threatened.

The norm repertoire of the Quebec of the sixties and seventies as reflected in fiction overlaps to a certain extent with the attitudes and values prevalent in the rest of Canada since World War II and even earlier. But these predominantly commercially determined norms are questioned not by reminiscence and nostalgia for an "ancestral" past, nor by commitment to an alternative culture, as in many English-Canadian novels, but in terms of their radical ideological negation as being exploitive and colonial. The social frame of reference is the sub- and counter-culture, constituted by asocial elements, revolutionary movements, and the artistic *avant-garde*.

Thus the *québécois* novels often describe the structures of consciousness of characters living beyond the margins of society: the destitute (*Le Cassé*),[8] the psychotic (*Un Rêve québécois*),[9] the counter-culture (*L'Hiver de force*),[10] the child and adolescent (*Une Saison dans la vie d'Emmanuel*,[11] *L'Avalée des avalés*,[12] *Les Manuscrits de Pauline Archange*[13]).

The difficulties involved in trying to describe a corresponding normative formula for English Canadian fiction are familiar enough. They are usually seen in the cultural heterogeneity determined by ethnic and regional differences. On closer investigation, however, this cultural heterogeneity is not reflected in English-Canadian fiction by reference to multiple norm repertoires. The work ethic, economic success as the ultimate social norm (*The Edible Woman*,[14] *The Apprenticeship of Duddy Kravitz*[15]), and nostalgia for either the "old country" or the unbroken nature of the pioneers (*The Diviners*,[16] *The Blue Mountains of China*[17]), or both, are prominent features in the works of Anglo-Saxon and "ethnic" writers from all parts of Canada. Ethnic and regional particularities may play an important role in describing milieu, but they rarely seem to designate a separate normative system.

Following a period in the thirties and forties in which novels of urban and rural social realism predominated in both Quebec and in the rest of Canada (compare, for example, Quebec's *romans de la terre* with the prairie novels of Frederick Philip Grove, or the urban novels of Gabrielle Roy and Roger Lemelin with those of Morley Callaghan or Earle Birney), these 'parallel' lines of development were, by the middle of the century, running farther and farther apart. With growing secularization and nationalism in Quebec, writers like André Langevin and Anne Hébert began to be influenced by the modern existentialism and the *nouveau roman* emerging in France, although they used the philosophical and aesthetic concepts generated by these movements to communicate a fictional reality which remained, in its external features, unmistakably *québécois*.

Contemporaneously with the publication of Langevin's *Poussière sur la ville*[18] and Anne Hébert's *Le Torrent*,[19] however, Canadian writers writing in English seemed more concerned with exposing the social, cultural and moral deficiencies in the Canadian reality surrounding them than with ontological definitions and their aesthetic correlatives. Implicitly expressed in the earlier novels of Mordecai Richler, Hugh MacLennan, Rudy Wiebe and Margaret Laurence, for instance, is the desire to "correct" a given social reality by pointing out its weaknesses as a first step in eliminating them. The view reflected in these novels is essentially one which seeks to preserve the familiar world by the alteration of the attitudes and behaviour which are seen to be responsible for its deficiencies, while the existentialist novels written in Quebec challenge the reader to revolutionize the world by revolutionizing his perceptual experience of it.

Explanations for these diverging patterns in English-Canadian and *québécois* fiction of the forties and fifties must be of a speculative nature. One possible conclusion is that in spite of the ethnic heterogeneity of its authors, English-Canadian fiction reflects the tendency of the dominant majority culture to preserve its societal order by correcting or improving it. In the fiction emerging at approximately the same time in Quebec, on the other hand, the break with traditional literary conventions seemed to be accompanied if not determined by the will to a more radical change in the socio-political order.

This hypothesis is strengthened when one considers subsequent developments in Quebec literature. In the sixties and seventies the Quebec separatist movement grew more and more associated with the artistic *avant-garde*. As the perceptual process itself came to stand in the foreground of art as a communicatory act, a number of Quebec writers chose to dramatize the socio-political situation in Quebec by equating their political and aesthetic insights as part of a generally emancipatory movement. This is particularly the case in the novels of Hubert Aquin and Jacques Godbout. As this equation of political separatism and the *avant-garde* became so firmly established that it took on almost a normative cultural role itself, it was challenged as a new power "establishment" by some younger novelists, notably Réjean Ducharme.

A surprisingly large number of English-Canadian novels written since 1945 still reveal what Iser calls an "oppositional" arrangement of perspectives, one which opposes the norms presented by one perspective to those represented by another, each exposing the deficiencies of the other. What is more, this perspectival system as it occurs in relatively recent English-Canadian novels has a narrative function similar to that which, according to Iser, it fulfilled at the time of its most frequent and typical occurrence, in the eighteenth century. If one accepts the premise that such narratological features are closely interrelated with the societal attitudes from which the texts emerged, it becomes clear to what extent the English texts in question still seek to achieve a "corrective" effect upon the society they represent. As such a "corrective" effect relies heavily upon drawing the reader's attention to certain problematic aspects of the social norms governing the fictional world presented (which in most cases is to be seen as paradigmatic for the reader's own empirical reality), the relatively high degree of determinacy of novels in which oppositional perspectives occur is a prerequisite.

Other structural features also play a part in creating the high determinacy required for this kind of "corrective" novel to achieve its intended effect upon the reader. These are the awareness possessed by the hero and the secondary characters, and the degree to which they communicate their insights to themselves or one another and thence to the reader.

In the majority of English-Canadian novels, the main characters possess qualities which, in the typology described by Stanzel, would situate them closer to Henry James's "central intelligence" than to the other extreme on the scale represented by characters who, like "dull or opaque mirrors, reflect an unclear, incomplete, often even distorted because ununderstood image of the world."[20]

Not only the central perspective of the hero and/or narrator, but also those of the secondary characters tend to be reliable and articulate both in revealing their own deficiencies and in their mutual evaluation. The insight and increased self-awareness achieved at the end is usually coupled with the exposure of the deficiencies of the social system itself.

The absence of a cohesive movement in English-Canadian fiction in the early years following World War II makes the occurrence of these oppositional perspectival arrangements in the novels of writers not otherwise related all the more remarkable. Yet in the decade following 1945, a considerable number of novels reveal a perspectival pattern which demands that readers unequivocally embrace the norms and values embodied by the hero, and that they reject the views of those characters representing the aspects of the system that are seen to threaten them.

Although the yes/no decisions the reader is to make are often complicated by a certain degree of problematization in the main characters, the normative function of the marginal figures is usually simply

to illustrate what is more or less explicitly negated by the main characters. Opposition remains the principal perspectival structure.[21]
English-Canadian novels of the forties and fifties tend to have reliable
omniscient narrators whose sympathies are unequivocally with their
heroes and the norms they represent.

The significance of these narratological features emerges more
clearly when one examines the ideological elements that they communicate in the individual texts. Generally speaking, the English-
Canadian corpus of the forties and fifties reveals the desire and need
for a national identity, both social and cultural: a fear of American
social, economic and cultural hegemony; a certain uneasiness vis-à-vis
the increasing urbanization taking place at the time, and its effects on
Canadian socio-cultural values and perceptions. These quasi-
ideological components, to function "correctively," require a consensual and programmatic response on the part of readers. Such programmatic consensus-seeking, in turn, involves close control of the appropriate reader responses, in other words, the creation of a relatively
passive role for the reader. The non-contemporary's involvement,
particularly, is restricted not only by the high determinacy of the text,
but by the selected norms themselves. The alternatives presented are
already familiar elements of the repertoire, since changes in those
elements of the system called into question by the novel have already
taken place. From the non-contemporary point of view, the patterns of
negation and affirmation proposed by the novel thus tend to represent
fixed formulas which have been either assimilated by the system itself,
or have been transcended by history.

ONE

Social Norms and Perspectival Patterns

1. Oppositional arrangements of perspective

Three novels, all of which may be regarded as constituting important items in the Canadian literary canon, illustrate the pattern described above: Hugh MacLennan's *Two Solitudes*,[22] Ernest Buckler's *The Mountain and the Valley*,[23] and Ethel Wilson's *Swamp Angel*.[24]

In Hugh MacLennan's *Two Solitudes* the oppositional perspectival structure is underlined by two explicitly designated complementary normative extremes, the colonial, money-manipulated values of upper-middle class "English" Montreal, and the nationalistic, rurally structured and clerically manipulated cultural traditions of Quebec. The degree to which the characters conform to the respective systems determines their place in the normative hierarchy outlined in the novel. The most objectionable (secondary) characters most rigidly uphold the old order, while the central characters with whom the reader is to identify and sympathize illustrate the old order's deficiencies and deliberately break its norms.

The norm opposition of the two societies is underlined by a marked symmetry in the double configuration formed by the characters. Only the feudalistic servant and community structure surrounding the Tallards at St. Marc, and a few incidental characters who seem to have been introduced to demonstrate certain norms presumably absent in English Canada, lack English-Canadian counterparts.

The most objectionable characters in the novel are Janet Methuen, Huntly McQueen, Father Beaubien, and Marius Tallard. While Father

Beaubien's prejudices and moral aberrations are determined by his ignorance and his literal conceptions of the doctrines involved in his faith, and Marius's fanaticism can be explained by childhood traumas, Huntly McQueen has only the impoverished small-town gentility of his pius mother to explain his financial ambitions and personal eccentricities.

Janet Methuen, however, is without a doubt the villain of the piece. With no alibi in her background except a snobbish finishing school (and, it is suggested, a pretentious and ambitious mother), she is the typical upper-class *parvenu*, slavishly devoted to the family whose money and social status she has married into. Ashamed of her own modest family and background, she perpetuates the values resulting from her new social status by inculcating them in her children. Although she seems psychologically repressed to the point of neurosis, this aspect remains anecdotal and illustrative of her unpleasant character. She epitomizes the prejudices, conventionality, social activity and personal emptiness of the society matron, exaggerating them almost to the point of caricature.

Huntly McQueen, while aspiring to (and ultimately achieving) social access to upper-class Montreal (represented by the Methuens) can nevertheless not shed his small-town middle-class background. Very much a self-made man, he constantly betrays that his tastes and manners are his by acquisition only. Huntly McQueen represents the North American oligarchy, combining an unshakeable faith in progress and economics with middle-class hypocrisies, prejudices and pompousness. Infallible in questions of finance, he strives toward a consolidation of his influence in other spheres by implementation of his financial methods. Although in his own terms still effective, he miscalculates when he and Tallard become partners. The dam and factories are built, but at the price of Tallard's ruin and the corruption, exploitation and self-alienation of the community of St. Marc.

Father Beaubien, with whom the novel opens, combines most of the features constituting the English-Canadian cliché image of the French-Canadian priest. First and foremost, he feels "personally accountable for every soul in St. Marc" (p. 3). This naïvely literal interpretation of his calling lets him clash with the feudal authority of the anticlerical Tallard. He resembles Huntly McQueen, financial priest and confessor, both in his shrewd manipulations and in his immoral view of war. Corresponding to the English-Canadian's stereotyped image of the French Canadian as unenlightened peasant is not only his ignorance (he takes the prints of Voltaire and Rousseau in the Tallard library for old family portraits), but also his aberrations in taste (his new church is to be adorned with a 25-foot high bronze statue of Christ crowned with a halo of coloured lights).

Marius Tallard reveals himself as a fanatic, both religious and political, representing the excesses to which the enlightened but misled segment of Quebec's population is subject when aroused. Daphne Methuen, his counterpart in the hierarchy of characters, duplicates exactly the values of her mother Janet Methuen, whom she eclipses as she grows up not only in the brilliance of her marriage, but also in her prejudices, affectations, and pathological emotional sterility.

In contrast to these objectionable characters, Athanase Tallard and Captain Yardley represent those features of their respective cultures which the reader is to affirm, both by sympathy and inclination and by being able to identify with the positions they take in various situations involving the norms of their respective societies. The features characterizing Tallard demonstrate exclusively the "positive" aspects of his seigneurial role. His cultural sophistication and quasi-aristocratic background manifest themselves in the nobility of his appearance, in his benevolent authority over his illiterate, medievally superstitious and generally unenlightened and unemancipated servants, and in his social grace. The benevolent authority with which he rules over St. Marc is legitimized by his function as elected Member of Parliament, formalizing his representation of the best interests of the community. On the other hand he votes against the public opinion of St. Marc in the conscription issue, so that the reader credits him with his moral courage in taking the "right" side and showing political as well as social responsibility. Even his weaknesses add to the reader's identification and sympathy with him. His ineffectuality in dealing with McQueen, which in the end ruins him and his family and, in a way, destroys the community of St. Marc, is due to his own moral incorruptibility and lack of opportunism. His extra-marital affairs not only are legitimized by his first wife's excessive religious fervour and sexual frigidity, but they also prove to the reader that Athanase is a "whole" man and not sensually deficient.

Captain Yardley, it seems, has no weaknesses at all. With his wooden leg and sailor's yarns, he is even more stereotyped than his friend Athanase Tallard. He is the decent, brave, good-humoured, modest, loyal, unprejudiced, fair, child-loving seaman who is not above manfully revealing his emotions by noisily blowing his nose.

As the main characters, Paul Tallard and Heather Methuen negate more or less in their entirety the normative systems in which they have been raised. Class- and culture-specific values are replaced or modified by transcendent human ones such as tolerance, respect, and the mutual nourishing of the other's inherent creativity. With the importance of wealth, power and authority abolished by the relationship between Paul and Heather, the legacies of Janet Methuen and Huntly McQueen go unclaimed. So, of course, does that of Athanase Tallard.

In the end, it is Captain Yardley's pragmatism that lays the cornerstone of the future Utopia of Canadian unity.

The only character with an ambivalent place in the novel's hierarchy is Kathleen, Tallard's Irish Catholic second wife. Hers is clearly a catalytic role. At first seen positively by the narrator (and hence by the reader) in that she brings emotional and sensual warmth into the Tallard household, she degenerates after Tallard's death into selfish, lower-class commonness, falling back into the life-pattern she followed before meeting Athanase. Her easy-going adaptability on the one hand and moral unawareness on the other, however, are not problematized either at the psychological or social levels. She merely falls from the reader's favour in the course of the novel due to her conduct, which the text unmistakably asks that the reader condemn.

The reader's affirmative and negative responses to the various characters are reinforced by direct narrative intervention that exegizes even unambiguous action. Thus Marius, rifling through his father's papers looking for money, is described as "secretive," "devious," and "obsessive." The sole common denominator of Father Beaubien and Athanase Tallard is omnisciently identified by the narrator: "They were both Normans, and they were both notably stubborn" (p. 19). The narrator's disapproval of Kathleen's sensuality and seductiveness is betrayed by a tell-tale conjunction: "Her voice had a husky, pulsing quality, *but* it was friendly, warm and frank" (p. 37; my italics). Her seductiveness is also indicated by the fact that her lips are "generous," her breasts "full," but her hips are "slender."

With these epithets, the narrator makes stereotypes of two potentially ambiguous characters, psychologically rather more differentiated than the others: in the case of Kathleen, that of the harmless and proverbially good-natured whore. Marius, in spite of his problematic childhood and adolescence, becomes, as a result of narrative explication, a dangerous fanatic entirely undeserving of reader sympathy.

In *The Mountain and the Valley* (1952) the conflict lies between rural attitudes and values oriented towards preserving the past and the traditional, and the urban way of life which is seen not only as implying a break with the past and the traditional, but also as morally disintegrating and corruptive. The hero and his family represent the rural and traditional, while the figures representing the urban and progressive are marginal. Their main role in the plot is to reveal the subversive corruption of certain members of the family, for instance Toby's influence on David and particularly on Anna. The rural-urban opposition is complicated by the rural anti-idyll represented by Rachel and her daughter Charlotte. Rachel is characterized by life-denying Puritan values which she piously exploits to manipulate other characters. Charlotte surreptitiously lives out her adolescent sexual urges with Chris Canaan, resulting in a forced marriage, but she lacks the self-will to dissociate herself from her mother. In the absence of any positive qualities attached to them, Rachel and Charlotte become the most unambiguous and offensive characters in the novel.

Although the opposition between the two families—who live in the same community—is not expressed as rural versus urban, Rachel and Charlotte are drawn in strong contrast to the members of the Canaan household which, throughout the novel, is seen as exemplary of the rural community. Although in this novel, too, the hero and his family represent norms that contrast positively with those represented by the other secondary characters, the plot itself reinforces the mutual negation of the two perspectives by revealing the inadequacy of the norms perceived as positive ones by the reader. In this novel, it is the reader therefore who is induced to motivate the ultimate failure of the hero (in terms of both the normative systems presented) and also perhaps to formulate a corrective.

In *Swamp Angel* (1954) the heroine Maggie Lloyd and her aging friend Mrs. Severance represent two alternatives to the mediocrity of a conformistic, materially oriented urban existence, while the heroine's husband Eddie Vardoe and the lodge-owner's wife Vera Gunnarson represent conformity to the system. As in *Two Solitudes*, the hierarchy of norms represented by the characters is relatively fixed. The heroine represents the norms to be affirmed, i.e. she negates certain elements of the system, while the secondary characters illustrate varying degrees of failure to conform to the alternative system proposed by the text (through the perspective of the heroine). The secondary characters' position in the hierarchy is indicated by their emotional and spiritual proximity to the heroine herself, or to old Mrs. Severance.

Clearly, these novels have little in common with regard to what they intend to communicate. *Two Solitudes* hardly deviates from the romance formula, while in *Swamp Angel*, though the heroine is rewarded and the villains are punished, the fact remains that the novel's conclusion is open-ended (albeit unconvincingly so, since the reader has every reason to believe that Maggie will preserve the serene self-harmony she has achieved). *The Mountain and the Valley*, on the other hand, records a human tragedy representative of the social and cultural hiatus between the lost rural idyll and its invasion by urban disillusionment. But the paradigmatic pattern is complicated in that the idyll itself is called into question, and in that the hero David Canaan is an artist *manqué*.

Similar oppositional patterns are to be found in the earlier novels of Morley Callaghan, which stress the moral problem of socially rather than emotionally or spiritually determined relationships. Robertson

Davies's Salterton trilogy, particularly the first two novels (*Tempest Tost*[25] and *Leaven of Malice*[26]) also presents an oppositionally structured hierarchy of characters. Unlike Davies, Callaghan demands the unequivocal affirmation of the perspectival views presented by his heroes (though not of the heroes themselves), who tend to be representative types; but, like Davies's central figures, they are sufficiently complicated to induce their differentiated evaluation by the reader.

Thus in spite of their similar perspectival structures Davies's and Callaghan's earlier novels differ from the three novels discussed above in two ways. One difference lies in the problematization of the central characters alluded to above. The other consists in that neither the Davies nor the Callaghan novels seem to intend a corrective effect. In Callaghan, the social problem is personalized not as an illustrative principle, as in novels of social realism, but in the transcendent sense of personal salvation. Davies's satires of provincial Ontario, though they present the microcosmic social panorama of the social realists, have little in common with that genre. The exposure of cultural deficiencies achieved in large measure by the parodying of romance patterns is as unconcerned with their correction as are the classic comedies of the theatre, whose character hierarchies Davies's novels evoke. The governing dialectic is not that of class society and the individual, but, as in the great theatrical comedies, that of folly and wisdom.

2. Graduated perspectives: Margaret Atwood's *The Edible Woman*

In the majority of both English-Canadian and *québécois* novels, the intended effect lies not in the unequivocal affirmation or negation of a particular perspectival view and the norms it represents, but in the reader's calling into question the norms invoked and recognizing either their deficiencies or those of the perspectival view indicating them, or both. The predominant structuring principle in these novels is not oppositional but graduated; that is, both hero and secondary figures demonstrate the problematization of the selected norms.

The "echelon" or graduated arrangement of perspectives is the most prevalent in the history of the novel. Iser considers it to be characteristic of the genre from Thackeray to Joyce, and indeed it is still dominant in some form in much of contemporary fiction. As a narratological vehicle this type of perspectival arrangement permits much more latitude in reader response: there are more characters with whom the text permits sympathetic identification, that is, the normative value of the various characters and the perspectives they represent are not necessarily hierarchized. While many "graduated perspective" novels still seek a consensual response from their readers, the programmatic element is not always present; when it is, it is far less prominent than in an oppositionally structured novel.

In the more realistic and easily accessible novels of the graduated perspective type, the text repertoire still overlaps to a large extent with the reader's own experience of reality, or at least offers multiple points of tangency with it. As in oppositionally structured novels, the communicatory intention usually lies in the exposure of deficiencies immanent in the normative system designated by the text repertoire, which is generally taken to be paradigmatic for the reality in which the reader dwells. But, unlike the oppositional novel, the graduated-perspective novel leaves the reader multiple possibilities and fragmented versions of how the questions posed in the novel are to be resolved. The formulation of the questions themselves as well as their resolution is more problematic. It is up to the reader to formulate a composite "corrective" which accommodates the variables allowed for in this much less determinate type of novel.

The fictional world presented in Margaret Atwood's *The Edible Woman* is hardly unfamiliar to readers, who recognize in it a great number of normative elements determining their own everyday lives. The process undergone by Marian is recognized and formulated because the problematic elements overlap to a great extent with those of the reader's real world.

At the same time the graduated arrangement of perspectives permits a distribution of the problematic norms (norms to be contested or called into question) amongst the various characters in a linear/sequential rather than vertical/hierarchical fashion. Although the problematic norms are readily identifiable, the reader still must recognize and group them as they occur in the various perspectival views. It is also up to the reader to "assemble" the valid responses of the various characters to the deficient norm system presented in the text, in order to arrive at a composite "corrective." The validity or deficiency of a given textual perspective is by and large determined by reference to the reader's own extratextual reality. Thus it is the graduated arrangement of perspectives and the extensive overlapping of text and reader repertoire that largely determine the effect of the novel.

In *The Edible Woman* the norms the reader is to negate are clearly indicated. They involve the commercial, social and ideological manipulation of human needs. The heroine's crisis stems from her inability to distinguish real needs from manipulated ones, and so her attitude becomes life-denying in a curiously literal sense: Marian gradually becomes unable to eat. The crisis is overcome not when the figures threatening to "consume" her are eliminated, but when she herself learns to relativize her own perceptions. Her alignment with Duncan is part of this process, for unlike the commercially, socially, or ideologi-cally determined and fixed self-image masks of the others, his views are erratic and self-contradictory. Thus in her relationship with Dun-can, Marian is constantly forced to modify or negate the validity of her previous responses to him, breaking her own behavioural consistency with her outer image. Not until this image has been thoroughly destroyed does her identity emerge and assert itself in the conscious creation of an image: a cake in the shape of a girl, whose ultimate destiny and *raison d'être* is, precisely, to be consumed.

In spite of the fact that most of the novel is written in the first person, and that the narrative voice also represents the central per-spective of the heroine, the perspectival views of the various figures are clearly conveyed to the reader. Except for Duncan, and to a certain degree Marian's friend Clara, none of the secondary characters con-tradict the heroine's view of them as initially presented, so that her views tend to be accepted as valid by the reader throughout the novel.

The normative system as a manipulable commercial production-consumption cycle is outlined by allusions to Marian's job as market-ing consultant, but also by references to the norm-forming commercial activity in advertising. The context of need manipulation established by these allusions determines recognition of the elements motivating the perspectival views presented by the secondary characters, and enables the reader to perceive how commercial manipulation of human needs eventually affects emotional and social interaction.

Thus Peter, Marian's fiancé, is characterized solely by the attrib-utes of advertising images and bestseller heroes. Since his appearance, actions, and reactions remain consistent with these commercially determined norms throughout the novel, the reader perceives him as a human commercial product, or rather the advertising image of a pro-duct, whose social and personal motivations are indistinguishable from his commercial success-oriented ones. In Peter, social, personal, and emotional motivations are all ultimately commercially induced. They are as indistinguishable from one another as his personal identity and social mask. Since he persists in trying to create the female counterpart of a commercially determined success-image out of Mar-ian, his declared emotional motivation in his involvement with her is called into question. The reader thus recognizes, long before Marian does, that Peter sees her merely as an enhancing attribute of his own image.

Marian's colleagues, the Office Virgins, represent female counter-parts to the perspectival view represented by Peter, but at varying stages of perfection. Furthermore they illustrate their inability to fill the prerequisites of prevailing social norms since they lack the most impor-tant (female) attribute of social success: (successful) male partners. The views represented by the three office girls focus more upon the social norm of woman's role as wife than on the commercial success norms foregrounded in the perspective represented by Peter, but this traditional social norm is heavily reinforced commercially: Peter is perceived as the perfect mate (by and for all three of them).

Ainsley, Marian's room-mate, is observed by the reader as short-circuiting the system by negating and breaking the success norms incorporated by Peter, Len, and the Office Virgins. Her reversal of socially determined (and commercially reinforced) sexual roles—by reducing the male role in the reproductive process to a necessary instrument in the achievement of her own self-fulfilment—exposes the victimization of the female underlying the socially sanctioned male pursuit of self-realization. Her justification of her behaviour, however, does not indicate to the reader a deeply felt need, for it contains the same unquestioning prescriptive elements already recognizable in the commercial slogans and traditional adages constituting the norms represented by the other perspectival views. The reader thus perceives Ainsley's self-fulfilment ideology as a mere variable in the commercial conditioning of human needs.

The only perspective which stands in outright opposition to the prevailing system is that represented by Duncan. His favourite activities are the non-productive ones of washing and ironing. His manipulation of clothes as disembodied extensions of their owners tends to be evaluated by the reader as a harmless eccentricity, given the established context of various forms of manipulation of human beings themselves. His substitution of washing and ironing for the "productive" role expected of him as a graduate student of English (namely the writing of term papers on original topics) invokes the problem of original scholarship in a mass-university system, itself illustrative of a culture that is intellectually hypertrophied.

The views Duncan represents not only reveal the deficiencies of the norms demonstrated by Peter, Ainsley, and the other secondary figures, but also correct Marian's own perceptual deficiency. His is the only perspective whose validity overrules that of the heroine. This is indicated to the reader not only by the diametrical opposition of the two views represented by Peter and Duncan, but also by the fact that Marian constantly opts for the alternative norm system Duncan represents.

Aside from the multiple metaphorical and symbolic reinforcements of the consumption-production theme, several metaliterary elements explode the realistic framework of this early novel, creating the kind of indeterminacy to be found in Atwood's later works.

One is the shift in narrative voice. In the three-part novel the first part is written in the first person, the second in the third, and the third in the first again. The fact that the shifts are intended to reflect the heroine's self-alienation, or the loss and restoration of the heroine's identity, is indicated not only through the plot and the perspectival views presented, but also by the narrative voice, which explicitly draws attention to the shifts and their significance: "Now that I was thinking of myself in the first person singular again I found my own situation much more interesting than his [Duncan's]" (p. 290).[27]

Another metaliterary feature drawing particular attention to itself is the unformulated allusion to the production-consumption metaphor at the end of the novel. It also constitutes a reference to its previous occurrence in a seemingly banal context near the beginning. The full significance of the Peter-Marian-Duncan triangle seen at the end (in the discussion between Duncan and Marian as to who was trying to destroy whom) does not emerge unless the reader recollects Duncan's previous allusion to a mythological triangular constellation. At their first meeting, in which Marian interviews him for a beer survey, Duncan's response to the slogan "Healthy hearty taste" is the invocation of a cannibalistic pattern occurring in the *Decameron* and in Grimm's tales: "the husband kills the wife's lover, or vice versa, and cuts out the heart and makes it into a stew or pie and serves it up in a silver dish, and the other one eats it" (p. 48).

The interchangeability of roles indicated by Duncan's allusion to the pattern suggests that the significance of the cake episode at the end is ambiguous. This ambiguity is underlined by the symbolic displacement of the mythical elements: both Marian and Duncan eat the cake, while Peter is shocked by the implications of doing so and refuses it. On the other hand Marian's rejection of the symbolic significance of her cake ("Nonsense. It's only a cake.") seems to negate the validity of the allusion recognized by the reader. At the end of the novel, the heroine's "normalization" is indicated by her negation of externally induced images, commercial, social or psychological, and the affirmation of inalterable human needs, represented by the ingestion of food. The thesis and antithesis represented by the apparently opposing views of heroine/narrator and reader at the end are resolved by the reader's recognition that the heroine's rejection of symbolic interpretation of the consumption act with which she frees herself from manipulability (at least temporarily) is communicated through symbolic structures. Thus while the text exposes the degree to which people can be manipulated by commercially exploited images and symbols, it asserts their validity by making the reader aware that the same images and symbols make this recognition communicable.

––––––––––

In the novels discussed so far, a preoccupation with the social repertoire of norms and a relatively high degree of textual determinacy can be observed. The effects of these novels are created in large part by the way in which the perspectives in a given novel are arranged, and by the considerable overlapping of text and reader repertoires. Furthermore, both the high textual determinacy and the focus on the social norm repertoire have been observed as being more characteristic of the English-Canadian novel than of works of *québécois* fiction.

High determinacy itself as an intended effect in English-Canadian novels may be seen in this context as an attempt to define or even create a national literary identity on the one hand, and as a means of correcting a given social reality on the other. Only by alluding to the reality determining a collective identity can any given aspect of it be thrown into relief or called into question. A number of the English-Canadian novels discussed or mentioned above have been concerned with first creating a consensus as to the kind of reality to be represented; in doing so they have fallen back on the historical conventional models which characterized the emergence of the novel as genre.

In *québécois* novels of the forties and fifties, both kinds of identity—national and literary—are pre-established. The fictional reality presented, though not necessarily familiar, is readily recognizable, since it is set off against a social and cultural reality the nature of which is already predefined.

Thus in two classics of *québécois* realism, Gabrielle Roy's *Bonheur d'occasion*[28] and Roger Lemelin's *Au pied de la pente douce*,[29] for example, the hermetic worlds represented by St. Henri and Westmount in the one and the *haute-* and *basse-ville* of Quebec City in the other enable the reader to recognize the entire fictional world of the novels, not because it *is* necessarily familiar to the reader, but because it is alluded to as if it were.

This implied consensus between text and reader concerning the kind of reality to be represented and the conventions invoked in doing so (those of social realism) forms a background of anticipation against which the features to be communicated are thrown into relief. It is perhaps because of this existing consensus, which the English-Canadian novel has first sought to establish by using oppositional arrangements of perspective and other elements contributing to high textual determinacy, that we find no incidences of similar perspectival arrangements and a correspondingly high degree of textual determinacy in the *québécois* novels of the same historical period. *Bonheur d'occasion* and *Au pied de la pente douce* are novels "without a hero" in the sense that each of the main characters presented illustrates different elements of the fictional world of the respective novels, and exposes the deficiencies of various aspects of the social and moral system upon which it is built, thus corresponding to what Iser calls an "echelon" arrangement of perspectives.

Although most of the perspectives presented in the latter two novels indicate the characters' own perceptual deficiencies, insofar as (with the exceptions of Jean Lévesque and Denis Boucher) they are unable to understand the complexity of the social apparatus outside the small world which in a sense determines their lives in St. Henri or the *basse-ville*, the communication of these deficiencies is nevertheless unproblematic. As in *The Edible Woman*, the reader's attention is focused upon the way in which representative character types will act and react to clearly indicated social problems. The unmediated representation of the perspectival views, however, induces reader sympathy and identification with the figures of the novels, while awareness of the larger social problems which the figures themselves do not wholly perceive and hence to which they cannot adequately respond leads the reader to formulate both the problems and alternative solutions to those sought by the characters. In addition to creating a sense of sympathy and identification in their readers, these novels induce social *engagement* precisely by making the readers themselves formulate the deficient norms involved and relate these to the individual problems of the various characters.

Marie-Claire Blais's *Une Saison dans la vie d'Emmanuel* reveals the same preoccupation with the social norm repertoire characteristic of Quebec society in the early fifties (as witnessed in the novels of Gabrielle Roy and Roger Lemelin alluded to above). But in Blais's novel the prevalent social norms of Quebec are thoroughly alienated by the fictional reality in which they are represented. This alienation is effected in part by the way they are seen to function, and in part by the serial arrangement of perspectives, where the multiple views presented disorient the reader to the point where the perspectives themselves are difficult to identify.

The calling into question of the normative system invoked is far more radical than in the novels previously discussed. While Blais's novel, too, challenges the system on social, ideological and moral grounds, it also exposes the noxiousness of normativity itself. Thus two important principles of the genre of social realism are here carried to extremes: in addition to certain individual social norms, it is normativity itself that is called into question. Secondly, the de-hierarchization of perspectives, which in novels of social realism still permits the orientation of the reader, here gives way to a disconcerting disorientation, which is due to the serial arrangement of perspectives and to the ironic partial disclosures of the capricious narrative voice. In its radicalization of both the thematic elements and the narratological devices of the genre it invokes, *Une Saison dans la vie d'Emmanuel* may be seen as a work which is eminently parodic in its effect.

3. An instance of "serial" perspectivisation: Marie-Claire Blais's *Une Saison dans la vie d'Emmanuel*

Une Saison dans la vie d'Emmanuel presents a series of perspectival views behind each of which stands the ironic presence of an anonymous narrator. The inversion, or perversion, of cultural and social values in the day-to-day life of rural *québécois* society is communicated to the reader in part by the apparent irreconcilability of these values with the quasi-mythical fictional world of the novel. This fictional world is itself perceivable by the reader only against the background of the external norms and values commonly held in the society alluded to. Each perspectival view represents the problematization of a given norm, not so much by negating it but rather in conforming to it, thus demonstrating the discrepancy between its letter and its spirit.

By revealing the characters' unawareness of this duality of external norm and norm content, the novel exposes the irrationality (at least from the perspectives of the figures involved) latent in the norms themselves. This element, together with the figure of Grand-Mère Antoinette, whose benevolence and malevolence are both arbitrary and unpredictable (and so, in a sense, irrational) lets the life of the characters in the novel appear to be determined by erratic forces which eventually assume mythical dimensions.

The symbolical statement behind this *univers mythique* has been variously interpreted. Proponents of literary sociology such as Jack Warwick,[30] Michel Brûlé,[31] and Lucien Goldmann[32] have recognized it as representing the old and new orders of Quebec society. Genre-oriented critics like Dominique Aury[33] and Jacques Chessex[34] have identified it as a modern literary incarnation of ancient myth, legend, folk- and fairy-tale. Quebec critics, on the other hand, have tended to view *Une Saison dans la vie d'Emmanuel* primarily as a novel of social comment.[35]

Despite these varying interpretations, there is a consensus, however vague, that *Une Saison dans la vie d'Emmanuel* forms part of a movement in Quebec fiction which a French reviewer described as being led by a group of "jeunes terroristes du roman."[36] However objectionable academic critics may find the term *terroriste* in this context, it expresses the resistance of the novel to any attempt to render harmless the radical exposure of the demonic forces—demonic in both the social and mythological sense—which are seen to determine human existence in the fictional world it presents.

The process by which the reader is led to recognize and formulate the perversion of the normative system, and the demonic mythology which is in a sense seen to be responsible for and even equated with it, constitutes the focus of the following analysis. In their parodistic handling of the conventions of social realism, the narrative strategies involved are largely unprecedented in both English-Canadian and *québécois* novels, although since its publication similar patterns have emerged, notably in the novels of Roch Carrier.

The opening of the novel, presenting the perceptions of a new-born infant of the world around him, creates a contradictory effect by drawing the reader into a reality both familiar and improbable. The familiar world is that represented by grandmother and babe alone in a poor family's farmhouse kitchen, a scene evoking the "milieu" of the social realism novel, while not lacking a certain idyllic quality. The improbable lies in the perspectival presentation of Emmanuel the new-born infant perceiving and narratively articulating his observations of himself and his surroundings. These observations rapidly transform the peaceful kitchen scene into an anti-idyll, characterized by the abject poverty and moral and physical depravity accompanying it.

But the contradiction of the reality principle implied in the infant perspective is itself undermined by an anonymous narrator, whose ironic presence manifests itself in the communication of circumstances unknown to the perspectival view presented as Emmanuel's: "elle [Grand-Mère Antoinette] écartait Emmanuel de ce geste de la main qui, jadis, avait refusé l'amour, puni le désir de l'homme" (p. 9).

This narrator not only evokes the past, the secret, but also invokes the future, drawing the reader's attention even more overtly to an omniscient narrative presence: "Plus tard, il la verrait marchant ainsi au milieu des poules, des lapins et des vaches, semant des malédictions sur son passage ou recueillant quelque bébé tombé dans la boue" (p. 12).

This perspectival duality between Emmanuel's perceptions, sensations, and self-articulated needs and the narrator's revelations of knowledge beyond that possessed by the infant is further complicated by brief lapses into the consciousness of other figures.

> L'homme s'habillait au coin du feu. Grand-Mère Antoinette lui jetait des regards fugitifs à la dérobée. Non, je ne ferai pas un geste pour servir cet homme, pensait-elle. Il croit que j'imiterai ma fille, mais je ne lui apporterai pas le bassin d'eau chaude, les vêtements propres. Non. Non, je ne bougerai pas de mon fauteuil. Il attend qu'une femme vienne le servir. Mais je ne me lèverai pas. (p. 16)

> Pour la première fois, l'homme lève un regard obscur vers la mère et l'enfant: puis il les oublie aussitôt. Il regarde le bassin d'eau souillée sur le poêle. Il se sent de plus en plus à l'étroit dans sa veste. (p. 19)

The difficulty of attaching oneself to a single perspectival view is determined not only by the multiple perspectives which segment the reality presented and seem to converge in time, as in the two quotations above, but also as evidenced in the same quotations by variations in narrative tense. Like the narrator's allusions to past and future events, and references to habitual or repeated action evoked by an event or a gesture situated in the present, these rapidly alternating perspectives result in a temporal disorientation of the reader. This disorientation is increased by narrative elements that cannot be unambiguously situated in the consciousness of any of the characters presented, and therefore can be taken as manifestations of the narrator, whose irony further dissolves the realistic veneer of the novel. Often the narrator's observations are of an antithetical nature, creating ironies which range from the poignant—"De ses ongles noircis de boue, Jean Le Maigre tourne gracieusement les pages de son livre. Ravi comme un prince dans ses vêtements en lambeaux, il se hâte de lire" (pp. 18-19)—to the savage: "Théo Crapula [a sexual pervert attempting to corrupt Le Septième, who is referred to in this passage] venait au secours du jeune garçon pour le mettre avec honneur sur la trace du bien" (p. 167).

All of these narrative elements—the shifting perspectival views, the *invraisemblance* of the perspective presented as Emmanuel's, the temporal segmentation and the narrative irony with which idyll and anti-idyll are simultaneously evoked—contradict the linearity, consistency and narrative authority which the reader expects of the "social realism" aspects contained in the novel. The effect of this contradiction is to let the reader perceive the fictional world presented as an alienation or deformation rather than the "representation" that is anticipated. Since there is no one perspectival view to which the reader can hold fast, and the social realities described are all possessed of antithetical aspects invalidating their familiarity to the reader, the experience of the novel results in the giving up of both the reality categories to be found in traditional fiction and the glib social formulas of everyday experience.

This suspension of the habitual views of the reader is achieved through a number of narrative elements which it is the reader's task to evaluate and relate within the context of the plot and the various perspectival views presented. These elements are: the perspectival views of the figures themselves and the interaction between them; the equivocality of the system of norms alluded to; the incarnation of religious, mystical and mythical polarities in some of the characters; the irony of the narrator and the ironies of the plot.

The reader easily identifies the norms invoked by the perspectival views presented by the main characters. No doubt it is this socio-historical aspect of the novel that provoked certain reviewers and literary sociologists to regard it as reflecting the social changes in Quebec society, and others to use the term "naturalism" in connection with it.[37] In fact, the novel does negate the entire system of premises upon which societal consensus is built.

First and foremost among the social and moral norms to be thematized and rejected in the fictional reality of the novel is the notion that life is the highest value, and that humanity, uncorrupted by society, is inherently good. Corollaries to it are presented in the values associated with social institutions, the family, the church, the state, whose collective civilizatory claim is concern for the welfare of the individual. More specifically still, the religious and secular authority vested in the institutions by virtue of this claim is seen as constituting a moral authority and so as guaranteeing the validity of the prescribed norms, such as the work ethic, the desirability of health, the immorality of non-reproductive sexuality, and the acceptance of death as liberation from disease and as a manifestation of divine will.

Each of the "authority" figures demonstrates certain aspects of this normative system and reveals, in interaction with the other characters, the disparity between formalized norm and norm content.

The prime authority figure throughout the novel is, of course, Grand-Mère Antoinette. While she is characterized by her triumphant "immortality," her unchallenged authority both in the family and in the religious and secular community reveals the manipulability of the norms involved. She represents the supreme authority of the worldly and divine orders of her own cosmogony, and she also conforms to the prescribed norms, but she does so not out of acknowledgment of their moral validity but out of self-interest (which often negates their validity). Thus for instance she accepts the death of others not out of pious resignation to the will of God, but as a proof of her own immortality. She accepts the numerous deaths among her grandchildren because they reduce the number of mouths to feed. Furthermore, funerals are festive occasions on which the family enjoys the luxuries of cleanliness, order, and sufficient food: *M. le Curé* showers the generosity of the parish treasury upon those bereaved. The same self-interested thinking motivates her to "dedicate her grandchildren to God": their entering novitiates and convents has the double advantage of guaranteeing both their spiritual salvation and physical survival, and temporarily reducing the brood to be fed and lodged at home. Accordingly, Héloïse's excessive piety is indulged not out of tolerance or religious conviction, but out of the same kind of pride and self-interest: "Qui sait, pensait-elle, c'est peut-être une sainte?" (p. 36).

The mother, on the other hand, whose parental role denotes authority in the social consensus (though secondary to that of the father) possesses no voice at all in determining the lot of the family. She is represented as the long-suffering beast of burden who mutely acquiesces in the decisions taken by Grand-Mère Antoinette. The conjugal relationship, in the socio-religious system indicated, is characterized by mutual consent, while birth of a child is seen as the ultimate fulfilment of the marriage relationship and also as proof that the latter is God-willed and God-blessed. In *Une Saison dans la vie d'Emmanuel*, the invalidity of these norms is indicated by the fact that the mother is raped nightly by her husband, and involuntarily produces an annual child which the family is not in a position to want or support.

The authority role of the father and husband is similarly undermined in the novel. Aside from sharing his wife's stuporous dullness, the father cringingly endures the humiliation of Grand-Mère Antoinette's household supremacy, compensating for his denied virility by the sexual abuse of his wife and the corporal abuse of his children.[38]

The function of the village *curé* as moral and spiritual authority in the societal structure becomes, in the reality of the novel, at worst one of parasitic self-interest and, at best, benevolent self-indulgence. His pious encouragement of the incessant child-bearing described in the novel assures not only the size of his congregation, but also the filling of convents and novitiates. If he nevertheless occasionally gives Jean Le Maigre Latin and geography lessons (although he has no inkling of the latter) this seems to be less in fulfilment of his role as cultural leader of the community than out of a kind of jovial vanity.

If Héloïse's convent and Jean Le Maigre's novitiate represent religious institutions (and so elements of authority) that seem relatively humane, in that the novices are well cared for, they are nevertheless highly repressive. Furthermore, they are also a direct source of evil: it is through the rituals of the convent that Héloïse's aberrant sexual fantasies are nourished, while in Jean Le Maigre's monastery Frère Théodule, though mindful of Jean Le Maigre's well-being (for reasons of his own), exults in his approaching death in anticipation of the fulfilment of his necrophilic desires.

Secular authority, finally, appears in the figure of the director of the *maison de correction* to which Le Septième and Jean Le Maigre are sent for setting fire to the school. In direct opposition to the term *correction*, the institution is corrupting and the director barbarous by the norms of the very society in whose name the two culprits are condemned.

An analysis of the three central figures reveals the same kind of disparity between norm value and norm function.

Jean Le Maigre, tubercular, constantly coughing, loves his disease whose fever he cherishes as the source of his visions and dreams, recording them in numerous manuscripts which he hides about the house and in the outdoor latrines. Nor is this the only instance in which the desirability of physical health and wholeness is called into question as a norm. Among his limited amorous experiences, his favourite is Marthe, a hunchbacked classmate. His preference, though ostensibly influenced by the generosity with which she offers him gifts, seems determined by her infirmity: "je suppose que toutes les petites bosses vieillissent très vite. Moi, ce sont celles que je préfère" (p. 33).

Jean Le Maigre's artistic temperament is inspired not by lofty idealism, but by a fascination with evil, with the aesthetic dimension of the demonic. Thus he is filled with admiration for the lazy, bald, fat, beer-swilling *curé* most of all for his ears: "Les plus beaux péchés de la terre ont coulé dedans" (p. 59).

Héloïse, both chaste and passionate, goes from convent to brothel. The sensuousness of the occult, the rites of the church, and the luxury of adequate meals and privacy she experiences at the convent nourish her passion, to which she succumbs by fasting and fervent prayer. It is this excessive passion that she sees herself as expiating in the brothel, "doing good" as a prostitute by "helping those in need," and also by sending the money thus earned home to her family.

Le Septième, thief and pyromaniac, is often beaten for the misdeeds of Jean Le Maigre, over whom Grand-Mère holds a sheltering hand. Whereas Jean Le Maigre is sent to a novitiate to relieve the crowded conditions at home, Le Septième and his brother Pomme are sent to the city as apprentices in a shoe factory. Pomme loses three fingers at a machine, while Le Septième, who, through Grand-Mère Antoinette's determination for self-improvement, has been sent for lessons to a tutor, is savagely beaten and left for dead by the latter for denying himself as a partner in his erotic fantasies. The tutor is none other than Frère Théo, who has hastened Jean Le Maigre's death in the novitiate. While the case of Pomme demonstrates the invalidity of the work ethic, in that it reveals industrial labour as a form of exploitation rather than as a decent way of earning one's living, the experience of Le Septième (like that of Jean Le Maigre) with Frère Théodule evokes the demonic as an anti-human force taking on the appearance of a friend to man.

The reader, constantly tempted to attribute the shocking physical and moral depravity presented through the experience of Jean Le Maigre, Héloïse and Le Septième to extreme social circumstances, is as persistently reminded of the corruptibility and latent malevolence of the institutions representing the entire social system. The fact that, throughout the novel, supposed salvation (through norm-conforming) seals the characters' doom is due not only to a defective functioning of the norms alluded to, but also to the antithesis inherent in the norms themselves. It is this revelation of the demonic, the taboo, as a counterpart and in a way a consequence of the sanctioned norm that constitutes the moral irony of *Une Saison dans la vie d'Emmanuel*. The norms presented are so intricately intermeshed, and contain so completely their own antithesis, that any attempt at an alteration of circumstances inevitably activates corollaries to the particular norm to be negated or undermined and is thus self-defeating. The social panorama alluded to through the perspectives of the central figures goes beyond a critique of a particular society at a given time; the effect of the novel is thus not exhausted in revealing the enormity of the moral contradictions in the designated socio-cultural system.

Perhaps the most striking and obvious example of the moral irony created by this dialectical opposition of external norm and norm content is to be found in the perspectival view presented through Héloïse. Her rigorous conformity to the rules of the convent, which she ingenuously equates with those of Mme Octavie's brothel, reveals not so much her moral obtuseness as the demonic antipole virtually present in the Catholic cult. The analogy is communicated to the reader through the symmetry of the elements determining life in the convent and in the brothel, but also in the interchangeability of Christ the Bridegroom and the sadistic demon lover in Héloïse's sexual fantasies and dreams.

This perversion of norms by their own latent antithesis is recognizable in every other element of the novel as well. Jean Le Maigre's consistent recognition of the aesthetic dimensions of socially negated conditions (such as disease and sin) is expanded and confirmed precisely at the point when he decides to reform. Tempted by the smell of broth issuing from the kitchens of the novitiate, Jean Le Maigre resolves to stay and become a convert. "J'aurai des apparitions, les saints me parleront dans mon sommeil, et les anges" (p. 60). In the refectory soon afterwards he suffers a haemorrhage (accompanied by a sudden sense of well-being) and is transferred to the infirmary, where Frère Théodule (identified by Jean Le Maigre as *le diable*) takes over his care.

In the autobiography Jean Le Maigre writes from his infirmary bed, this principle of reversal manifests itself in a rhetorical *tour de force*, a sort of parody of a portrait of the artist ("Dès ma naissance, j'ai eu le front couronné de poux!"), but also in the evocation of fictitious domestic circumstances which are diametrically opposed to those existing in Jean Le Maigre's reality ("Un poète, s'écria mon père, dans un élan de joie," p. 65). It is in Jean Le Maigre's final vision that the significance of the norm perversion which characterizes the authority of both the world order and the divine order in the novel fully emerges. The two systems come together in a sinister climax as the central figure of the vision pronounces judgment over Jean Le Maigre in the form of *monsieur le Directeur*, who simultaneously evokes the barbaric *directeur* of the *maison de correction*, and the divine justice of God. Consistent with the equivocality of good and evil suggested throughout the novel, Jean Le Maigre is instructed by *Monsieur le Directeur* to strike a posture which denotes equally prayer and execution.

This exposure of the antithesis latent in human norms, will, and experience would remain highly abstract if the reader were unable to recognize the extreme moral situations presented in the novel as in some way representing a dramatization of empirical reality. One of the elements which determine this recognition is the reader's own sense of the gap between norm value and norm function in the reality of everyday life. The fictional world of the novel and the everyday world of the reader converge in the moral ambivalence created by this gap, and this socio-cultural aspect represents an important condition for reader identification throughout the novel.

A second element determining the reader's identification with the strange world of the novel lies in its mythological evocations. The myth as the metaphorical depiction of the universal human experience is alluded to in the text by the mythological features of certain characters.

The most obviously mythological figure is Grand-Mère Antoinette. The associations she evokes have been imaginatively described by Dominique Aury:

> cette ogresse des anciens contes, qui nomme les nouveau-nés, suppute sans chagrin la date probable des enterrements, est-ce la Grand-Mère de la tradition, ou bien une incarnation nouvelle, moitié mythe et moitié cauchemar, de la *Magna Mater*? Oui, avec caparaçons de corsets, de jupons, de bottines lacées, elle est bien la Bonne Déesse qui vous porte, vous châtie, vous nourrit et vous berce, de votre incompréhensible naissance à votre mort vite effacée. Elle est la force vive, la sérénité silencieuse et sans raison au coeur du tourment, la vie acceptée malgré tout quand c'est la mort qu'il faudrait choisir.[39]

The parent figures, too, may be recognized as wearing mythical features. The mother in her involuntary fertility, with the inevitable infant at her breast, in mournful dialogue with the images of her deceased children, bears traits of pre-Christian fertility figures as well as of the *mater dolorosa*. The father, on the other hand, a creature of habit and instinct, demonstrates the masculine principle as an acultural, almost bestial one. The elements connected with the father are those of pre-civilized man.

Another mythical allusion may be recognized in the intervention of the divine. As seen by the figures of the novel, divine intervention is both ambivalent and malicious, and may thus be interpreted as ironically referring to the capriciousness of pre-Christian deities. When Le Septième is born, he appears so unhealthy that Grand-Mère

Antoinette observes: "Si ce n'est pas la méningite, c'est la scarlatine, mais celui-là n'en sortira pas vivant," to which M. *le Curé* ambiguously responds: "Dieu bénit les nombreuses familles" (p. 68), making haste to baptize Le Septième (who, of course, survives). Similarly, Héloïse functions as a sort of *deux ex machina* in preventing the suicide of Jean Le Maigre and Le Septième: "nous avons tenté des suicides que nous n'avons jamais réussis jusqu'au bout, car Héloïse nous trahissait toujours par un cri de joie avant que l'un de nous ait franchi le seuil de l'éternité" (p. 73).

Like the mythical extensions described above, plot-extraneous elements such as the visions, dreams, poems and jingles alienate the familiar features of the fictional reality presented. In addition, they underline the effect of the temporal and perspectival juxtapositions observed earlier, segmenting the linearity of the novel as interpolations from a plane of reality which refers to, but lies outside, the narrative reality itself.

Fragments such as the macabre *Pivoine est mort/Pivoine est mort/A table tout le monde* (p. 66) or Le Septième's homesick letters (*Et la vache Clémentine grand-maman/Et le petit veau grand-maman*, p. 139) are typographically set off in the text, representing rhetorical formalizations which suggest to the reader that, like Jean Le Maigre's poetry, they are not formulated by the designated perspectives themselves.

These features, like the evidence of knowledge exceeding that of the characters, draw attention to the role of the non-dramatized narrator. The effect of these "intrusions" of an otherwise unidentifiable narrator who, nevertheless, refuses to mediate between the reality of the text and the reality of the reader, is to undermine the illusion of immediacy which characterizes novels of social realism, and thus to alienate the presented reality, pointing to the self-consciously aesthetic elements of the text. This self-conscious aesthetic distancing also occurs in the plot, and is always in some way connected with Jean Le Maigre. Its function is to draw the reader's attention to the transforming power of the aesthetic, which, like all the other elements of the novel, has a demonic aspect as well as an edifying, solacing, or divine one. Not only do Jean Le Maigre's visions, dreams and poems reveal an inner life remote from that which surrounds him, it is his poetry and the music performed at his funeral that permits detachment from the circumstances occasioning them. Grand-Mère Antoinette, listening to the novices singing the *Kyrie eleison*, "ne put maîtriser un frisson d'espérance" (p. 112). So spellbound are Le Septième and Pomme at the elaborate musical framing and the pomp and circumstance of Jean Le Maigre's funeral that "il leur arrivait d'oublier le mort qu'ils pleuraient avec tant d'ardeur" (p. 113).

The fact that Jean Le Maigre's *prophéties de famille* all come true in the end may be seen to demonstrate the inevitable consequences of intolerable social conditions, but it also suggests the validity of the ancient notion of the poet as seer. His poetry describes visionary experiences expressing truths which emerge only in the recreation of inarticulate reality. Thus the one element to be affirmed as a possibility of transcending the realities described, the novel seems to propose, is art. It is in the aesthetic reshaping of reality as manifested in the manuscripts of Jean Le Maigre, rather than in the "correction" of reality, that the reader recognizes an escape from the oppressive existence described, an escape that is not only temporary and intermittent, but also illusory.

There are critics who insist that the ending of *Une Saison dans la vie d'Emmanuel* is optimistic.[40] They refer to the symbolic significance of winter's end and approaching spring, to Grand-Mère Antoinette's reiterations that *tout va bien*, and, somewhat astonishingly, even to *l'oncle Armandin*'s evaluation of Pomme's future: "Vendre les journaux est un bon métier" (p. 174). This interpretation can be (as it has been) countered by reference to Le Septième's criminal ambitions, Héloïse's continued prostitution, Pomme's hopeless situation, Jean Le Maigre's death and, finally, the inalterability of the described conditions suggested by the cyclical implications of *saison* as metaphor. This latter interpretation would see Grand-Mère Antoinette's optimism charged with irony for the reader.

It is presumably the intention of the novel that either interpretation of the ending can be validated by the text. In the context of the present study, however, the latter seems the more convincing. Since the principal strategies of the novel are aimed at the disorientation of the reader's own habitual social and literary perceptions, the invocation of both social and literary norms, values and conventions must be taken to have an ironic function. The effect of these strategies then is to let the reader recognize the ironic reversal of norm intention and norm function on the one hand, and the formal ironization of the conventions of social realism on the other.

Reference Notes to Part I and Chapter One

1 This situation is described in Booth's definition of the reliable narrator: "For lack of better terms, I have called a narrator *reliable* when he speaks for or acts in accordance with the norms of the work (which is to say, the implied author's norms), *unreliable* when he does not." Wayne C. Booth, *The Rhetoric of Fiction* (Chicago: University of Chicago Press, 1961), pp. 158-59.

2 For a general overview concerning theories of perspective, see Françoise Van Rossum-Guyon, "Point de vue ou perspective narrative," in *Poétique*, 4 (1970), pp. 476-97.

3 Cf. Norman Friedman, "Point of View in Fiction: The Development of a Critical Concept," in *PMLA*, 70 (December 1955), pp. 1160-64.

4 A rough equivalent to the French phrase used by Van Rossum-Guyon to quote Kayser. The statement alluded to, in its original version, reads: "geht man nun so

weit, den Erzähler aus dem Roman überhaupt zu verbannen,—man hat es im 20. Jahrhundert theoretisch gefordert und praktisch versucht—so beraubt man den Roman seines bedeutsamsten Wesenszuges, dann muß er verkümmern." Wolfgang Kayser, "Wer erzählt den Roman?" in *Die Vortragsreise* (Bern: Francke Verlag, 1950), pp. 82-101, 98.

5 Cf. Iser, *The Act of Reading*, p. 100.

6 Cf. Iser's analysis of *Tom Jones* in *The Implied Reader*, pp. 46-56.

7 Max Dorsinville, *Caliban Without Prospero: Essays on Quebec and Black Literature* (Victoria, B.C.: Press Porcépic, 1974).

8 Jacques Renaud, *Le Cassé* (Montreal: Parti Pris, 1964).

9 Victor-Lévy Beaulieu, *Un Rêve québécois* (Montreal: Éditions du Jour, 1972).

10 Réjean Ducharme, *L'Hiver de force* (Paris: Gallimard, 1973).

11 Marie-Claire Blais, *Une Saison dans la vie d'Emmanuel* (Paris: Grasset, 1966).

12 Réjean Ducharme, *L'Avalée des Avalés* (Paris: Gallimard, 1966).

13 Marie-Claire Blais, *Les Manuscrits de Pauline Archange* (Montreal: Éditions du Jour, 1968).

14 Margaret Atwood, *The Edible Woman* (Toronto: New Canadian Library, 1973).

15 Mordecai Richler, *The Apprenticeship of Duddy Kravitz* (Toronto: McClelland and Stewart, 1969).

16 Margaret Laurence, *The Diviners* (Toronto: McClelland and Stewart, 1974).

17 Ruby Wiebe, *The Blue Mountains of China* (Toronto: McClelland and Stewart, 1970).

18 André Langevin, *Poussière sur la ville* (Montreal: Le Cercle du Livre de France, 1953).

19 Anne Hébert, "Le Torrent," in the volume of *nouvelles* entitled *Le Torrent* (Montreal: Beauchemin, 1950).

20 Franz K. Stanzel, *Typische Formen des Romans* (Göttingen: Vandenhoek und Ruprecht, 1964), pp. 43-44, my translation; the original quotation reads, in context: "die Skala der Möglichkeiten läßt sich ungefähr abstecken, wenn man an ihrem einen Ende die *central intelligence* eines Henry James ansetzt. Am anderen Ende der Skala begegnen Charaktere, die wie matte oder trübe Spiegel nur ein unklares, unvollständiges, oft auch verzerrtes weil unverstandenes Bild ihrer Welt reflektieren."

21 Robertson Davies, *Fifth Business* (New York: New Americaan Library, 1971).

22 Hugh MacLennan, *Two Solitudes* (Toronto: Laurentian Library, Macmillan of Canada, n.d. [1945]).

23 Ernest Buckler, *The Mountain and the Valley* (Toronto: New Canadian Library, 1969).

24 Ethel Wilson, *Swamp Angel* (Toronto: New Canadian Library, 1950).

25 Robertson Davies, *Tempest Tost* (Toronto: Clarke Irwin, 1950).

26 Robertson Davies, *Leaven of Malice* (Toronto: Clarke Irwin, 1954).

27 This narrative intervention notwithstanding, the voice shift remains structurally unmotivated. It does not indicate changes in the structure of consciousness of the heroine, nor in the perspectival view she represents. Her self-alienation and "recovery" represent a gradual linear process throughout the novel, so that the points at which the shifts occur appear arbitrary. Furthermore there are no elements withheld from the first person narration which manifest themselves in the third person, or vice versa. The change in voice, aside from making explicit a process which begins long before the change in voice, has little communicative effect.

28 Gabrielle Roy, *Bonheur d'occasion* (Montreal: Beauchemin, 1965).

29 Roger Lemelin, *Au pied de la pente douce* (Montreal: Éditions de l'Arbre, 1944).

30 Jack Warwick, "Un Cas typique de l'application de la méthode sociologique: les écrivains canadiens-français et leur situation minoritaire," in *Revue de l'Institut de sociologie de Bruxelles*, fascicule 3 (1969), pp. 485-502.

31 Michel Brûlé, "Introduction à l'univers de Marie-Claire Blais," in *Revue de l'Institut de sociologie de Bruxelles*, fascicule 3 (1969), pp. 503-13.

32 Lucien Goldmann, "Note sur deux romans de Marie-Claire Blais," in *Revue de l'Institut de sociologie de Bruxelles*, fascicule 3 (1969), pp. 515-23.

33 Dominique Aury, "Vive le Canada," in *La Nouvelle Revue française*, 28, no. 168 (décembre 1, 1966), pp. 1066-70.

34 Jacques Chessex, "Marie-Claire Blais: *Une Saison dans la vie d'Emmanuel*," in *La Nouvelle Revue française*, 14, no. 168 (décembre 1, 1966), pp. 1093-94.

35 Cf. Madeleine Greffard, "*Une Saison dans la vie d'Emmanuel*, kaléidoscope de la réalité québécoise," in *Les Cahiers de Sainte-Marie*, No. 1 (Montreal), pp. 19-24; see also Vincent Nadeau, *Marie-Claire Blais: Le noir et le tendre* (Montreal: Les Presses de l'Université de Montréal, 1974). Nadeau formulates his thesis as a symbolical analysis, but seems to view the novel chiefly as a reflection of the social panorama of rural Quebec; cf. also Suzanne Paradis's section on Marie-Claire Blais in *Le personnage féminin dans le roman féminin canadien-français de 1884 à 1966* (Quebec: Éditions Garneau, 1966), pp. 177-97.

36 Jean Onimus, "Les jeux de l'humour et du roman," in *La Table Ronde*, no. 230 (mars 1967), p. 129.

37 Cf. Yves Berger, "Zola au Canada," in *Le Nouvel Observateur*, no. 77 (mai 4 and 10, 1966), p. 31; also J.-C., "L'Enfer de Marie-Claire," in *L'Express*, no. 776 (mai 2 and 8, 1966), p. 114; cf. Robert Buckeye, "Nouveau Roman made easy," in *Canadian Literature*, no. 31 (Winter 1967), pp. 67-69.

38 In the society of rural French Canada, the authority role of husband and father is also challenged from another quarter. As Vincent Nadeau observes, the father plays "le rôle effacé qu'y jouent les hommes autres que les religieux ayant officiellement renoncé à leur virilité" (*Marie-Claire Blais: le noir et le tendre*, p. 19).

39 Aury, "Vive le Canada," p. 1068.

40 Michel Brûlé, for example, justifies the interpretation of an optimistic ending saying: "*Une* saison: ce qui implique l'avenir; d'autre part, le nom d'Emmanuel a une connotation d'espérance" ("Introduction à l'univers de Marie-Claire Blais," p. 512).

TWO

Relationships between Social and Literary Norm Repertoires

Qu'on le veuille ou non, ... une nouvelle littérature se précise. Elle n'est plus française, elle n'est plus canadienne. ... Elle ne sera pas joual. ... Ce qu'elle sera, ... importe peu. Nous sommes sortis du mimétisme littéraire qui n'était utile qu'aux critiques. Ça leur permettait de porter des jugements de valeur sans risquer de se tromper.

Laurent Girouard

Aussi paradoxal que cela puisse paraître, le mouvement qui s'est dessiné ces dernières années commence par la prise de conscience des limites d'un art pseudo-réaliste, voué à l'expression pure et simple du réel, et se termine par l'évasion, d'abord rêvée puis matérialisée, du milieu.

Clement Moîsan

In the novels discussed so far, it was the social norm repertoire presented in the fictional reality that constituted the central interest. Although the explicit invocation of certain elements of the literary repertoire can be observed in these novels, such references usually remain relatively oblique. The Rilke allusion (in the title of *Two Solitudes*) and, in the same novel, the Homeric allusions recognizable in the description of Paul Tallard's journey around the world, at the end

Reference notes for Chapter Two are found on pp. 71-73.

of which Heather Methuen, a faithful Penelope, awaits him in Montreal, are two obvious examples of explicit intertextual invocation. But at no point do such references occur to demonstrate the violation of a previous or existing literary convention, as is the case in the novels we are about to examine. Even in Marie-Claire Blais's novel, the conventions of social realism are invoked only to expose their inadequacy in describing those aspects of the human condition that the social norm repertoire itself conceals. The reader's focus remains fixed upon these darker aspects of the human condition rather than upon the violation of the narrative conventions through which they are communicated.

In *Fifth Business*, *L'Hiver de force*, and *Poussière sur la ville*, recognition of deviations from the patterns and conventions of the literary genre they invoke plays a central role in the way the reader experiences the text. These deviations manifest themselves in a number of ways, two of the most important of which are manipulation of the traditions of first-person narrative (deformation of the familiar literary repertoire) and the increasing defamiliarization of the social norm repertoire presented.[1] The resulting changes in the relationships between the various repertoires—that between text and reader repertoire on the one hand, and that between social and literary repertoires on the other—are, to a large extent, interdependent.

The effect of *Two Solitudes*, *The Edible Woman*, and *Une Saison dans la vie d'Emmanuel* depends to a large extent upon the reader's familiarity with the social repertoire of norms to which they allude. The "overlapping" of the norms predominant in the fictional reality of the text and those determining the reader's everyday experience is a necessary precondition for the intended literary communication, exposure of the deficiencies of a normative system very much like the reader's own.

In André Langevin's *Poussière sur la ville*, Réjean Ducharme's *L'Hiver de force*, and Robertson Davies's *Fifth Business* the relationship between text and reader repertoires may be described as "tangential" rather than as overlapping. For the effect intended by these novels is to reveal the unfamiliar world which lies behind the reader's own everyday experience: subconscious and unconscious motivations and the mechanisms governing interaction with one's environment. Here, the points of tangency between text and reader repertoires, or those elements which at first are taken to be familiar, serve as points of orientation as the reader enters the unfamiliar world of the text. On the other hand these familiar items are transformed in the unfamiliar context, in a process which Iser calls depragmatization.[2] This type of novel—that is, a novel whose repertoire is presented as tangent to that of the reader rather than as overlapping with it, but which presents an "intelligible" central perspective—de-automizes the reader's response to the familiar by simultaneously designating and alienating the familiar. The familiar elements (i.e. those shared by text and reader) direct the reader towards the recognition and motivation of unfamiliar relationships and processes.

This "defamiliarization" of the familiar repertoire is to a great extent dependent upon the invocation of familiar literary conventions and reader recognition of their deformation. Inevitably, the process of literary communication itself emerges more and more into the foreground of the readers' consciousness as they go about reading these novels.

As the "defamiliarization" of the familiar social repertoire and the "deformation" of familiar literary conventions represent conditions to be fulfilled if the intention of the text is to be communicated, narrative elements with functions differing from those recognized in the novels discussed earlier begin to emerge. Thus with the novels of André Langevin, Réjean Ducharme and Robertson Davies, the relevance of perspectival arrangements becomes secondary to the significance of other narrative processes involving "type" and "consciousness" of the narrator and/or central perspective.

As these categories imply, the novels are concerned with the perceptualization of the central figures' experience of the fictional reality described, rather than with calling into question the social norms governing that reality. These novels place the perceptual norms in the foreground. Since the reading experience itself represents a perceptual process, one of the effects of these texts is to make readers conscious of their own habitual patterns of perception, and so induce a questioning of the way they experience everyday reality as well as the fictional reality in the text they are reading.

In all three novels, the manipulation of certain conventions governing the first-person novel constitutes the principal narrative strategy, focussing on the perceptual process as the intended object of communication. But since in the different novels different conventions of the genre are alluded to, and the manipulation of the conventions themselves takes the reader in very different directions, it may be well to review the distinctive features of the first-person novel as a narrative genre.

In his discussion of the first-person novel (in his typology of "narrative situations"),[3] Franz K. Stanzel distinguishes between the role of the first-person narrator standing at the periphery of the events (this is frequently the case, for instance, in Dostoievsky's novels) and the quasi-autobiographical novel. In the former type of first-person narrative, "perspectivization" and "mediation" represent central functions of the first-person narrator.[4] In the latter type, which follows the "confessional" tradition, the focus of interest is on the tension resulting from the first-person narrator's experiences of the events on the one hand and the narrator's telling of the story on the other. The essential feature of the latter type of narrative is, according to Stanzel, that the first-person narrator tells the story "after having experienced a transformation effected through repentance, conversion or insight."[5] Stanzel presents numerous examples of how this relationship between the first-person narrator as teller of the story and as the central figure experiencing the events has been varied in modern fiction. Thus he identifies, for example, quoting Hans Robert Jauss, the interrelationship between the memory of the first-person narrator and the first-person narrator in the act of remembering as the "secret principle [underlying] the composition of Proust's *A la recherche du temps perdu*."[6]

When the representational focus lies on the narrator experiencing rather than recounting events, the effect can be, according to Stanzel, on the one hand the reader's heightened interest in "plot" and "character," which is the case in the adventure novel, and on the other hand the reader's access to and involvement in the "inner world" or the inner consciousness of the first-person narrator.[7]

Fifth Business, at least at first glance, appears to fall neatly into the "confessional" category. The narrator retrospectively telling his story mediates between the past reality in which the story is situated and the fictional present of the narrative frame. Following the pattern of the *Bildungsroman*, the novel presents the dual perspective of the narrator as hero experiencing the events and the narrator as teller recounting them with his retrospective awareness and insight. But although it corresponds in structure to the paradigmatic elements of the *Bildungsroman*, *Fifth Business* invokes the genre to problematize it. The reader's attention is drawn not so much to the "transformation" of the narrator as manifested in his dual perspective, but rather to the principle of perceptual selectivity which brings it about. The effect of the novel hinges upon the reader's recognition of the principle of selectivity as determining not only what is to be communicated in the work of fiction, but as governing the processes involved in everyday perception as well. By itself pointing to the virtual aspects of the experiences described in it, the novel induces the reader to acknowledge these aspects and so to recognize more fully the significance of the actualized alternatives.

In *L'Hiver de force* and *Poussière sur la ville*, the narrator(s) constituting the central perspective do not mediate between a present frame of fictional reality and past events, but describe the events in the present and as they occur. These two novels describe not the acquisition of insight through the amassing of experience, but a process of alienation from the familiarity of past experience. Indeed, the structures of consciousness of the main characters are foregrounded in such a way that their respective backgrounds of experience become in various ways deformed. In the perception of the reader, these deformations are so extreme that the interrelationships, the interaction, between the individual and the "other" in the form of society becomes in some sense absurd.

Inevitably, this more radical defamiliarization of a familiar repertoire increases textual indeterminacy; that is, readers are forced to become more actively involved in constructing relationships and motivations, and also in interpreting the significance of events, than in novels in which they are asked merely to affirm or negate the positions presented by the various perspectives. In the two *québécois* novels, the alienation of the main characters from their reality as a function of defamiliarization is largely responsible for the textual indeterminacy, while in *Fifth Business* the critical self-awareness of the first-person narrator/hero results in an overdeterminacy in describing persons and events that itself contributes to the general indeterminacy of the text.

Thematically, each of the three novels marks a kind of historic milestone in English-Canadian and *québécois* fiction. *Poussière sur la ville* is widely held to be the first existential novel to be written in Quebec; *L'Hiver de force* may be seen almost as a documentation of the political and cultural co-opting of the 1960s revolutionary movement; *Fifth Business* may be read as the individual manifestation of the experience of growth and self-awareness, of the maturing and cosmopolitizing of Canadian society as a collective whole. With regard to the effects they produce in the reader, these texts also mark the emergence of various trends in the English-Canadian and *québécois* novel which have in common an increasing preoccupation with the processes underlying literary communication itself.

Thus the following study of André Langevin's *Poussière sur la ville* focuses on the text's lack of narrative mediation and perspectival relativization and on its metafictional, self-referential quality, rather than on its thematic status as an existentialist *roman à thèse*. Réjean Ducharme's *L'Hiver de force* is examined more in terms of the strategies by which the sense of meaninglessness, ideological hollowness and exhaustion of the *avant-garde* in the post-sixties era are communicated, rather than for these thematic elements themselves. In Robertson Davies's *Fifth Business*, the effects of the novel are seen to be brought about by the strategies invoking the virtual aspects of the characters and events described as opposed to the actualized alternatives. Thus it is not so much the thematic of the novel, but its overdeterminacy (a form of indeterminacy) that brings about the reader's (as opposed to the characters') heightened sense of self-awareness.

1.   **First-person narration as a function of alienation: André Langevin's *Poussière sur la ville***

While *Bonheur d'occasion* and *Au pied de la pente douce* give what in traditional criticism is called a "representative view of life," a *tranche de vie*, the inner worlds dwelt in by the central figures of *Poussière sur la ville* are determined by metaphysical experiences which let the external world take on the irreality of a nightmare. It is no longer a question of exposing the personal dilemmas and inadequacies of the various characters or the deficiencies of the system of norms that are seen to determine them; Langevin's novel reveals the innermost depths of experience of the central figures, characterized precisely by their inability to perceive the inner reality in which the other lives, or to communicate their own inner reality to the other.

Speaking of the characters in Dostoievsky's novels, Nathalie Sarraute describes their ultimate motivations as an attempt to "establish contact." Her description expresses with a singular precision certain features governing the behaviour of the two central figures of *Poussière sur la ville*.

> C'est [un] besoin continuel et presque maniaque de contact, d'une impossible et apaisante étreinte, qui tire [les] personnages comme un vertige, les incite à tout moment à essayer par n'importe quel moyen de se frayer un chemin jusqu'à autrui, de pénétrer en lui le plus loin possible, de lui faire perdre son inquiétante, son insupportable opacité, et les pousse à s'ouvrir à lui à leur tour, à lui révéler leur plus secrets replis.[8]

In its representation of voluntary death as the ultimate liberation from the subjectivity of the human consciousness, whose incommunicability determines the isolation and alienation of the individual, *Poussière sur la ville* (1953) may be seen to have initiated French-Canadian fiction into the then existentialist *avant-garde*. If the novel nevertheless seems to be less an existentialist *roman à thèse* than, say, *L'Étranger* or *La Nausée*, this is perhaps due in part to the fact that it has not entirely renounced certain conventions of the so-called "psychological" novel and its antecedents. While abstaining from that hallmark of the "psychological" novel, the interior monologue representing a stream of consciousness, the way in which the external world is perceived by the consciousness of the first-person narrator results in a symbolic structure in which this consciousness itself is reflected.

The reader's difficulty in construing an external world which would reveal the nature of its representation by Alain lies in the fact that both the events of the novel and the milieu in which they take place are communicated to the reader by the manipulation of certain conventions governing the first-person novel. If the traditional motivation to use the first-person narrative was to lend authenticity and credibility to the story, and thus to verify the objective existence of the world presented in the novel, it is used here to "verify its subjectivity, its reality as the matter of the consciousness of the first-person narrator, or rather as an ultimately inseparable combination of the objective . . . external world and the subjective . . . internal one."[9]

Throughout the novel, only one perspective is available to the reader, and that is the narrator's. The reader is submerged in an alien reality unrelativized by conflicting perspectival views or other forms of mediation. Furthermore, the novel deprives the reader of the double dimension of the narrator as the one who tells his story on the one hand and the one who experiences it on the other. This double dimension, traditionally created by a narrator recounting past experience out of the heightened perceptual and moral awareness manifested by the narrator as "teller," creates a dual frame of reference in which two different views are perceived as interacting to allow the intended message to be communicated to the reader. In *Poussière sur la ville*, no alternative frame of reference is available to the reader, neither that of temporal distance constituted by allusion to the past, nor that of an alternative perspective. The first-person narrator relates the story in the present tense and denies the reader any knowledge lying beyond the (subjective) experience of the moment.

Thus readers perceive the narrator's experiences from the standpoint of a consciousness simultaneously familiar (in their inevitable identification with Alain) and alien (in their awareness of the deformation of an external reality unavailable to them). The reader's necessary acceptance of the narrator's views is thus always conditional, because it is undermined by the former's recognition of the latter's subjectivity. In this sense the reader is always reading against the text, for reader resistance to the narrator's subjectivity cannot be dissolved until the event of Madeleine's suicide at the end of the novel. Even then this resistance remains diffused, since there is no alternative reality (except the act of suicide itself, which lacks the context of Madeleine's own subjective consciousness) to which the reader can attach it in order to justify it.

The norms invoked by the text are thus indicated not by the presentation of a number of contrasting perspectival views, but by their elimination. The dialectic process by which previously held views are altered or renounced takes place within the isolated consciousness of the narrator himself. Accordingly, in attempting to understand what has brought about the narrator's situation, namely the marriage crisis, his isolation from the community, and his self-alienation, the reader is constantly forced to rest in the negative, since there is no perspective view to overrule that of the narrator, which is both deficient and self-contradictory.

The uncertainty and doubt in which the novel leaves its readers is a result of their recognition that the narrator's "novel," so eloquent in its articulation of the experiencing consciousness, has a virtual and complementary counterpart. This is the "novel" of Madeleine, or, put differently, penetration of the consciousness of Madeleine, which represents the supreme and impossible goal of Alain. The impossibility of this contact is expressed both by the events of the novel and through the narrative strategies themselves, in their presentation of the human consciousness as a prison of subjectivity of all perception, the escape from which in rare moments of mutual revelation, of communication with an alien consciousness, is inevitably illusory.

Against the background of the subjectivity of human consciousness, however, Madeleine's suicide represents an act of liberation, self-determination, and unambiguous communication; its effect in the novel is to let Alain seek to achieve contact with his fellow human beings in his understanding of the isolation resulting from the human condition.

The thematic aspects of *Poussière sur la ville* demonstrating its significance as one of the first existentialist novels to be published in Canada have been discussed extensively in other studies of Langevin's fiction,[10] and need not be dwelt on here.

It should be pointed out, however, that in connection with its invocation of perceptualization as a normatively determined process it may be seen as a highly self-referential novel as well, anticipating the subsequent development of the *québécois* novel in this direction. This self-referentiality is at its most explicit in the illusory transformation of external reality through light, snow, or dust, which may be seen as analogous to the experience of the illusory and "alienated" fictional reality of the novel. It can also be observed in the analogous relationship between Alain's effort to seek access and "establish contact" with Madeleine and the reader's attempt to "penetrate" the text as the manifestation of an alien, external, and therefore "opaque" consciousness.

Other metaliterary allusions, referring to the relationship between text and reader, can be recognized in the novel's repeated instances of communicatory failure and in the multiplicity of possible motives for Madeleine's suicide. While failed communication may be seen to refer to the conditions governing all processes of communication, which would include the interaction between text and reader in the reading process, the motivation of Madeleine's suicide represents a specific act of interpretation by the reader. Consistent with the thematic of the novel, various conjectures can be validated to some extent by reference to the situations and events described. But like the "meaning" of the novel, as the product of an alien consciousness, the motive for

Madeleine's suicide remains ultimately as ambiguous and elusive for the reader as it does for Alain. Indeed, this uncertainty and ambiguity may be seen to conceal a potentially absurd dimension of the unequivocal act. Confronted with Madeleine's suicide, Alain reflects: "Au fond, c'est peut-être tout simple. Madeleine n'a peut-être jamais cru réellement au revolver" (p. 193).

The metaliterary and auto-referential elements of the novel, together with the ambiguity and "opacity" of the consciousness of its central figure, characterize the increasing degree of indeterminacy to be found in many of the *québécois* novels which have appeared since *Poussière sur la ville*. Though less radically indeterminate than some of the more recent novels, it may be seen to mark the definitive "emancipation" of *québécois* fiction from the resolutely realistic novel characteristic of the decades preceding its publication.

2.   Réjean Ducharme's *L'Hiver de force* and the decontextualization of narrative

In Réjean Ducharme's *L'Hiver de force*, as in *Poussière sur la ville*, solitude, alienation, and the difficulty of communication may be said to constitute major themes. But the inadequacy of these concepts in describing the effect of *L'Hiver de force* points to the increasing preoccupation in *québécois* fiction with the complex relationship between social and literary norm repertoires, or what Wolfgang Iser has more technically called the "system of equivalences" designated by the text.[11]

In *Poussière sur la ville* the individual living-out of subjectivity as an existential problem, and in *Une Saison dans la vie d''Emmanuel* the problematization of a given socio-cultural system, were presented through communicatory strategies whose deviation from certain traditional conventions allowed the given thematic complex to emerge as such. *L'Hiver de force* presents an account of contemporary reality whose sense of immediacy is due not only to its apparent familiarity to the reader, but also to its "documentary" form, to the seeming absence of any literary frame of reference. *L'Hiver de force* declares itself (through the narrator) as a kind of non-selective account of everyday life ("On va se regarder faire puis je vais tout noter avec ma belle écriture," p. 15) in what the reader readily recognizes to be the counter-culture of the early 1970s (*la Contre-Culture de Consommation*, p. 194). But the narrator is not only the narrator, who describes his text as *notre vie enregistrée*, he is also half a couple which collectively constitutes the central perspective of what, on the cover of the book, is called a *récit*.[12] Furthermore, the final authority as to the communicatory intention of *L'Hiver de force* does not lie with the narrator, but with the implied presence of an extra-textual perspective which betrays its existence in the mystifying epigraphs, section headings and footnotes.[13] The reader is thus faced from the outset with a mass of contradictory "instructions" as to how the text is to be read, and is forced to suspend the habitual literary expectations determined by the genre being invoked and the nature of the reality it is intended to convey. The reading of the text itself, then, represents an act of acquiescence and complicity with the narrator, while the reader remains wholly in the dark as to where this complicity will lead.

The very first sentence indicates that this initial effect is to be somehow related to the kind of reality presented by the narrator. *L'Hiver de force* opens with what sounds like a resounding cliché: "Comme malgré nous (personne n'aime ça être méchant, amer, réactionnaire), nous passons notre temps à dire du mal" (p. 13). This apparently banal statement, however, fulfils a variety of functions in creating an initial relationship between text and reader. As the subject of what seems to be presented as a universal truth, the pronoun *nous* refers to the reader as much as to the speaker/narrator, evoking an identification psychologically reinforced by the apologetic *comme malgré nous*. But it is the rhetoric between parentheses that motives the statement itself. The parallel adjectives read like a formula to describe undesirable elements of human behaviour. The ideologically coloured final adjective thus seems to indicate the ideological position of the narrator. At the same time the rhetorical context of the word *réaction-naire* creates an ironic distance between the narrator and what he is saying. For in implicitly equating *méchant* and *amer* with the leftist catchword *réactionnaire*, the narrator reduces the parenthesized state-ment itself to a cliché, this one, however, situated not in the psychol-ogistic truisms of conventional society, but within the counter-culture of the protest movements. To perceive the three adjectives in paren-theses as a formula or cliché describing an undesirable attitude is, however, to perceive the statement as both morally and ideologically normative. The reader's formulation of the norm thus initiates the reader's own participation in the text by inviting a response, which, in its equivocal evocation of conventional and leftist ideologies, cannot, at this point, be reduced to mere affirmation or negation of the pre-sented stance.

The statement, then, provokes readers of the novel not only by implicitly attributing to them a stance which they do not necessarily have, but also by disorienting them with respect to the kind of identifi-cation with the narrator expected of them. The adequacy of their response is bound up with their being able to situate the position of the narrator, and their uncertainty in doing so determines their anticipa-tion of what is to follow in the text.

The effect of this opening sentence may be seen to illustrate one of the central strategies governing the entire novel. The attitudes and values of the leftist *avant-garde*, later defined more specifically as the *avant-garde* of Quebec, form the socio-cultural frame of reference for the central perspective of the novel. In confusing the values of conventional society with those of the counter-culture, and in setting the central perspective in opposition to both, the novel does two things. First of all, it exposes the revolutionary *avant-garde* as being as rigid and prescriptive as the conventional system, for it demands the same kind of conformity by imposing the same kind of sanctions on those who remain ideologically outside it. Secondly, it disorients the reader by presenting the perspectival views of the central figures as equivocal and so withholding positions which could be recognized as valid and with which the reader could therefore identify. These two effects are achieved by processes which may be referred to, respectively, as the *ideological disqualification of the socio-cultural repertoire* and the *decontextualization of narrative*.

The ideological disqualification of the socio-cultural repertoire

As has already been indicated, the principal social frame of reference in *L'Hiver de force* is the counter-culture, which is presented as a closed and highly normative system. There is little or no field of conflict between it and the conventional systems, the possibility of whose validity is thus more or less excluded by the central perspective presented in the text.

An alternative to the social and cultural alienation determining modern life (i.e. that of the counter-culture as well as that of conventional society) is formulated early in the text, in Nicole's proposal to create an existential void ("Faisons qu'y ait plus rien," p. 14). But having already indicated to the reader that "En tout cas, on mène une vie platte" (p. 15), the narrator deflates the anticipation generated by the implied negation of both the conventional systems and the counter-culture in much the same way that the reader's literary expectations have been cancelled by the withholding of a generic context. The text thus initiates a certain curiosity as to how the central figures will go about creating their *néant* (and also as to how the text will go about communicating it), only in the subsequent chapter to submerge the reader in the minutest details of their everyday life, in other words, in the seemingly undiscriminating "chronicle."

The central figures' desire to abolish the reality surrounding them can only be motivated by the intolerability, inalterability, and absence of an alternative characterizing their day-to-day life. The text supplies this motivation by disallowing the invocation of any alternative reality or alien cultural context. In this sense, too, André's "chronicle" of his and Nicole's everyday life presents a sort of documentary, the individual elements of which constitute the daily experience not only of André and Nicole, but also that of the reader. The consensus between

text and reader achieved by the allusion to a common everyday repertoire is broken only in the individual response to it.

Initially, text and reader repertoires seem to overlap to a large
extent. But because of this high degree of apparent overlapping the
behaviour of André and Nicole—which is seen as a response to and as
a consequence of their reality—emerges as an absurdity, the possible
motivation of which holds out the only promise for the emergence of
its meaning. Unlike the novels of Samuel Beckett, in which the central
figures inhabit a world in which not only the meaning of present culture, but its very existence, seems to be denied, *L'Hiver de force* makes
use of the socio-cultural repertoire to expose its own absurdity, which
is therefore seen to generate the absurd behaviour of its central figures.

This exposure of the absurdity of the socio-cultural repertoire is
achieved first and foremost by the ideological disqualification of both
conventional and *avant-garde* values. This disqualification is communicated to the reader not only through the explicit aversions to both
expressed by the narrator and Nicole, but also through ridicule created
by parodistic inflation. In order for the reader to be able to perceive the
world represented in the text—which appears as one largely coincid-
ing with the reader's own—as a totality stripped of cultural context,
the text presents long catalogues of elements constituting a kind of
socio-cultural inventory: "Nous disons du mal ... de tous les hippies,
artistes, journalistes, taoïstes, nudistes, *de tous ceux qui nous aiment,*"
and: "Mille masses en mouvement, armées de micros, de typos, de
photos, de labos se disputent notre petite idée" (p. 13). But undercutting both the narrator's declarations and the parody itself is the equally
explicit ambivalence of the central figures toward their own position in
the reality they describe. In the views they present of themselves, the
reader recognizes the negation of both the socio-cultural apparatuses
striving to swallow them up under pretext of knowing "où est notre
bien," but also the degree to which they have internalized the values of
social belonging, public success and system-functioning shared by the
two socio-cultural streams. Their non-conforming to these values lets
them feel *jaloux, incapable, peureux, crachés, solitaires, malsains et
malpropres* (pp. 13-14). Yet it is this sense of alienation and failure that
guarantees André and Nicole's incorruptibility by either system, for
though pretending to reject the *avant-garde* as well as the conventional
system, they are in fact rejected by both as failures. The "straight"
norms subvert the counter-culture to co-opt precisely its foremost
opponents by their very function as leaders. Success remains the
primary norm, and its achievement coincides with the corruption and
betrayal of the revolutionary values of the *avant-garde.*

The exposure of the counter-culture myth as an alternative to
conventional systems is most clearly illustrated by Petit Pois, the beau-

tiful separatist-writer-actress-filmmaker and unchallenged queen of Montreal's *avant-garde* set, and her husband Roger, leader of a political Marxist-separatist group, editor of a newspaper and author of diverse propaganda tracts. In spite of Roger's holding what is obviously a key position in the media, fraternal communication with the masses to be liberated and revolutionized is, presumably, impossible. Like many of the secondary figures, Roger, the leading representative of Quebec's art-and-politics scene, speaks trendy Parisian.

While battling the "system" to achieve the liberation of Quebec, abolition of the social hierarchy and economic equality, Roger and Petit Pois inhabit a luxurious house in Outremont, keep a cleaning woman and frequent chic, expensive restaurants. Roger has a fashionable office downtown and an appropriately snobbish secretary. He reveals himself as a master of business psychology: when he requests the services of André and Nicole to proof-read a 400-page volume on Marxism, a proposal which André and Nicole, with their feelings of insecurity, interpret as an act of charity, Roger doubles their ridiculously low asking-fee of $25, concealing, in good capitalist tradition, his exploitation of his destitute friends behind what appears to be a gesture of generosity.

If Petit Pois and particularly Roger Degrandpré represent the living-out of what may be somewhat anachronistically termed an ideological double standard, the mechanism by which this double standard is produced is illustrated through Laïnou, André and Nicole's aging, ugly, love-starved artist friend. Having for years reiterated her contempt for official policies of aesthetic evaluation ("Leur gloire je l'ai de travers dans le cul; ma gloire c'est quand ils vont tous être d'accord pour dire que mon oeuvre vaut pas de la marde" p. 17), she is *délirante* at her triumph at the *concours international de Québec*. The reader recognizes, along with André and Nicole, that there is no better way of co-opting a dissident than by bestowing success upon him.

It is through Laïnou, too, that the aesthetic validity of the *avant-garde* is questioned. Laïnou's *taches*, according to André, represent a simplistic symbolism describing the painter's emotional state: "Laïnou est peintre-spécialiste. Spécialiste de deux sortes de taches: les bleues et les jaunes. Le jaune symbolise la joie; le bleu c'est le contraire" (p. 18).

But it is the commercialization which pervades all aspects of modern life—the counter-culture as well as the conventional system—that is perhaps the most persistently invoked element throughout the novel. It manifests itself in the exploitive price policies of a marketing system ruled by advertisers: the narrator often quotes prices, and they are inevitably those familiar tolerance-threshold figures of $1.87, $5.99, etc. Conversely, whenever André and Nicole are obliged to sell anything, they invariably get round sums—$10 for the radio, $15 for the stove. More subversive still is the effect of a consumer-duping system on language itself. Commerce enters every-day language in the puns of advertising slogans; trademarks become the metaphors of ordinary discourse: "Te brosses-tu les dents avec le même Crest que les autres, toi?" (p. 103).

This deformation of language is presented not only as a result of the commercialization of almost every aspect of modern life, but also as a consequence of modern communication and media. Petit Pois's tele-gram is an abstruse jumble created by the mindless processes of automated encoding and decoding; national bilingualism results in gross redundancy. This deformation of language itself has as conse-quence a corresponding deformation of that which it signifies. To avoid sullying their own utterances by a language thus corrupted, Nicole and André resort to deformations of their own ("twistesse") and to foreign languages ("*grosser Lärm*").

Many elements of the everyday reality described in *L'Hiver de force* reflect aspects of the reader's own day-to-day life. The communicatory mode of the novel, for instance the rhetorical inflation with which both the counter-culture and a society conditioned by the consumer manip-ulation of an automated technocracy are described, may make the reader aware of the limited possibilities to resist the *Zeitgeist* which is being invoked. Similarly, the reader may be more apt to recognize the deformation of language itself by the imperatives of the consumer culture, through the occurrence in the novel of brand-names and trademarks to designate objects, a kind of metaphor readers are unac-customed to in literary texts. The jargon of the counter-culture reflects the same kind of linguistic reductivity, as in Petit Pois's use of *halluciner* to describe all negative experiences and *flipper* to describe those she considers positive.

These features of the text, though they may heighten the reader's sensitivity to manifestations of the same phenomena in the empirical world, are nevertheless self-motivating because of the reader's famil-iarity with the ideologies from which they spring. What actively involves the reader in trying to determine the communicatory inten-tion of the text is, on the one hand, the necessity of explaining the alien responses of the central figures to the reality presented, and, on the other, the attempt to identify the position of the extra-textual narrator whose presence is indicated by the mysterious epigraphs which pre-cede the novel proper, by the section headings, and by the "explan-atory" footnotes.

While the reader is constantly assembling elements from the social reality presented in the text which might account for the behaviour of the central characters, there is never any assurance that this is the kind of "explanation" meant by the text. To perceive the central figures' behaviour merely as a response to their reality would be to ignore those elements of the text designating the literary repertoire—implicitly present in the reader's recognition that it is being withheld.

Yet the social repertoire presented through the reality of the text provides a considerable range of possibilities for motivating the attitudes and actions of the central characters. Each episode of the novel illustrates their alienation from a reality determined by mass movements. Thus their painful impotence in responding to the "lows" and "highs" of their adored Petit Pois may be seen to represent their victimization by the emotional self-indulgence of a society conditioned by popular self-help psychology. In André and Nicole's disapproval of Laïnou's *taches* and her lover P.D.'s "bijoux de boîtes à surprise qu'il trempe dans l'acrylique et qu'il revend à des prix de fou avec ses initiales gravées partout" (p. 19), and in the quasi-commercial sexual relationship between the two, artistic and sexual self-indulgence are evoked as demonstrations of the triumph of cleverness and novelty over talent and work, and of the deterioration of sex to a commercially available commodity.

The record-disposing incidents can be interpreted as a negative response to the universal availability of mechanically reproducible aesthetic events (films, TV, records) which has replaced the uniqueness and also fragmented the totality of aesthetic experience. The discarding of a record after listening to it only once may be seen as a symbolic if futile attempt to restore wholeness and uniqueness of effect to the aesthetic event.

Like throwing away records, watching entertainment films for the *n*th time *pour les toffer* may be seen as a negation of culture as a commercial commodity. In the manner of Godard heroes, André and Nicole turn their heads away when commercials interrupt the films they are watching in order not to get them *pleine face*, a gesture which, like seeing the films themselves, is futile and perceived by no one but themselves.

If there is any one episode in *L'Hiver de force* which defines individual alienation from a culture characterized by profit and convenience, it is perhaps to be found in Nicole's carefully sealing her orange peel in an old telegram envelope to see if it will *finir par faire quelque chose* (p. 183). Predictably, the paper of the envelope fades and the peelings inside dry, "on sent qu'ils se pulvériseraient sous la moindre pression" (p. 183). This banal experience of the transitoriness of material things increases the reader's sense of the deterioration of the central figures' relations with the reality surrounding them, and synecdochically expresses their own sense of their empty and therefore perilous existence. The envelope, having served its one-time purpose, is stripped of its original function—is decontextualized—and becomes an empty and purposeless shell whose original content, like that of the orange peel inside it, has been "consumed." Both are useless and to be discarded, and, as a gesture, the episode may be seen as a fulfilment of Nicole's exhortation at the beginning of the novel: "Faisons qu'y ait plus rien."

The decontextualization of narrative

The reader's difficulty in motivating the behaviour of the central figures is in part due to its eccentricity: André and Nicole's throwing their long-coveted Boris Vian record out the window after playing it only once—having spent months watching and waiting for it to be reduced in price so that they could afford to buy it—is a case in point. But there is a more general difficulty confronting the reader which is determined by a structural feature of the novel. Traditionally in the journal, the chronicle, and other narrative forms in which the first-person narrator also represents the central perspective, reader identification with the central/narrative perspective could be depended upon to mediate between the reader's own world and the alien reality presented by the text; this principle is reversed in *L'Hiver de force*. The fictional reality it describes is by and large familiar and similar to the reader's own, while the erratic behaviour of the central figures frustrates the reader's attempts to identify with them. For in the reader's previous reading experience, identification with the hero or heroine has been created by the ability to understand and sympathize with their behaviour, and was instrumental in the ability to grasp the communicatory intention of the text. The reversal of the habitual pattern presents a crucial problem. While the reader can readily identify with the non-conforming hero of past literature and even with the anti-hero predominating in the literature of this century, since their behaviour represents a recognizable reaction to a given aspect of the described reality, the unusual and alienating behaviour of André and Nicole is baffling. The only context available by which it can be explained is the presented reality in its totality, yet it is a reality very similar to that in which the reader himself dwells. Furthermore, since most of their erratic actions are neither public nor directed "at" any specific individual or institution, they seem to have no goal except for the achievement of the action itself. The reader, then, is deprived of a causal structure into which the actions of the central figures might fit as reactions to given situations. The reader's activity throughout the reading of the text is therefore directed towards the construction of a dialectical system by which the behaviour of the central figures might be interpreted.

Here, however, the reader faces a curious dilemma: the generic hybridism of the text. The vivid if parodistic invocation of the reader's own everyday reality indicates that it is to be perceived as part of an interaction with the central figures, and so brings up the question of the "validity" of André and Nicole's behaviour. At the same time this behaviour is often so unusual that the reader is reminded of the absurdity of some of Beckett's heroes, whose fantastic reality, however, bears little or no resemblance either to the reader's own or to that dwelt in by André and Nicole, and precludes the question of validity of interaction with it.

Apart from the behaviour and attitudes of André and Nicole, there is a difficulty on the part of the reader in trying to establish a motivation for the narration itself. This involves not only André's diffuse "chronicle," but also its implied frame (indicated by the epigraphs, section headings and footnotes). All of these features contribute to what may be described as the *decontextualization* of the narrative. André's recording of his and Nicole's day-to-day experience remains undefined by any articulated purpose. As a record or document, it goes one better than the descriptive "documentary" (the genre it invokes) whose purpose is to measure the subject "documented" against the present culture, or the consensus of values producing it. In *L'Hiver de force* the point is that the reader is denied any such context. The day-to-day reality of the present culture constitutes the "subject" of the documentary, which remains unrelativized by any reference to a larger reality which could provide a focus. G.-André Vachon has described this decontextualization in a comparison of the novel to a cubist painting:

> Comme une toile cubiste, sans horizon ni marges, qui accumule jusqu'au bord de son cadre objets et fragments d'objets hétéroclites, *L'Hiver* recenserait, s'il le pouvait, et dans un ordre toujours linéaire, l'infinité des paroles et des choses dont est faite une quelconque "tranche de vie."[14]

This feature communicates the sense of meaninglessness of the world described in the text as much as the platitude- and cliché-ridden language with which it expresses itself, and of which the bizarre and futile gestures performed by André and Nicole form an essential part.

Though the views presented by André (who as chronicler declares the unanimity of his views and those of Nicole) represent a negation of the CCC (=*Contre-Culture de Consommation*) in which they dwell, their behaviour never suggests the possibility of a reality beyond the daily manifestations of this CCC-determined one. Since André declares that he is recording his and Nicole's observations of their day-to-day life, whose purpose is to *faire qu'y ait plus rien*, allusions to history, myth, art, literature, music or film are perceived as items of the cultural inventory to be discarded, and as such they fail to represent an alternative context to the reality described by the text as world.

Even the *Flore laurentienne* and *l'encyclopédie Alpha* (*la Mémoire du Temps*), in which André and Nicole seek refuge in the form of ritual readings whenever an immediate experience seems to threaten their goal to *faire qu'y ait plus rien*, have no function other than sheer escapism. As Gilles Marcotte puts it, they read "comme s'ils voulaient se désinstruire, détruire en eux-mêmes, par ces lectures dérisoires, toute idée d'acquisition intellectuelle et de participation émotionnelle. Ils lisent pour faire le vide."[15]

Nowhere is this phenomenon of decontextualization more explicit than in the non-specification of the relationship between André and Nicole. The unanimity of their views deprives the reader of any possible contrasting perspectives between the two, while ignorance of the nature of their relationship (husband and wife? brother and sister?) cancels any attempt to attribute their collective alienation to some aspect of the relationship itself. Readers accustomed to incestuous brother/sister relationships from other Ducharme novels (notably *Les Enfantômes*), here are as constantly denied the concept of sexual duality as *altérité* as they are denied reference to other forms of alternative reality or fantasy. The "unisexuality" of the "double" narrator is alluded to in one of the epigraphs ("C'est tous des jaloux, ces hosties-là"—Carpinus)[16] as well as in the second section heading [*L'Amarente Parente* (*Amaranthus Graecizans*)].[17] Its implications have been speculated upon by Vachon as eliminating sexual duality and polarity as an essential category of human conceptualization and perception.

> Solidairement, Nicole et André sont le narrateur. ... Ce qui, au centre immobile du récit, tente de se "posséder soi-même," est double. Comme Christ ou Bouddha, qui *est* deux sexes et deux natures, l'Un serait-il Deux? Faut-il comprendre que l'être, qui est un, n'est pas Un? qu'il est secrètement Deux? et, contre toute évidence, que deux n'est pas Deux? qu'il est, secrètement, Un?[18]

As Vachon's hypotheses concerning the sexual ambivalence of the central figures demonstrate, this withholding of context has the effect of eliminating construed "meaning" as a possible resolution of the "illogicalities, conflicts, and indeed, the whole contingency of the world" indicated or implied by the text.[19] The decontextualization results in the constant cancellation of the reader's anticipation of an emerging resolution. Though the narrator's "documentation" of the banality of everyday life seems to indicate a negation of the social and cultural norms which determine it, the absence of a superimposed context which the reader could relate to the day-to-day episodes described deprives the reader of any formulation of meaning which would transcend the world presented.

The role of the text-extraneous elements

The epigraphs, like the section headings, take on significance for the reader only retrospectively, after reading the text. Even then, they do not add up to a consistent schema summing up the theme or the structure of the novel or its individual parts, but seem rather to draw attention to the arbitrariness of their own function.[20]

While the genuine quotation constituting the first of the epigraphs seems to represent the simplistic ideological formula underlying the Quebec counter-culture described in the text, the second challenges the reader's credulity in a double sense: first of all in the incongruity between the erudition suggested by the Latin name of the "writer" supposedly cited, and the banality of his "wisdom" which, furthermore, is expressed in unmistakable *québécois*. In fact, *Carpinus* does not designate a historical figure but a botanical species (of North American birch), characterized by its uni- (or bi-) sexuality and its ability to survive severe winters. The "quotation" itself, then ("C'est tous des jaloux, ces hosties-là!") may be recognized by the reader as an allusion to the undifferentiated sexual relationship between André and Nicole which, together with the fact that they function as unanimous "narrators," lets them appear inseparable (as one). The *Carpinus* characteristic of winter survival may be recognized as another reference to the life of the couple, given the title and the conclusion of the novel.

The final epigraph may be seen as the ironic reversal of the human concept of its own supremacy, by superimposing an un-human (and implicitly feline) perspective on the events of the novel. At the same time this sentence invokes the interdependence of the relationship between the human and the pet, with its connotation of the proverbial exhortation (to the dependent pet) not to "bite the hand that feeds it." The implications of this epigraph, too, are ambiguous. Does it refer to André and Nicole's pet cat, which refuses its freedom and chooses to remain with its owners, and if so, does it indicate its selfishness (its demand to be fed) or its fidelity? Or does it refer to André and Nicole, "pets" cultivated by and dependent on representatives of the counter-culture (Roger Degrandpré) as well as on those of the *petite bourgeoisie* (the Lithuanian *concierge* and the Greek grocer)?

It seems obvious that none of the epigraphs resolve the ambiguities confronting the reader in the reading of the text and even at its conclusion: if anything, they multiply the ambiguities created by the text, and evoke possibilities of interpretation which lead in several different directions at once. Nor do the epigraphs or section headings provide a key to the communicatory intention of the text (as is the case, for instance, in *Fifth Business* or *The Second Scroll*). Like the puns and inconsistencies of the "footnotes," they entice the reader through their traditional function as a source of enlightenment, only to result in further mystification.[21]

In thus denying the reader the possibility of formulating meaning to resolve its ambiguities and contradictions, the text dissolves the traditional equation of meaning and aesthetic experience as a manifestation of the "wholeness" and "harmony" of the work of art; it challenges the reader, instead, to seek and find either one in the banal reality of everyday modern life.

Le monde du sens et le sens du monde

An incident which begins as an Arcadian idyll and ends as a Beckettian nightmare concludes the novel. Having spent days in a bucolic retreat on Ile Bizard with Catherine, whose caprices have induced in them alternately ecstasy and desperation, André and Nicole find one morning that their idol has disappeared. They find her sleeping, naked, under a dead elm, a sight which moves them to cover her with masses of the wild flowers blossoming profusely all about her. But Catherine's charming abandon, unlike the situation in the pastoral idylls it evokes, has been pharmacologically induced (she is tightly clutching a bottle of Valium). André and Nicole, overeager for her to awaken and express her appreciation of their gesture, overeager also to "repossess" her, for their parts contribute to the transformation of the scene into an anti-idyll. André catches a frog and lets it walk over Catherine's face. Catherine's awakening in disgust (and taking more Valium) are elements which complete the parodistic deformation of the Arcadian idyll.

Catherine's ultimate disappearance from their lives finally seems to produce the void André and Nicole have been attempting to create. While this void is at times seen as giddying, at others it is perceived as an absence, as irrevocable loss: "Tantôt je sens l'absence de tout et la tête me tourne et ça me fait rire. Tantôt je sens tout ce qu'il n'y aura plus et ça me serre à la gorge et je prends une grande respiration" (p. 281).

The disappearance from their lives of Catherine seems to represent the ultimate separation of André and Nicole from reality, and thus in a way seals off their world from that of the reader. This mutual alienation of subject and world represents another form of decontextualization which is recognized by the reader not only in the resulting equation of Catherine's vanishing and the disappearance of "meaning" for André and Nicole, but also in its syntactic expression:

> Puis demain, 21 juin 1971, l'hiver va commencer, une dernière fois, une fois pour toutes, l'hiver de force (comme la camisole), la saison où on reste enfermé dans sa chambre parce qu'on est vieux et qu'on a peur d'attraper du mal dehors, ou qu'on sait qu'on ne peut rien attraper du tout dehors, mais ça revient au même. (pp. 282-83)

As in Beckett's novels, one part of a sentence negates the other, resulting in an equation of contrary realities, the motivation of which the reader recognizes as representing a possible resolution of the non-sense they denote. The question formulated in G.-A. Vachon's study—"Entre les premières pages du livre ... et la dernière, quelque chose a-t-il bougé?"[22]—seems of less significance in determining the intention of the text than the effect produced by the Beckettian conclusion. Wolfgang Iser has pointed out that Beckett's consistently self-contradictory novels reveal the fictive nature of any meaning the reader could impose upon the text (the implication being that all such meanings represent projections of the reader).[23] Similarly, *L'Hiver de force* presents a series of episodes all of which point toward the abolition of a reality in which life has been divorced from culture—has been "decontextualized"—and therefore from meaning. The achievement of a *néant* which seems to be indicated by the conclusion remains illusory, for the *peur* out of which the *néant* has been sought as a refuge persists, both as memory and as anticipation.

With *L'Hiver de force*, Ducharme postulates the conservation of *la mémoire du temps* by a civilization for whom this memory itself has lost its meaning. The world evoked at the end of the text, not least through the equivocality of the syntax, represents a cultural amnesia of Beckettian dimensions. The central figures as narrator document their own cultural and social disorientation as a consequence of the rupture between "meaning" and everyday life, itself a function of the disembodiment of culture in its role as a carrier of meaning in day-to-day human experience.

Indeed, the documentary form chosen to recount the experience of the first-person narrator seems to testify, as a quasi-documentary, to the validity of the view of present western culture described by Fernand Dumont, whose study entitled *Le Lieu de l'homme* has been regarded by some critics as the theoretical structure underlying *L'Hiver de force*: "S'il est, en définitive, quelque caractéristique essentielle de la culture actuelle, elle semble résider dans le sentiment d'un déchirement irréductible entre le monde du sens et celui des formes concrètes de l'existence."[24]

3.   Overdeterminacy as a strategy of defamiliarization: Robertson Davies's *Fifth Business*[25]

In spite of numerous allusions to the norm repertoire of early to mid-twentieth-century rural eastern Canada, the intention of Robertson Davies's *Fifth Business* is not to expose the weaknesses or even the causal background of this repertoire. The long view of the intellectually aware narrator-hero looking back on his childhood, adolescence and young adulthood relativizes the significance of a given norm even while it is seen to determine the characters' attitudes and actions in the retrospectively recounted story.

The reader's involvement throughout the novel is thus determined not by attempts to recognize and evaluate social norms, as in Davies's earlier novels, but by the multiple possibilities of motivating plot elements and the development of the lives of the figures occurring in the novel over a period of fifty-five years.

Three textual elements presented at the beginning of the novel determine the reader's anticipation of the following text and prestructure reader response to it. These three features are the epigraph defining the term "fifth business," the narrative frame of the novel (a "report" to the headmaster of Ramsay's school), and the fact that the key incident is recorded in a sort of prologue preceding Ramsay's direct address to the headmaster.

The epigraph, defining a term of theatre jargon which is the title of the novel itself, causes the reader to anticipate that the traditionally marginal will be foregrounded in the text. As a result of this anticipation, the reader's response to a situation described by the first person narrator (who represents a "fifth business" function throughout the novel) is determined by the reader's evocation of the way the narrator probably appears to the other figures. Each view presented by the narrator therefore simultaneously invokes alternative perspectival views indicated by the other figures, yet not expressed in the text.

This multiple focus is built up and illustrated by the narrator's description of his motivation to write to the headmaster. The narrator feels misunderstood by the teacher who wrote the "tribute" to him on his retirement. In his attempt to invalidate the latter's perceptions he proceeds to give an account of his life, beginning from his boyhood, in which his own views and those of the other figures are shown in interaction. The reader thus has available a multiplicity of perspectival views to invoke in response to any given element of the text: Ramsay's subjective view of himself, the way he is seen in old age by younger colleagues at his school (and, by implication, the way his pupils experience him), and the roles designated for him by the other figures involved with him throughout his life, from childhood on.

The communicatory function of the "prologue" may be seen as illustrating the notion of "fifth business" as defined in the epigraph. Each of the figures involved in the snowball episode function as a "fifth business" depending upon which figure is taken to be the "hero" or "heroine." In thus drawing the reader's attention to the perceptual subjectivity involved in determining the roles of the various figures, the text makes the reader aware of the multiple perspectival views virtually present whenever a particular view is foregrounded in the text.

As a literary convention, the prologue expresses the substance of what is to follow in the main part of the text. In this sense it represents a sort of miniature of the text, itself containing the message it announces. In *Fifth Business*, this prologue describes the archetypal structures which are seen to predetermine the personalities of the figures themselves, as well as how they interact. Their respective roles in the snowball episode, and the way they experience and react to the incident, essentially characterize what becomes of them in later life.

The apparent overdeterminacy created by the first-person narrator (who also constitutes the central perspective), a sensible, intelligent man and professional historian viewing persons and events from the distance of a lifetime's experience, induces a credulity and complicity on the part of the reader which is constantly undermined by the text itself. For the trustworthiness, the reliability which the reader is inclined to see in the narrator's view of other figures and, most of all, of himself, is called into question by his perception of the way others experience him, as well as by his limited access to the inner lives of others. The reader's calling into question the narrator's views is thus less a result of conflicting views between the perspectives (all of which are filtered through the consciousness of the narrator) than of the reader's growing awareness that all the elements presented by the narrator are possessed of dimensions of which the narrator himself seems to remain unaware. The dialectic pursued by the reader throughout the novel is that of the insight and blindness determining the relationships between the figures of the novel, and also that of the narrator's own quest for self-knowledge. The reader's recognition that the narrator's authority (only seemingly validated by his personal and professional integrity and reliability) is inevitably illusory increases reader awareness that growing knowledge is accompanied by its dialectical opposite: it is knowledge that generates mystery.

This strategy of simultaneous enlightenment and mystification is most readily recognizable when one considers the entire trilogy of which *Fifth Business* is the first volume. It is not the perspectival segmentation as such (the central perspective in *Fifth Business* is Ramsay, in *The Manticore*[26] it is David Staunton, while in *World of Wonders*[27] it is Magnus Eisengrim, though in the latter Ramsay is again the first-person narrator) but the mass of information available from the various perspectival views which both add to the reader's knowledge of certain figures and events and at the same time deepen the mystery surrounding them. The overdeterminacy created by this mass of information creates a complicated web of moral relationships, motivations and causalities which the reader attempts to unravel both retrospectively, in terms of what has been read, and prospectively, in anticipation of what is to follow. Although the "mystery" attached to figures and events is always yielded up, in that at some point withheld information is unexpectedly made available, this information from which the reader has expected the resolution of the mystery in fact only exposes deeper-lying aspects, leaving the reader with a sense of the ultimate elusiveness of the truth.

The strategy described above is perhaps best illustrated by the stone-in-the-snowball episode, with which *Fifth Business* opens. The effect of the incident brings about the premature birth of Paul Dempster, the madness of his mother Mary, and the death of Boy Staunton. It is also responsible for all the contingent events, thus indirectly determining the lives of all the Deptford characters throughout the entire trilogy; for example, Mrs. Dempster's copulation with a tramp, the subsequent ruining of her husband's career as a Baptist parson, and her barbaric isolation from the outside world, contact with which is henceforth reduced to the length of the hemp rope with which she is restrained. Paul's secret visit to the fair, after which he disappears with Wanless, is made possible due to her reduced condition, which thus in a way determines her son's future life. Ramsay's lifelong involvement with saints and the problem of evil seems to be a direct result of this initial involvement with Mary Dempster, itself brought about by Paul's premature birth, Mrs. Dempster's derangement and its effects already described.

The roles of the two boys in the incident—Boyd Staunton threw the snowball, Ramsay deliberately dodged it—determines their subsequent relationship, each in his consciousness of the other's role. Ramsay accepts his guilt which he attempts to expiate in his involvement with the Dempsters; Boyd Staunton denies his guilt, but his role as Ramsay's financial adviser, to which Ramsay in large measure owes his comfortable circumstances, may also be seen as a form of relief of conscience. Boyd's death, however, seems to be a direct consequence of his boyhood act: he is found dead in his car, which he has apparently driven off a Lake Ontario pier, the snowball stone clenched firmly in his mouth.

Certain initially withheld elements elucidating the events gradually emerge. The reader learns that Mrs. Dempster's "act of mercy" with the tramp has actually led to his "redemption": he has henceforth reformed and headed a home and mission for outcasts such as he had been at the time. The "mystery" of the circumstances of Paul Dempster's disappearance is resolved by Magnus Eisengrim's description of his seduction and kidnapping by Willard. It is Magnus Eisengrim, too, who describes the motivations behind Boyd Staunton's suicide.

These "revelations," like the causal logic with which the snowball incident precipitates subsequent events, are elements which the reader is inclined to believe and accept since they correspond both to the familiar causal patterns of everyday life and the conceptual framework of the reader's moral-cultural background: the notion of original sin as the cause of evil in the world, and that of man's descent from the mythological figures personifying human conflict and historical causality, Adam and Eve.

Both the causal logic of the chain of events and its moral implications represent repertoire elements shared by text and reader. But this common ground is only the point of departure for what is to be communicated to the reader. What emerges, against this normative background shared by text and reader, is *the virtual text of designated but unexpressed alternatives to the perceptions formulated by the respective perspectival views.*

How is the reader's attention drawn to the existence of this "subtext," to borrow a term from one of the novels? And how does the text initiate, control, and "validate" the reader's recognition and interpretation of it?

The strategies determining the reader's response to the text involve certain features of the figures themselves, the alternatives they select in the interpretation of their reality, which are in turn determined by their own predispositions, the development of the plot, the symbolic significance of certain objects and proper nouns, such as personal or place names.

The main figures of *Fifth Business* are non-conforming in terms of their indicated normative backgrounds. They live out the dialectical opposite of the sort of lives the reader would expect them to lead on the basis of the fictional world created by the text, many features of which coincide with the reader's perception of the latter's own real world. Dunstable Ramsay, Canadian small-town Scots Presbyterian, devotes his life to the care of a demented woman and the study of saints, the ultimate goal of which is to have Mary Dempster canonized; in his old age he retires to a secluded Swiss mountain retreat in the company of the monstrously deformed patron of Magnus Eisengrim, who pursues the anachronistic minor art of illusioning.

Boyd Staunton, though helped by his father's initial success in the sugar-beet industry, is a self-made man of obscure ancestry who has made his fortune in junk food. His social pretentions and political ambitions can be explained by his desire to overcome the aura of the *parvenu* which still clings to him and his family. His role model, however, is none other than the Prince of Wales, his emulation of whom eventually motivates his suicide. The paradox in Boy Staunton's life is that he attempts to eradicate the traces of his small-town background, while his ultimate goal in doing so is to live out the fantasies characterizing such a background: to achieve proximity to the glamorous royalty of the sensationalist press, to become, in a sense, royalty. His efforts at realizing what is at the same time a childish fantasy (to live out a fairy-tale) and a fantasy of the lower classes (to live out the society reports of the rainbow press) are thus seen to underlie his attempt to abolish the realities of the childhood and lower middle-class background which he so resolutely rejects.

Magnus Eisengrim, the former Paul Dempster, achieves a synthesis out of the curious morality of the superstitious world of the theatre and the Bible-thumping fervour of his childhood religion, the elliptic formulation of which in a Bible quotation may be seen to refer to the "subtext" of the autobiography he has recounted: " 'I am become as a bottle in the smoke: yet do I fear thy statutes' " (*World of Wonders*, p. 340). Born the son of a fervent Baptist parson and a girlish, domestically ineffectual mother, educated with a sense of the literalness of the Biblical word, he is involuntarily apprenticed to an art and a way of life which, in terms of the background described, are the devil's own. Paul Dempster alias Magnus Eisengrim thus invokes most dramatically of all the dialectical opposition of being and becoming.

For the reader, the three figures represent worlds that are both familiar and unfamiliar: familiar in the predispositions assumed to be created by their thoroughly provincial bourgeois childhood, unfamiliar in their living out of fantasies which seem to have their roots in facets of personality inexplicable in terms of their respective backgrounds.

This recognition enables the reader to perceive that the perspectives presented by the figures themselves are always of an implicit duality. In the presentation of a given view the reader's attention is simultaneously drawn to the motivation of that view and to the features it excludes. The reader not only identifies the selection involved in a given perspectival view, and motivates that selection, but also formulates alternative (not presented) views on the basis of textual features which have already occurred. The validity of a given perspectival view as opposed to the virtual alternative one formulated by the reader represents a decision to be made by the reader. But since the virtual elements are as clearly designated as the explicitly presented perspectival views, the ambiguity of certain textual elements is never wholly resolved. It is this inability to formulate the "truth" about an incident or figure in the novel—and the more information becomes available, the more problematic this formulation becomes—which causes the reader to call into question even those elements which initially were felt to be familiar. Thus while the familiar constitutes a point of access to the unfamiliar, the intuitive and cognitive processes involved in the reader's attempting to grasp and so make familiar the previously unfamiliar result in a reversal: in the light of the unfamiliar aspects of the familiar world, this familiar world itself becomes defamiliarized, and inalterably so, since the reader can no longer even invoke the authority of the reader's own (familiar) experience.

This strategy, equating the validity of the unfamiliar with that of the familiar, can be illustrated in almost every element of the three novels. Two examples may serve to illustrate the principle.

The snowball incident already described has the effect of disorienting Mrs. Dempster, not only by Deptford norms but also by those governing the reality of the reader's world. Ramsay's guilt and a good part of his subsequent experiences are determined by his certainty that the snowball with the stone inside has set in motion the chain of events described in the trilogy. The notion that this causal chain may be invalid is indicated by the text, but never formulated with the explicitness of Ramsay's causal views: Mrs. Dempster is presented even before the incident as an outsider to Deptford society not only because she does not conform, but also because of her romantic temperament. Since she is described as an emotional, highly sensitive girlish nature, one of her implied attributes seems to be a certain vulnerability. Thus though her fall and Paul's premature birth are certainly to be seen as a consequence of being hit by the snowball, the possibility remains that the blow and the fall created shock and hysteria, which in turn effected the premature birth and her own subsequent derangement. The question arises whether Mrs. Dempster, given the predispositions of her own nature, might not inevitably have gone mad and given birth prematurely, either spontaneously or because of some other event. This possibility is suggested by Ramsay's mother, a forthright, no-nonsense Scotswoman, who has expressed the view that "Mrs. Dempster was really no different from what she had been before, except that she was more so" (*Fifth Business*, p. 23).

The effect of the stone-in-the-snowball can thus be interpreted teleologically as well as causally. The incident can be seen as instrumental (rather than causal) in bringing about a state of affairs which would inevitably have come about due to certain predispositions latent in the figures themselves. Similarly, Ramsay's guilt may be seen as a feeling adequate to the situation, particularly in view of his Calvinist-Presbyterian upbringing. But it is also instrumental in his quest for self-knowledge, and thus in the self-realization he achieves from his study of saints and evil which he ultimately owes to the causal role he attributes to himself in the incident.

The same kind of unconscious complicity with fate—or history— is suggested in the incident that leads to Paul Dempster's seduction and kidnapping by Willard. As Magnus Eisengrim first tells the story, fifty years after it happened, he watches Willard's tricks, by which he is overwhelmingly impressed, and then, to impress him, performs a few of his own, after which Willard gags and rapes him in the latrine.

Ramsay is later privileged to be told a detail Magnus Eisengrim has omitted from his first version: little Paul Dempster rewarded Willard's first surreptitious sexual caress in the tent with a smile. His sense of guilt at this indication of sexual complicity, it is suggested, is what binds him to Willard. The reasoning behind the view presented by Eisengrim is causal, like that of Ramsay in the snowball episode. But just as Ramsay's sense of guilt "apprentices" him to the lifelong study of sainthood and evil, Paul's experience apprentices him to an art for which he has already shown a natural talent and which ultimately yields deep fulfilment and self-realization. The teleological view is presented as having the same validity as the causal. In both cases the "truth" remains ambiguous and, in a sense, irrelevant.

The development of the plot reinforces the duality suggested by the explicit and implicit perspectival views. For while the pragmatic considerations of everyday life, i.e. the demands of the fictional reality in which they live, seem to be the motivating force behind the actions of the figures of the novel, the experiences they make involuntarily seem to be those which they consciously or unconsciously seek. Ramsay's ceaseless search for the little madonna which "appeared" to him during the war (wearing the face of Mary Dempster) finally bears fruit. He finds her in a Salzburg exhibition. In his quest for the madonna, however, he twice chances to meet Paul Dempster, alias Jules LeGrand, alias Magnus Eisengrim: once in the Tyrol, and once in Mexico. In both cases the illusions performed are recognized by the reader as representing archetypal features of the central figures of the novel (though never identified as such by Ramsay). Furthermore Ramsay's experiences with Liesl and Faustina, both of whom he meets through Eisengrim, represent dimensions of the feminine which coincide with those attributed to Mary Dempster and thus, by extension, with those represented by the little madonna: it is Ramsay himself who identifies the Faustina illusion as illustrating the Gretchen/Venus symbiosis of spiritual and profane love, while it is Liesl, of ambivalent sexuality, who is revealed to be the intelligence behind the whole show. While such coincidences are self-exegetically identified in a G. K. Chesterton quotation (in *The Manticore*) as " 'a spiritual sort of puns' " (p. 281), their role in determining the reader's response to the text consists in drawing attention to features which have been previously indicated but whose full significance the reader has not realized. Thus the figure of Mary Dempster, which has loomed large in Ramsay's life due to the sexual and spiritual experiences associated with her, is related retrospectively in the mind of the reader with the stage attributes of Faustina. Similarly, the mental derangement of Mary Dempster and the physical deformation of Liesl, both of whom act as mentor figures to Ramsay, are seen as archetypal links between the two women.

The plot itself is thus perceived by the reader as being determined and motivated by half-conscious predispositions of the figures themselves, not only in what they do, but also in what happens to them.

This convergence of causality and teleology manifests itself not only in the perspectival views of the central figures and the development of the plot, but also in the *nomen est omen* principle operative throughout the three novels. The three central Deptford figures undergo a name change indicating the achievement of an already pre-established identity. Dunstable is "rechristened" Dunstan by Diana Marfleet, his English hospital nurse, whom he resists the temptation to marry. Ramsay's mock imitation of St. Dunstan's resistance to the devil who appears in the form of a woman is evoked by the reader in a later incident with Liesl, whom Ramsay "exorcises" during a physical struggle by violently twisting her nose, thus living out the allusiveness of his name.

The change from Boyd to Boy (Staunton) may be seen to designate its bearer's rejection of advancing age, but even more it reinforces the regression characterizing Boy's psychological development, modelled after the archetype represented by the Prince of Wales: the crown prince who becomes king only to abdicate. "Staunton" contains "taunt" and "staunch," both of which have situational contexts validating their appropriateness to its wearer. In *The Manticore*, however, the origin of the well-sounding family name is revealed by genealogical research. As an unwed mother, Boy's grandmother, a domestic in a pub, chose it to taunt the father, who claimed that her son's paternal origin was indeterminable. Since he said that all of the village of Staunton could claim to be the father, and she wanted him to "carry his father's name," this is what she christened him. It is a variation of the Staunton village arms, designed by a co-student of David's as a joke, that graces the coffin at Boy's funeral, so that the irony resulting from the pretentious intentions of using the arms and what they actually mean represents a final "taunt" to Boy's snobbishness, bigotry, and above all ignorance of himself.

Paul Dempster's name change, on the other hand, indicates a reversal rather than the progression suggested by Ramsay's rechristening and the regression implied in Boy's self-chosen epithet. The double biblical allusion in Paul's name invokes the extremes of faith undergone by the apostle Paul as well as the spiritual *redemption* which represents a central doctrine of the Christian church. His assumed name Magnus Eisengrim, or the great wolf, simultaneously evokes the nobility and evil associated with the wolf as symbol in Germanic legend. The reversal suggested by the name change is thus from Christian to pagan, from a state of grace to the incarnation of the demonic. Like so many other elements of the novels, the mythological associations evoked by *Paul Dempster* and *Magnus Eisengrim* respectively represent patterns of polarity (as in Christian dialectics) in the mind of the reader, the validity of which is cancelled by the fictional reality of the text. Thus combined in one figure, the presented patterns of polarity are recognized by the reader as intrinsic to the human personality rather than as representing definitive moral choices.[28]

Even excluding *The Manticore* and *World of Wonders*, which may be considered as Jungian *romans à thèse*, the reader of *Fifth Business* experiencing the effect of the strategies described above approaches the formulation of the central teachings of Jung. The reader is constantly made aware of the selectiveness with which experiences are made and communicated, of the significance of the non-selected items, and their virtual presence in the selection itself. Furthermore, the teleological view of the predetermination and development of a personality represents a problematization of that development itself, influenced by individual self-awareness. The Jungian model also manifests itself in the readily recognizable archetypes alluded to by the central figures of the novels, whose interaction complicates their respective archetypal functions. Finally, the novels abound in parapsychological phenomena, such as Mary Dempster's "miracles" and the Brazen Head's "oracles," which correspond to the Jungian concepts of the way in which psychic energy manifests itself in the reality of day-to-day experience.

But whether or not the reader invokes Jungian psychology in the reading of the novel, its communicatory strategies draw attention to themselves as representing the perceptual and historical processes underlying all human experience.

The narrative strategies involved in *Poussière sur la ville*, *L'Hiver de force* and *Fifth Business* reflect a shift in focus from the realistically presented accounts of problems arising out of the social norm repertoire of a given socio-cultural system witnessed in *Two Solitudes*, *The Edible Woman* and *Une saison dans la vie d'Emmanuel*. The interest in Langevin's, Ducharme's, and Davies's novels centres around the exploration of human consciousness and the way it experiences the world. Furthermore, human experience is not, in these novels, seen to be determined exclusively or even primarily by the social norm repertoire of the represented system, but rather by the conflicts arising between it and deeper-lying aspects of the human condition: humankind's imprisonment in its subjectivity, the inalterability of the human condition, and, in the case of *Fifth Business*, the amoral and irrational desires, instincts and motivations that have given rise to the archetypes of both ancient myth and modern psychology.

To make communicable to the reader elements of human experience characterized precisely by their incommunicability, these novels inevitably depend to a far greater degree upon individual patterns of the literary repertoire than is the case in the novels dealing with a primarily social thematic. The literary conventions invoked in the novels of Langevin, Ducharme and Davies may vary greatly not only in type and function, but also in the degree to which they deform familiar narrative patterns. In all three cases, however, the narrative strategies used to communicate the experiences of the central figures work to draw the reader's attention to the problematic nature of the communicatory process itself.

Reference Notes to Chapter Two

1 Iser refers to the transformation of familiar repertoire elements, effected by their occurrence in an unfamiliar context, as "depragmatization." He considers this process to be an essential feature in determining the reader's response to all literary texts (cf. Note 2). My use of the term "defamiliarization" in the present context is rather in the sense of "deliberate alienation."

2 Wolfgang Iser sees this "depragmatization" as characteristic of the way the fictional reality is presented in all literary texts: "The literary text . . . takes its selected objects out of their pragmatic context and so shatters their original frame of reference; the result is to reveal aspects (e.g., of social norms) which had remained hidden as long as the frame of reference remained intact" (*The Act of Reading*, p. 109). This depragmatization also creates textual indeterminacy: "The depragmatized norms and literary allusions have lost their familiar context; their depragmatization creates a blank which, at best, offers possibilities of connection." Ibid., p. 184.

3 Stanzel, *Typische Formen des Romans*, pp. 27-31.

4 Ibid., p. 31.

5 Ibid., p. 31. The original sentence reads: "Das Entscheidende . . . ist, daß die Ich-Figur ihr Leben erzählt, nachdem sie eine Wandlung durch Reue, Bekehrung oder Einsicht durchgemacht hat."

6 Ibid., p. 33.

7 Ibid., p. 37.

8 Nathalie Sarraute, "De Dostoievski à Kafka," in *L'Ère du soupçon* (Paris: NRF, Callimard, 1956), pp. 33-34.

9 Stanzel, *Typische Formen des Romans*, p. 30; my translation; the original quotation reads in its full context: "Die Ich-Erzählsituation verifiziert also nicht die Objekt-Existenz der Welt, von welcher der Ich-Erzähler berichtet, sondern ihre Subjektivität, ihre Realität als Bewußtseinsinhalt der Ich-Gestalt, oder vielmehr als eine letztlich unauflösliche Vermengung von objektiver, dinglicher außen- und subjektiver, ideeler Innenwelt."

10 Cf. for example: Jean-Charles Falardeau, "Le héros chez Langevin," in *L'Évolution du héros dans le roman québécois* (Conférences J. A. de Sève, 1968), pp. 20-33; André Gaulin, "La Vision du monde d'André Langevin," *Études littéraires*, 6, no. 2 août 1973), pp. 153-67; Roger Godbout, "Le Milieu, personnage symbolique dans l'oeuvre d'André Langevin," in *Livres et auteurs canadiens* (1966), pp. 198-203; Pierre Hébert, "Forme et signification du temps et du discours immédiat dans *Poussière sur la ville: le récit d'une victoire,*" *Voix et Images*, 2, no. 2 (décembre 1976), pp. 209-30; Pierre Hébert, "Le Discours immédiat: essai de modèle et lecture de *Poussière sur la ville* d'André Langevin," *Présence francophone*, no. 14 (printemps 1977), pp. 105-20; Jean-Claude

Tardif, "Les Relations humaines dans *Poussière sur la ville,*" *Études littéraires*, 6, no. 2 (août 1973), pp. 241-55; David J. Bond, *The Temptation of Despair: A Study of the Quebec Novelist André Langevin* (Toronto: York Press, 1982).

11 "The social and literary allusions that constitute the two basic elements of the repertoire are drawn from two quite different systems: the first from historical thought systems, and the second from past literary reactions to historical problems. The norms and schemata selected for the repertoire are rarely equivalent to one another—and in those few cases where they are, the text will cease to be informative because it will merely repeat the answers offered by an existing text, even though the historical problems will have changed. Generally, however, the two elements of the repertoire are not equivalent to each other precisely in the degree of their familiarity.... The nonequivalence of these two familiar elements does not mean that the principle of equivalence is absent from the text itself; its presence is signalized by the fact that the familiarity of these elements no longer serves to bring about correspondences" (Iser, *The Act of Reading*, p. 81).

12 Gilles Marcotte has pointed out the irony in Ducharme's decision to call *L'Hiver de force a récit*: "Les quatre premiers livres de Réjean Ducharme portent la mention 'roman'; le cinquième, *L'Hiver de force*, s'appelle 'récit.' Pourquoi, ce changement d'appellation? on se le demande avec d'autant plus de perplexité que Ducharme avait appliqué le mot 'roman' à des histoires proprement invraisemblables, voire à une épopée versifiée, et que *L'Hiver de force*, par contre, porte un coefficient de réalisme beaucoup plus élevé qu'aucun de ses autres livres. Si le roman, comme dit Mary McCarthy, est 'un livre en prose d'une certaine épaisseur qui raconte une histoire de la vie réelle,' en voilà donc enfin, un roman, un vrai, avec une histoire tout à fait vraisemblable." Quoted from the article entitled "Réjean Ducharme contre Blasey Blasey," *Études françaises*, 11, nos. 3-4 (octobre 1975), p. 279.

13 For an analysis of the function of the footnote in fictional texts, see Shari Benstock, "At the Margin of Discourse: Footnotes in the Fictional Text," *PMLA*, 98, pp. 204-25.

14 G.-A. Vachon, "Note sur Réjean Ducharme et Paul-Marie Lapointe," *Études françaises*, 11, nos. 3-4 (octobre 1975), p. 361.

15 Marcotte, "Réjean Ducharme contre Blasey Blasey," p. 281.

16 *Carpinus* is a member of the birch family, which bears both male and female flowers and is adapted to survival of the winter.

17 *Amaranthus Graecizans* may have male or female flowers or contain both types of reproductive structures. The *graecizans* variety referred to by the text is commonly known as "prostrate pigweed." Both the common and botanical names of the ornamental varieties of the *genus amaranthus* seem to represent a curious allusiveness to certain elements of the text: "love-lies-bleeding" (*Amaranthus caudatus*); "prince's feather" (*Amaranthus hybridus* variety *hypochondriacus*); "Joseph's coat" (*Amaranthus tricolor*).

18 Vachon, "Note sur Réjean Ducharme et Paul-Marie Lapointe," pp. 372-73.

19 This phrase is quoted from Iser, *The Act of Reading*, p. 223. Its immediate context is as follows: "Classical and psychological aesthetics have always been at one over the postulate that the final resolution of initial tension in the work of art is coincidental with the emergence of meaning. With Beckett, however, we become aware that meaning as a relief from tension embodies an expectation of art which is historical in nature and consequently loses its claim to be normative. The density of negations not only lays bare the historicity of traditional expectation—we obviously anticipate a meaning that will remove the illogicalities, conflicts, and, indeed, the whole contingency of the world in the literary work."

20 Whereas in some cases the footnotes offer a genuine if evaluative explanation of the phrases they refer to, others are merely "phonetic" transcriptions of English words. Two examples: *Joual* is explained as "Jargon montréalais raffiné par le théâtre puis

exploité par la chanson et le cinéma québécois" (p. 15), while *anyway* is annotated with *ennéoué* (p. 173).

21 The allusiveness of the title contributes to the reader's sense of the elusiveness of meaning. While Vachon has concentrated his analysis of the title on the word *force* (cf. "Note sur Réjean Ducharme et Paul-Marie Lapointe," p. 360), the title in its entirety, like other elements of the text, also seems to allude to Jacques Godbout's *Salut Galarneau!* in which François Galarneau, immured in his high walls of cement, declares: "Avec les feuilles rousses au plafond, dans le salon, et ces corneilles sur le mur de la cour, *l'hiver ne viendra pas*" (p. 141). The reference to *Rimbaud et la Commune*, on the fly-leaf of which Catherine writes her farewell note, evokes another seasonal allusion which can readily be connected with the title *L'Hiver de force*, namely to Rimbaud's own *Une Saison en enfer*.

22 Vachon, "Note sur Réjean Ducharme et Paul-Marie Lapoint," p. 361.

23 Cf. Iser's analysis of negation in Beckett in *The Act of Reading*, particularly pp. 222, 224, 225.

24 Fernand Dumont, *Le Lieu de l'homme. La Culture comme distance et mémoire*, vol. 14 (Montreal: Editions HMH, Collection Constantes, 1969), p. 11.

25 Among the studies of Davies's Deptford trilogy, the following are of particular interest here: R. G. Lawrence and S. L. Macey, eds., *Studies in Robertson Davies' Deptford Trilogy*, (*English Literary Studies*, no. 20 [Victoria, 1980]); Nancy Bjerring, "Deep in the Old Man's Puzzle," *Canadian Literature*, 62 (Autumn 1974), pp. 49-60; Wilfred Cude, "Miracle and Art in *Fifth Business*," *Journal of Canadian Studies*, 12, no. 4 (November 1974), pp. 3-16; Gordon Roper, "Robertson Davies' *Fifth Business* and that Old Fantastical Duke of Dark Corners, C. G. Jung," *Journal of Canadian Fiction*, 1, no. 1 (Winter 1972), pp. 33-39; Patricia Monk, "Confessions of a Sorcerer's Apprentice: *World of Wonders* and the Deptford Trilogy of Robertson Davies," *Dalhousie Review*, 56 (1976-77), pp. 366-72; Anthony B. Dawson, "Davies, His Critics and the Canadian Canon," *Canadian Literature*, 92 (Spring 1982), pp. 154-59; Marilyn Chapman, "Female Archetypes in *Fifth Business*," *Canadian Literature*, 80 (Spring 1979), pp. 131-38; Gertrude Jaron Lewis, "Vitzliputzli Revisited," *Canadian Literature*, 76 (Spring 1978), pp. 132-34; Patricia Monk, *The Smaller Infinity: The Jungian Self in the Novels of Robertson Davies* (Toronto: University of Toronto Press, 1982).

26 Robertson Davies, *The Manticore* (Toronto: Macmillan, 1972).

27 Robertson Davies, *World of Wonders* (Toronto: Macmillan, 1975).

28 The significance of names occurring in the trilogy is not restricted to those of the characters. Ramsay's odyssey from Deptford (a homonym of Debtford) to Sorgenfrei (= care-free, *sans souci*) is transparently metaphorical in its allusion to Ramsay's own liberation from his past. At the same time Deptford accompanies him even to Sorgenfrei in the internalized form of past experience and of course in the person of Magnus Eisengrim, formerly Paul Dempster.

Part II

Aspects of
Indeterminacy

There are no more remote and easy perspectives, either artistic or national. Everything is present in the foreground. That fact is stressed equally in current physics, jazz, newspapers and psychoanalysis. And it is not a question of preference or taste. This flood has already immersed us. And whether it is to be a benign flood, cleansing the Augean stables of speech and experience, as envisaged in Joyce's *Finnegans Wake,* or a merely destructive element, may to some extent depend on the degree of exertion and direction which we elicit in ourselves.

Marshall McLuhan

It has always been recognized that the non-given, or those elements that are withheld or excluded, constitute an important feature in the process of communication. Furthermore, this withholding of information, and the resulting "blank" in the structure of the communication to be achieved, has—from Aristotle on—been closely identified with the aesthetic principle determining art as a process of interaction with the subject perceiving it.

What Walter Pater, in affirming that beauty is in the eye of the beholder, formulated as a purely aesthetic concept, has since been recognized by phenomenologists such as Sartre[1] and Merleau-Ponty[2] as describing a feature present in any act of perception. The substance of Pater's argument has re-emerged in its aesthetic-theoretical context in studies by Roman Ingarden (*Das literarische Kunstwerk*),[3] Hans

Reference notes for Part II and Chapter Three are found on p. 96.

Gadamer (*Wahrheit und Methode*)[4] and E. H. Gombrich (*Art and Illusion*),[5] the latter heavily influenced by Gestalt theory.

The function of indeterminacy as considered in these and other studies serves as a point of departure for identifying the role of this concept in the dyadic interaction between text and reader as described by Wolfgang Iser.

Referring to both speech-act and general systems theory, Iser argues that like linguistic action, "literary texts also require a resolution of indeterminacies, but, by definition, for fiction there can be no such given frames of reference [situational contexts]. On the contrary, the reader must first discover for himself the code underlying the text, and this is tantamount to bringing out the meaning. The process of discovery is itself a linguistic action in so far as it constitutes the means by which the reader may communicate with the text."[6]

Iser demonstrates that this "lack of an existing situation" characteristic of fictional texts "brings about two ranges of indeterminacy: (1) between text and reader, (2) between text and reality. The reader is compelled to reduce the indeterminacies, and so to build a situational frame to encompass himself and the text."[7]

It is precisely in this indeterminate condition of the text that Iser situates its aesthetic quality, which he defines as "an empty principle, realizing itself by organizing outside realities in such a way that the reader [can] build up a world no longer exclusively determined by the data of the world familiar to him."[8] In the present context, the most general aspect of Iser's detailed discussion of the "blanks" constituting indeterminacy may be summed up in the observation that a "blank" represents an "empty space which both provokes and guides the ideational activity of the reader."[9] In contrast to Ingarden's "place of indeterminacy," however, Iser's use of the term *blank* "designates a vacancy in the overall system of the text, the filling of which brings about an interaction of textual patterns. . . . The need for completion is replaced . . . by the need for combination."[10]

It is obvious that all texts contain a certain number of "blanks," or a certain degree of indeterminacy, for "there must always be an element of the non-given in the given, if the latter is to be grasped at all."[11] In other words, the non-given is essential in allowing the reader to determine the significance of the given as perceived against the overall structure of the text.

One kind of blank is created by the selectivity inevitable in the representation of the fictional world of the text. While the "ideational" activity of the reader is set in motion in the attempt to "picture" the figures and scenes described in the text, these mental images never correspond to the illusion of reality effected by photography or cinema. As Iser points out, the viewing of a film based on a novel provides an example of the discrepancy between the effect of the mental images created in the reader by a text and that of the visual images presented to a viewer of a film. In the film the type of blank described above has been filled by ready-made and explicit images, replacing the indeterminate mental pictures created by the inevitably schematic features provided by the text. (This may, Iser says, account for the generally prevailing sense of disappointment experienced by people viewing a film version of a novel that they have previously read.[12])

Another kind of blank present in all types of narrative fiction is that created by segmentation. The switching of perspectives, the alternation of narrative reflection and plotline, and temporal discontinuity (for instance the use of flashbacks) all result in blanks which, in order to be "filled," require the reader not only to connect the segments themselves by motivating their occurrence in a given context, but also to discover the relation of the way the text is segmented to the overall structure of the narrative.

In contrast to the conventions characterizing the functions of "blanks" up to the late nineteenth century, certain aspects of indeterminacy manifesting themselves in the novel since that time tend to draw attention to themselves by cancelling out any possibility for the reader to resolve them on the basis of previous literary experience, in the sense that the modern novel tends to invoke traditional literary conventions only to "violate" them. This radicalization of the function of indeterminacy has taken a number of different forms, one of which is constituted by the spatial and/or temporal disorientation of the reader, such as that effected by the suggestion of multiple identities of one or more of the characters, for example. Whereas traditionally allusion was responsible for creating extensions of the identities of certain figures, the contemporary novel juxtaposes and superimposes the historical and the contemporary, the immediate and the remote, often without any narrative mediation.

Since Joyce's *Ulysses*[13] and *Finnegans Wake*,[14] indeterminacy has taken on a highly radical function with respect to the responses it induces in the reader: beyond initiating the reader's "ideational" activity, and making the reader aware of the nature of this activity, indeterminacy tends to thematize the process of the communicatory act itself. "Blanks" are more and more likely to occur on the metaliterary level, due to deliberate confusion as to the identity of the narrator and/or hero, to perspectival ambiguities, or to the consistent deformation of a given reality by the consciousness perceiving it. Whereas in novels such as Graeme Gibson's *Five Legs*[15] or André Langevin's *L'Élan d'Amérique*[16] the high degree of indeterminacy is created chiefly by the blanks resulting from various figures' streams of consciousness and their divergent ways of experiencing the same events, in *Beautiful Losers*[17] these blanks arise not only out of the segmentation of plot, perspective and narrative, but also out of the superimposition of disparate realities.

In Aquin's novel, this segmentation and superimposition is taken even farther. *Trou de mémoire*,[18] as the title suggests, may be seen as a play on the notion of the "blank" itself. Like anamorphosis in painting, which it describes as a metaphor for itself, the novel creates an omnipresent "blank" by abolishing the central perspective entirely. Corresponding to the oblique perspective that reveals the hidden object of the anamorphosis, each successive segment of the novel abolishes the perspective that preceded it, in the perception of the reader actually transforming (rather than merely altering, contradicting, modifying or expanding) the elements initially presented into entirely different "objects."

While reader reception theory takes into account both the psychological and ideological aspects of indeterminacy as the *non-dit*, it focuses less on these than, say, the psychoanalytical or Marxist models. Whereas the latter tend to define the *non-dit* as that which is not said because it cannot be said, relating it to societal sanctions and sexual taboos, reader reception theory focuses on the communicatory function of textual indeterminacy. Thus in the following studies of Cohen's *Beautiful Losers* and Aquin's *Trou de mémoire*, indeterminacy is identified as the governing communicatory strategy of both novels, constituting the "empty principle" which requires active participation on the part of the reader to fulfil the communicatory and aesthetic functions of the text.

THREE

Segmentation and Super-imposition in Leonard Cohen's *Beautiful Losers*

While both English-Canadian and *québécois* novelists (such as A. M. Klein in *The Second Scroll*[19] and Hubert Aquin in *Prochain épisode*[20]) have provided variations of the Joycean paradigm in pushing to the extreme a multiplicity of allusive patterns, Leonard Cohen, in *Beautiful Losers*, has taken the phenomenon of synchronous identity in the direction of the fantastic.[21] As in Kafka's fiction, or in the stories of Jorge Luis Borges, the effect hinges upon the reader's recognition that the fantastic has in some way become identical to the fictional reality. The problem for the reader lies precisely in discovering how this transformation of his own mode of perception is brought about.

The equations of fantasy, myth, history and everyday reality demanded of the reader in *Beautiful Losers* become recognizable only through the constant interrelation of the multiple indeterminate structures presented in the novel. The various kinds of "blanks" indicated by these equations therefore condition virtually every element presented. Their effect, unlike that in "realistic" novels, lies precisely in the fact that the reader is made aware first of all of the indeterminacies themselves as structured "blanks," and secondly of the demands made upon the reader in resolving them. As in the classics of modern fiction, the resulting high degree of textual indeterminacy makes great demands on the performance of the reader in the reading process. Readers of the novel are constantly confronted with contradictory information; they are required to relate seemingly arbitrarily introduced and disparate elements; finally, they are made to reflect on their own role in the communicatory process taking place as they go about reading the novel.

Whereas all literature may be described as creating an experience for the reader which cannot be communicated as such in referential terms, *Beautiful Losers* thematizes this feature, making it the subject of the novel itself. It does so by revealing the inarticulate and frequently abstruse associations and equations that constitute individual experience to be a hallmark of the collective experience of human civilization. Since in order to be able to grasp the text the reader is required to formulate these associations and equations, the effect of the text is to make the reader aware of all the irrational and fantastic phenomena screened out in the habitual processing of day-to-day experience, but also of the collective experience which surrounds the reader as past and future history.

From the beginning of the novel, it is made clear that the reader is to bring together aspects of different kinds of reality that are habitually perceived as irreconcilable. The success with which this condition is imposed upon the reader depends upon a progression or series of "blanks" which one may describe as ranging from the loosely associative and suggestive equation of the "real" and the fantastic with which the reader is familiar from previous experience of literature, to the explicit and "literal" identification of various categories of reality as manifested, for instance, in the metamorphoses described.

The role of superimposition in creating indeterminacy

The cumulative effect of the novel is determined by the superimposition of everyday reality, ancient myth, history and pop culture, all of which are themselves transformed by the way in which they mutually absorb one another. It is true that the superimposition of multiple realities, or elements of various realities, is a principle operative to some degree in all literary works, if only in that implied by the different realities of the reader's world and experience and those of the work of fiction. It is also clear that superimposition of any kind represents an aspect of indeterminacy, the blank being constituted by the withheld but implied connection between the realities juxtaposed or superimposed. The thematization of the superimposition itself, however, is very much a characteristic of the modern novel, and represents a common denominator for novels as diverse in effect as the works of Proust, Joyce, Kafka, and Virginia Woolf.

Viewed in the context of the types of superimposition occurring in the modern classics, *Beautiful Losers* would seem to come closest to the Joycean pattern of superimposition created in *Ulysses*. The equation of the banalities of everyday reality (not excluding physiological functions) and transcendental truths of both mythical and mystical origin is an effect of both novels which derives from the superimposition. But unlike that in Joyce's *Ulysses*, where the superimposition is indicated outright by the title, the reading process in *Beautiful Losers* is determined by a progressive recognition of the cultural elements to be invoked and synthesized.

While in *Ulysses* parallel relationships are suggested or even more or less explicitly designated through the Homeric allusions, in *Beautiful Losers* these relationships must first be determined by the reader. The superimposition is a cumulative product of the reader's assembling of various related text elements and is not completed until the end of the novel. In *Ulysses* the superimposition is a given from the beginning, moving the reader between a constantly shifting foregrounding and backgrounding of the present text and its ancient model. In this sense the polydimensional reality created in *Beautiful Losers* (which results largely from the metamorphic relationships between Isis, Catherine, Edith and the blond woman with the moccasins), differs from the superimposition of such figures as Nausikaa and Gerty McDowell in that the latter mutually reveal latent or virtual aspects of one another, whereas in the feminine figures in *Beautiful Losers* the features they hold in common are foregrounded. In *Ulysses* the principle of the superimposition is deviation, while in *Beautiful Losers* it is similarity.

Consequently, a central function of the superimposition in Joyce is the mutual defamiliarization of the individual narrative elements. In *Beautiful Losers*, the superimposition is used to create a sense of *déjà vu*, mainly due to the multiple and seemingly random precedents available for each of the cultural elements invoked. As in Kafka, the sense of *déjà vu* induced in the reader through the superimposition of various kinds of reality is a precondition for the reader's acceptance of the manifestations of the fantastic.

A characteristic example of how in *Beautiful Losers* this principle of superimposition creates a sense of *déjà vu* reveals the double function of the latter phenomenon, namely to induce the reader's acceptance of the fantastic and to link different kinds of reality in the mind of the reader. In the following quotation, a variety of elements are invoked and immediately abandoned, only to recur later on in the novel in contexts which are unfamiliar and even "apocalyptic":

Is there a part of Jesus in every stamped-out crucifix? I think there is. Desire changes the world! What makes the mountainside of maple turn red? Peace, you manufacturers of religious trinkets! you handle sacred material! Catherine Tekakwitha, do you see how I get carried away? How I want the world to be mystical and good? Are the stars tiny, after all? Who will put us to sleep? Should I save my fingernails? Is matter holy? I want the barber to bury my hair. Catherine Tekakwitha, are you at work on me already? (p. 6)

Though too elliptical and briefly touched upon to be precisely remembered, each element invoked above contributes to the sense of *déjà vu* experienced by the reader as it recurs at a subsequent point in the novel. Thus the reference to the reddening maple, for instance, insidiously introduces the phenomenon of chromatic metamorphosis and so anticipates the apocalyptic effect of the little plaster acropolis F. covers with red nail polish.

Both the apocalyptic and the *déjà vu* effects are intensified in the account of Catherine Tekakwitha's spilling a glass of wine at a banquet, the purplish-red stain spreading until it has suffused the entire banquet scene and even the landscape outside the hall (pp. 124-25).

The associations evoked by this uncontrollable diffusion of a colour and a substance which connotes violence and emblematically represents blood sacrifice, passion, and life itself go in what the reader habitually perceives as two different directions, namely contamination and transubstantiation. The bloodshed of the Indian wars, blood sacrifice as a cultural ritual, and the implicitly cannibalistic aspect of the Christian doctrine of transubstantiation lose their culture-specific values as the reader recognizes, in the superimposition of the various realities evoked by the metamorphosis, a common mystical experience. The effect of the recognition, however, is not merely to expose the cultural relativity of deeply ingrained values and beliefs, but to problematize the phenomenon of transformation itself. By superimposing elements of the natural (the reddening maple), the supernatural (the diffusion of wine), and the metaphysical (the shedding of blood, the essence of life, as a source of power and redemption or salvation), the text draws attention to the process of transformation as the phenomenon determining all human perception. As the increasingly explicit transformations and metamorphoses multiply in the novel, they become more and more associated with the consciousness perceiving them. Readers of the novel, aware that they are entrusting themselves to a consciousness, or perspectival view, which is "unreliable" in the traditional literary sense, become increasingly preoccupied with the processes of transformation, induced by the text, in their own consciousness. Their own perceptual norms which they have tended to regard as the product of a cultural consensus begin to be called into question.

The element of superimposition as demonstrated in the multiple instances of chromatic metamorphoses determines one of the most crucial effects of the novel, namely the negation of the modern systematization of reality. Though the separation of myth from everyday reality is the most prominent feature to be called into question, it is the entire concept of polarization as an instrument of human thought th.. is ultimately invoked and rejected. Thus the chromatic metamorphosis described above evokes in the mind of the reader the acropolis scene in connection with the episode at the banquet, resulting in a corresponding association between the aesthetic quality of the former and the spiritual element of the latter. The effect of this association is to reveal to the reader the dimensions which are lost in the habitual fragmentation of experience.

Indeed, the novel renders two aspects of individual and common experience particularly suspect. One is the elimination of the irrational, instinctual or transcendental as motivation for civilized behaviour as it is contemporarily understood (variously designated throughout the novel by terms like *Magic, Miracle,* the *Impossible*), and the other is the separation of the experience of the erotic, sexual, instinctual from that of the intellectual and spiritual. Both aspects are linked with the converging identities of figures who not only exist in different categories of reality, but seem to represent positions of polar opposition to one another. The seventeenth-century Iroquois virgin, Saint Catherine Tekakwitha, becomes indistinguishable from *I*'s sensuous wife Edith, while the two merge in the anonymous woman who picks up the "old man" in the final part of the novel. The "old man" turns out to be both *I*, i.e. the narrator of the first part, and F., the correspondent of the second. In possession of both their identities he/they dissolve(s) at the end of the novel, in the setting of the *System Theatre*, into a movie depicting Ray Charles. This final metamorphosis, in which the Ray Charles movie enlarges until it fills the theatre and then the sky, is recognized by the reader as absorbing all the elements constituting the multiple superimpositions previously encountered. Though the chromatic element is missing, the metamorphosis itself evokes the previous events, and so creates in the reader a sense of universal apotheosis.

> Then he enlarged the screen, degree by degree, like a documentary on the Industry. The moon occupied one lens of his sunglasses, and he laid out his piano keys across a shelf of the sky, and he leaned over him [*sic*] as though they were truly the row of giant fishes to feed a hungry multitude. (p. 305)

In summary one may say, then, that the superimposition on the one hand results in the association and equation of categories which the reader habitually perceives as separate or even antithetical entities. The sense of universal apotheosis, on the other hand, is created by the association of banal and familiar elements with transcendental experience on the basis of their shared features, or the common element evoking the *déjà vu*. This dual effect depends upon the reader's recognition of the superimposition of multiple unfamiliar manifestations onto a single familiar feature. Though this is also true of complex poetic images, for example, the difference in effect lies in the segmented quality characteristic of the novel. Patterns of superimposition occur in the narrative, and are then seemingly abandoned, only to recur unexpectedly later on in the text, transforming the intermittent segments both prospectively and retrospectively, as the reader projects the effect of the superimposition on to the segment being read.

The superimposition of various kinds of reality on the basis of a common feature constantly reinvoked to create a sense of *déjà vu* represents only one of the thematic blanks to be filled by the reader in *Beautiful Losers*. Two other kinds of blanks occurring throughout the novel are to be found in the narrative segmentation and the interpolation of extra-narrative elements (the latter itself fulfilling certain functions of text segmentation). Both these features require that readers connect the individual segments, and in doing so, they are led to formulate the withheld elements constituting the blanks.

But the presented patterns of segmentation have another important overall effect. Because of the sequence in which they are presented, they also progressively create a predisposition in the reader to accept the fantastic elements of the novel. The fantastic elements increase in each subsequent segment, both in number and in the degree to which they deny the possibility of accounting for them within the framework of the reader's own everyday reality.

In addition to these general functions fulfilled by segmentation, four other strategies of discontinuity can be distinguished throughout the novel. One is the perspectival segmentation created by the three principal parts, or "Books." A second is the narrative segmentation constituted by the interweaving of the two main narrative strands (essentially the alternation of the reality surrounding the contemporary figures and the historical and "mystical" reality of Catherine Tekakwitha). Closely connected to these two strategies, and to some extent overlapping with them, is the segmentation of the plotline. Finally, there is the more radical segmentation created by the interpolation of extra-narrative elements, consisting of *I*'s "prayers," F.'s "invocations to History," and the excerpts from the English-Greek phrase book.

Perspectival segmentation

The first part of the novel, which bears the heading "The History of Them All," is narrated by *I*, an anthropologist specializing in Amerindian history and folklore. Through the perspectival view presented by *I*, the reader is confronted with a seemingly random collection of *faits divers*, scholarly knowledge, personal information, metaphysical questions, remembered episodes, and fantasy. Since each of these elements occurs in alien contexts, the reader's attempt to assemble and group individual features into traditional categories such as plot, character, fantasy and fictional reality, and narrative perspective is constantly obstructed.

Contributing to the reader's consequent disorientation is the narrator's own mystification by his "best friend," F. Since the narrator describes their relationship as that of pupil and teacher, the unavailability of F.'s perspectival view gives the reader a sense of the absence and withholding of a "superior intelligence" through which I's confused narrative of associations, reflections and experiences might be explained.

F.'s authority is built up with a series of references implying that he possesses an intelligence, originality, freedom of mind and spiritual sensibility which lets him fit all experience into a complex and all-encompassing system. This "system" is never coherently presented, but only alluded to in I's quotations from F. The apparent absence of an immediate context makes F.'s remarks extremely suggestive and "profound-sounding," lending them an aura of axiomatic truth: "We've got to learn to love appearances" (p. 4); "Oh, F.," says I, "do you think I can learn to perceive the diamonds of good amongst all the shit?—It is all diamond," answers F (p. 10).

In its equation of the aesthetic and spiritual experience symbolized by the acropolis with the physical experience of the sexual act, and an impossible and blasphemous one at that (namely "fucking" a long-perished saint), F.'s "system" challenges more and more elements of the reader's cultural repertoire and personal experience. By implicitly cancelling habitual historical and spatial categories, and the notion of the distinction of the moral, spiritual and aesthetic spheres from the physical and erotic, readers are left with a bewildering sense of alienation from the principles with which they have thought themselves familiar and with which they have identified themselves.

Further disorienting the reader is the fact that F.'s system resists even the most general formulation. How is the reader to grasp a system which exhorts (by exhorting I) to "connect nothing," an exhortation immediately followed by I in a description of the anarchic nature of human experience?

Like the other allusions to F.'s teachings, the "Connect nothing" speech occurs in the context of the sexual relationship between I and F. While F.'s "insights" seem to be associated with and even determined by his sexual experience, the epiphanic quality of sexual fulfilment felt by the narrator is called into question. The orgasmic moment as one of "universal comprehension" is exposed as an illusion: "F. said: Connect nothing. He screamed that remark at me while overlooking my wet cock about twenty years ago. I don't know what he saw in my swooning eyes, maybe some glimmering of a fake universal comprehension" (p. 20).

F.'s "system," then, seems to be a contradiction in terms. For what is a "system" in which nothing is to be connected? Why does F. deny *I* the validity of sexuality as an epiphanic experience when his own "system" seems to be derived from sexual activity as an experience which is at once spiritual, intellectual and aesthetic? Finally, why recommend to *I* to "fuck a saint," as an experience which will illuminate the system itself, if the two are not to be connected?

In *I*'s perception the superiority of F.'s inaccessible consciousness manifests itself not only in the breadth of cultural, intellectual and emotional elements encompassed by his system, but extends even to *I*'s personal experience and his areas of scholarly expertise. F.'s relationship with *I*'s wife Edith represents a conspiracy of experience from which *I* himself remains excluded. And while *I* is an anthropologist specializing in Amerindian folklore and history, it is F. who, knowing little about either, comes forth with cultural theories concerning the Indians and the ancient Greeks which *I* wishes he had hit upon himself (p. 11).

At the same time certain features cast the validity of F.'s system and his declared purpose of instructing *I* in it in a dubious light. The reader learns that "F. died in a padded cell, his brain rotted from too much dirty sex. His face turned black, this I saw with my own eyes, and they say there wasn't much left of his prick" (p. 4).

Furthermore, *I*'s accounts of his dialogues with F. reveal a curiously consistent pattern of factual unreliability. On the night of Edith's suicide, for example, F. confesses to *I* that he had "slept with Edith five or six times in the twenty years he's known her" (p. 8).

> − You lousy fucker, how many times, five *or* six?
> − Ah, grief makes us precise!
> − . . .
> − Listen, F., don't give me any of your mystical shit.
> − Seven.
> − Seven times with Edith?
> − Correct.
> − You were trying to protect me with an optional lie?
> − Correct.
> − And seven itself might just be another option.
> − Correct. (pp. 9, 10)

While this exchange calls the reliability of F.'s statements into question, its effect is not so much to expose this unreliability itself as to induce the reader to try to find out whether the truth lies in the statement or in its contradiction. For the contradiction, like the original statement, yields to challenge with a promptness which makes it all the more suspect. In another verbal exchange between F. and *I*, F. makes statements which *I* flatly denies as untrue, as for instance F.'s constatation that he is a "girl" who has had an operation. While these easily exposed "lies" of F.'s can be explained by reference to F.'s deliberate provocativeness towards *I*, ostensibly for purposes of *I*'s education, the reader is constantly attempting to determine in what this education consists, and in doing so to formulate the substance of F.'s teachings and the peculiar nature of the relationship between the two men. The constantly recurring references to the pupil-mentor relationship let the reader recognize F.'s didactic message as a system (for which the "System theatre" provides a symbol) into which to fit the whole of human thought and experience. All the individual episodes are therefore seen in the light of F.'s declared intention of bequeathing his "knowledge" to *I*, and require that the reader formulate their significance against the background of F.'s "system." The reduction of the symbol (owing to defective lighting the sign identifying the *System* theatre reads *Stem* theatre) becomes illustrative of the failure of the system, but may also represent an allusion to its ellipticism.

In the second section of the novel, "A Long Letter from F.," the reality categories which the reader was still able to cling to in *I*'s narrative are challenged with increasing persistence. The identicality suggested in Part I of Catherine and Edith becomes unmistakable, while F.'s nurse, Mary Voolnd, turns out to be an A., like Edith and Catherine, member of a victimized and almost extinct Indian tribe.

The increasing predominance of the fantastic in F.'s narrative—in the Danish Vibrator episode the sex machine has become an autonomous creature, Hitler disguised as an Argentine waiter bathes Edith and F. with a bar of "human soap," and Edith reveals, in Greek, that she is Isis—has a paradoxical effect. On the one hand, *I*'s allusion to F.'s mental disintegration and his resulting hospitalization, like F.'s capriciousness and the opacity of his teachings, can be invoked as rational explanations for his fantastic accounts. On the other hand, the reader is aware that many of the elements composing F.'s descriptions have occurred previously in some less fantastic context. The reader is thus predisposed to accept the fantastic as a symbolic extension of what has gone before, so that the significance of both the present element and that which it evokes is expanded.

In the DV episode, for example, the unequivocality of the function of the machine is called into question in much the same way that the function of the garment factory F. buys becomes transformed. Acquiring the factory for no other purpose than to keep it inoperative, it becomes a "playground" whose enjoyment presumably stems from

the absence of the necessity to produce, and from the contrast between
F.'s former menial work there and his present power role as owner.
Similarly, the DV becomes "emancipated" from its mechanical function
and reverses its role, itself seeking the sexual gratification it is designed
to produce. Eventually, it even deserts its partner. Significantly
enough, neither of these experiments of F.'s—i.e. the acquisition of the
factory and the use of the DV—works as intended. At the conclusion of
the factory scene F. cries, and he and *I* stand locked in a "forlorn
embrace" (p. 54). The Danish Vibrator, whose mechanical stimulation
is to restore Edith's capacity for human sexuality, turns out to represent the pinnacle of human experience.

Typically, the significance of the event is communicated to the
reader through an oblique literary allusion, namely to the Faustian
invocation of an unsurpassably beautiful experience to "stay."[22] The
effect of Edith's "stay" is heightened by the original Faustian context,
for Faust's invocation constitutes the condition of his pact with
Mephistopheles. As a result of the Faustian allusion, F.'s role in the DV
episode is rendered quite explicitly demonic.

Whether or not Edith's "stay" constitutes the climax of the novel
(as such it would involve a sort of three-way pun, since it also presumably expresses Edith's own orgasmic moment of highest ecstasy) is a
debatable point. Nevertheless for the reader who recognizes Edith's
exhortation as a Faustian allusion the relationship between *I* and F.
becomes associated with the Faustian dilemma: *I* becomes associated
with the Faustian quest, F. with the demonic force which holds out the
promise of its fulfilment and achievement. That the aesthetic "plausibility" of the fantastic in Cohen's novel is heightened in the allusion to
Goethe's phantasmagoria represents an additional effect. At the same
time the polarity suggested by the Faustian reference (*I* as the questing
scholar, F. as the false best friend, or Mephistopheles) leaves the reader
wholly unprepared for the converging of the identities of *I* and F. in the
"apocalyptic" epilogue in the third person.

In this epilogue, F. is said to have died of syphilis and sends *I* his
bequests from beyond the grave, but the "old man" of the epilogue,
whom the reader assumes to be *I*, bears F.'s distinguishing marks. The
old man being hunted down in the main Shooting and Game Alley is
an escaped terrorist and institution inmate (F.) and, like F., is missing a
thumb (F. lost a thumb blowing up a statue of Queen Victoria in
downtown Montreal). The blond woman who picks up the old man in
the epilogue wears moccasins (evoking Catherine) and, like Edith,
identifies herself, in Greek, as Isis ("Ἰσιζ ἐγῶ-," p. 296).

The novel's movement away from the realistic to the fantastic is
thus reflected in the sequence of the three perspectival segments. In
"The History of Them All" the *I* perspective presents a mixture of

reality, fantasy, and historical and pseudo-historical accounts. Inter-relationships between these categories are suggested by association and superimposition, but the categories themselves remain separable for the reader. In the second section, while the fantastic events described by F. in his "letter" are offset by a "realistic" frame, the occupational therapy room at the institution, by the end of this section this "frame" becomes as scurrilous and fantastic as the DV scene. Nevertheless the reader can still invoke F.'s capriciousness and the opacity of his "teachings" as a possible explanation for this deliberate confusion of the real and the fantastic in the text.

In the epilogue, however, no such recourse is left the reader. The narrative perspective remains anonymous (the description of the "old man") and becomes ambiguous (who is the *I* of the final page?). The narrative itself, therefore, presents no mediation between the fantastic and the realistic. Their equation, in Part III, is literal and explicit.

Narrative segmentation

The way in which the narrator's story is interwoven with and deter-mined by the seventeenth-century Indian girl Catherine Tekakwitha fulfils an expository function, introducing the complex intersecting patterns which become recognizable to the reader only later on in the novel. In the perspectival view presented by *I*, the reader recognizes certain preoccupations which, in subsequent parts of the novel, con-stantly recur. In the intensity and frequency with which *I* invokes them, they take on the urgent and compulsive qualities of obsessions.

The disparity of these obsessions at first baffles the reader. As they recur in new contexts, however, the reader begins to recognize certain connections between them. Thus *I*'s spiritual and erotic interest in Catherine can be explained not only as an offshoot of his scholarly research, but also by F.'s challenge to "fuck a saint" and by the curious coincidence that *I*'s sensuous wife Edith was an A., a descendant of the same tribe to which Catherine belonged. Similarly, *I*'s chronic consti-pation, a "disease" which can be seen as a physical manifestation of the involuntary retention of the past, may be seen to motivate certain other aspects of his obsession with Catherine. The references to legends which attribute to her the roles of miracle-worker and re-newer of life make clear the nature of *I*'s expectations, while they also expand the significance of his physical symptoms as the expression of a metaphysical dilemma.

These interrelationships between the reality of *I* and that of Cathe-rine designate two separate systems, both of which converge in the supervening system of F. *I* indicates his own situation *vis-à-vis* these systems in an image in which his physiological state seems to stand for a negation: "The straining man perched on a circle prepares to abandon all systems" (p. 48), but the object of the negation itself is not clear to the reader at this point. What it does designate, however, is an imminent act which indicates *I*'s will to manifest existence (through vital function). It is his inability to do so which lets him seek Catherine as a source of both purification and self-redemption: "I am the sealed, dead, impervious museum of my appetite. This is the brutal solitude of constipation, this is the way the world is lost. One is ready to stake everything on a river, a nude bath before Catherine Tekakwitha, and no promises" (p. 50). As the novel progresses, communion with Catherine becomes a more and more plausible necessity in implementing *I*'s will to manifest existence, not only in the process of physiological purging suggested above, but also in the spiritual release from solitude through communication. In assembling the described episodes and the perspectival views of *I* and F., and in relating them to those aspects of Catherine Tekakwitha's life which are invoked, it becomes evident to the reader in what *I*'s deficiency consists: *I*'s exclusion from the ritual intercourse between Edith and F., and his own orgasmic and communicatory impotence in his relationship with F., stand in sharp contrast to his retrospective desire and regret. By invoking Catherine, by turns, as an erotic figure—"I want to know what goes on under that rosy blanket" (p. 3)—as saint and miracle worker, *I* creates a figure who represents an expression of non-intellectual or irrational experience. This emerging figure of Catherine contrasts sharply with *I*'s inability to consummate present experience, as indicated in the sexual incident of the drive with F. to Ottawa, Edith's invitation to transformation in the grease-paint episode, and his exclusion, more or less voluntary, from F. and Edith's "telephone dance" and "drug experiments" (the latter consisting of the injection of a mixture of water from Lourdes and water from Tekakwitha's spring). Catherine, as invoked in the narrative, represents the "magic of the moment," the immediate realization of the impossible which is attempted and only fragmentarily achieved in the activities of F. and Edith, and at which *I* himself miserably fails.

Throughout the novel, Catherine is simultaneously associated with Edith, the Holy Virgin, and Isis, representing, like Molly Bloom, a composite figure pointing to the feminine principle as it appears in large segments of Western culture. She is therefore perceived by the reader to constitute the "other," the alien, communion with whom would release *I* from his solitude.

Nowhere is the Joycean influence more in evidence in *Beautiful Losers* than in the individual episodes counterpointing the narrative. The rich evocations of an event are unexpectedly deflated by the banality of the event itself, or, conversely, an initially banal situation turns out to carry universal and metaphysical significance.

Thus for instance the description of Edith's suicide takes an entirely unexpected and ironic turn: Edith has been foiled in her intention in committing suicide by a mere fluke of chance. Intending to become a "literal victim" of her husband, and so letting him experience what he has hitherto only known vicariously ("fictional victims," p. 8), she is killed not by her husband, as she has anticipated, but by a boy delivering Bar-B-Q chicken somewhere in the building who mistakenly takes the elevator down to the basement. This "tragic irony" is immediately undercut by the description which follows:

> We ordered chicken from the same place and we talked about my poor squashed wife, our fingers greasy, barbecue sauce drops on the linoleum. (p. 8)

The reader's initial "appropriate" response, then, is contradicted not only by the flippancy of *I*'s reference to Edith's death, but also by the "barbaric" behaviour of *I* and F. subsequent to it.

Another incident achieves a similar effect by a kind of reverse strategy. A comic-book ad for Charles Axis's body-building method is inflated to enormous proportions by a three-page description of the comic-book images and text, only to be exploded by a sort of Joycean epiphany:

> Charles Axis is all compassion, he's our sacrifice! He calls the thin but he means both the fat and the thin; he calls the thin because it is worse to be fat than thin; he calls the thin so that the fat can hear and come and be named! (pp. 91-92)

The shock effect of this incident is twofold. On the one hand, the reader is made to view the idealistic conceptions of modern life as a commercially created mythology consisting of (illusory) Messianic and Utopian notions (in the promise of redemption through physical power). Thus readers are confronted with the absurdity of their own deeply ingrained beliefs. On the other hand the text's description of the ad and its effect (it almost drives F. to suicide) represents a horrifying demonstration of the power of both images and language. Furthermore, the constant inflation and deflation of myth and banal commercial reality illustrates their inseparability in the mind of the consumer as a cultural being.

This kind of antithesis is one of the points of virtually every episode of the novel, including the tale of Catherine. The result is the revelation not only of the forces underlying modern mythology, but also of the tension between that which is articulated and that which is suppressed in human culture, myth, and history. It also points up the hermeneutic problem of any historical view as alluded to by the title of the novel.

The interpolation of extra-narrative elements

In addition to its patterns of superimposition and structural discontinuity, a feature Cohen's novel shares with Joyce's *Ulysses* is its consistent auto-referentiality. In Cohen's work, this feature represents the most complex level of indeterminacy since it results in the thematization of the communicatory act itself.

There are repeated allusions throughout *Beautiful Losers* to this kind of metaliterary "blank," as in F.'s enigmatic references to an undetermined "it" in his admonishments to *I*: "Your teacher shows you *how it happens*" (p. 234), and, more explicitly still, "Watch the words, watch *how it happens*" (p. 235). A clue as to what is meant by the pronoun *it* which seems to have no antecedent is provided by a passage preceding F.'s first exhortation: "it was I who pointed you to a place where I cannot go. I point there now—with my lost thumb" (p. 234). Given the context of what has gone before in the novel—the numerous metamorphoses, Catherine's miracles, and the moments of "apocalypse"—*it* becomes recognizable to the reader as that aspect of a transformational process which is invisible but nevertheless perceivable due to the communicability of its experience. The non-verbal element is suggested by F.'s missing thumb, which is to be perceived by *I* as "pointing," while the verbal one is indicated by the undetermined pronoun *it*, which is nevertheless present because it is constituted by the synthesizing activity of the reader.

This kind of metaliterary indeterminacy is present throughout the text, but it grows densest in the "interpolation" of extra-narrative elements whose indeterminate function is increased due to the necessity of relating them to the narrative itself.

In *I*'s "prayers," a multiplicity of seemingly unrelated elements are jumbled together in an abstruse mixture of curiously formulated banality ("In The Midst of Molecular Violence The Yellow Table Clings To Its Shape"), irrelevant and unverifiable observations ("There Are Old Eggs In The Gobi Desert"), and poetic and spiritual invocation ("Be With Me As I Lose The Crumbs Of Grace") (pp. 68-69). The consistent use of capital letters underlines the apparently random equation of material fact, the imaginary perception of the unperceivable, and the anguished appeal of the speaker for divine solace. Are these "prayers" the expression of a tormented mind half-crazed with grief, or do the elements alluded to form a sort of sample catalogue of the human situation and man's way of apprehending it? While the reader's response may be to decide that they are both, there remains the difficulty already alluded to of how the "prayers" are to be connected to the narrative. As with the other extra-narrative elements— the coupons, ads, phrasebook, F.'s "Invocations to History"—the "prayers" presuppose a reality which lies beyond everyday experience. The various realities represented by these elements are determined by the subject's belief in their existence; the coupons for gaining or losing weight, like the ads for Charles Axis's body-building method or for the healing powers of beads containing water from Lourdes, promise miracles, which can only be achieved by acts of faith on the part of the subject. F.'s invocations to history expose the traditional conceptions of history—as "faith" in history—as an illusion whose effect is not to bring the past into the present, but, like a drug, to induce forgetfulness (cf. F.'s "Invocation to History in the Middle Style," p. 238).

The Greek phrasebook represents the most direct allusion to the blank as an indeterminate structure created by language, for it invokes language itself as the most problematic of communicatory processes. Full of hypothetical situations and unidiomatic expressions which no one would under any circumstances utter ("I want this costume to be cleared," p. 177), the phrasebook in its very ineffectualness reveals language itself to be an act of faith. If the everyday discourse of banal commercial transaction presents difficulties in transformation from one language to another, how can any metaphysical experience—such as that presented in the novel—be communicated? The phrasebook demonstrates that communication as an act of will presupposes a receptive consciousness whose ability to respond to the given message rests solely on convention and common experience. Under any other conditions, the phrasebook seems to indicate, communication fails. The precarious nature of the communicatory act is further underlined by the link established between the phrasebook and the act of prayer.

As he bequeathes the phrasebook to *I*, pressing it into his hand, F. says: "It's a prayer book. Your need is greater than mine" (p. 7). It is F. himself who expresses the precariousness of communication illustrated by the phrasebook as one common to all communicatory situations, even that of man communicating with himself: "Prayer is translation. A man translates himself into a child asking for all there is in a language he has barely mastered" (p. 71).

If prayer is a translation of the self, and literary communication the translation of non-selective, uncontexted everyday experience into a fictional reality which makes common experience meaningful, the "miracle" clearly lies neither in one or the other of the entities translated or to be translated but in the transforming process itself, which takes place through language. Since the meaning produced in response to a literary text (or any linguistic utterance for that matter) can never wholly coincide with the intention of the author (or speaker), it is readers themselves who transform the world in that they "bring something into it"—a meaning—which was not there before.

The reader is induced to formulate this definition of meaning by plot contexts as well as by the extra-narrative elements already described. Edith, covered with red grease-paint and greeting *I* at the door of their flat, hands *I* the paint tube, saying "let's be other people." After her death *I* reflects: "Perhaps she meant: Come on a new journey with me, a journey only strangers can take, and we can remember it when we are ourselves again, and therefore never be merely ourselves again" (p. 18).

Transformation as a collective experience is also invoked through allusion to a cultural-historical event. The box of firecrackers, part of F.'s posthumous bequest to *I*, may be recognized as a Promethean allusion, letting the reader perceive *I*'s experience with F.'s "assort-ment" as a modern illustration of the consequences of the mythical Promethean gift. Elements of the Promethean myth become displaced onto the various figures of the novel, and constitute a significant aspect of the collective chronicle made up by the unwritten reverse side of human history, namely that of the "beautiful losers": *I* burns himself with F.'s firecrackers, F. himself loses a thumb in a dynamite explosion; both are driven to the verge of madness by the brilliance of the insight encapsulated in F.'s "system." The Indians are all but annihilated by the firearms of their white conquerors, who, in turn, are numerously burned at the stake by the Indians. The musician Ray Charles is blind, but his image is composed of the reflected light of a projection beam, and "explodes" its frame, the screen, and the theatre (an image of world), to absorb the light of the celestial bodies, the moon and the stars, themselves reflectors of light and symbols of infinity.

By focusing the reader's attention on its own indeterminate struc-tures, *Beautiful Losers* makes the reader conscious of the elements involved in the transformational process initiated not only by the participation generated as the reader perceives a work of art, but by all quotidian human experience as well. This subtle and elusive transfor-mation of the self through experience (and the determination of experi-ence by the self) is represented as a constant, a given of human existence, and a process of which the self often remains unconscious. Nevertheless the text also invokes the phenomenon of consciousness transformation as a moment of apocalypse, which demands the sus-pension of habitual patterns of perception and behaviour. Refusal to abandon everyday reality in the quest for the "miracle," or "apocalyp-tic experience," is, ultimately, a deprivation and, in a way, life-denying. This feature is illustrated by *I*'s refusal to engage in the eccentric transcendental experiments of F. and Edith, but it is also posed as a challenge by the text to the reader, since in order to be understood the text demands that the reader abandon habitual percep-tual categories. With its elements of the fantastic and the grotesque, the text may, like Edith's greasy disguise, be seen as an invitation to transformation as a conscious experience of self.

When it was first published in 1968, *Beautiful Losers* elicited shock, bewilderment and disapproval not only in general readers, but in some critics as well. As Michael Gnarowski's collection of Cohen criticism[23] demonstrates, this response was not in the first instance due to the breaking of sexual or moral taboos, at least not in the case of the critics. Reviews and essays revolved around the demands the novel makes on the reader: the breadth of its cultural allusions, the complexity of the characters' relationships, the shattering of conventional norms of novelistic representation—all these elements made the novel as "journey" a strenuous and even awesome one for Canadian readers of the sixties to experience. It was perhaps this unaccustomed strain imposed on the reader that led to a relative isolation of *Beautiful Losers* in the classic surveys and critical collections which, at that time, largely determined the English-Canadian literary canon.

To younger Canadian readers who may take the enthusiastic critical (and indeed general) reception of recent post-modernist works (such as Robert Kroetsch's *The Studhorse Man* or *Alibi* or Timothy Findley's *Famous Last Words* or *Not Wanted on the Voyage*) as a matter of course, some of the criticism in Gnarowski's volume must seem strangely dated. For the dissent generated by Cohen's novel represents a conflict still apparent in some Canadian criticism as to the nature of literary communication. In the Gnarowski collection the principal issue in Cohen's novel is still the high degree of indeterminacy: while *Beautiful Losers* is evaluated positively by some critics *because of* its indeterminacy, which is seen to break open the fixed structures of realistic fiction governed by traditional literary norms,[24] others regard it as breaking what they consider to be fixed aesthetic norms such as wholeness, harmony, and coherence.[25]

Whatever the critical tenor, all the essays seem to recognize indeterminacy as a predominant feature of *Beautiful Losers*. The striking evaluative disparity may be an indication of the degree to which Canadian fiction has remained bound to traditional novelistic forms until the appearance of Cohen's novel. Sheila Watson's *The Double Hook*,[26] published in 1954 and technically unprecedented in Canadian fiction, nevertheless maintained the traditional features of character and plot, albeit in highly alienated and stylized forms. But while the effect of *The Double Hook* could still be accounted for by its use of symbols and myths, and had a paraphrasable plot and differentiated characters, *Beautiful Losers* resists any attempt at thematic analysis in the traditional sense because its "theme" is, precisely, the uncommunicable associations constituting the individual experience of life. This incommunicability of experience is both indicated and demonstrated by the "blanks" segmenting the text. It is by inducing the reader's perception of the "blanks" and of their communicatory function that the text renders communicable the inarticulate nature of both everyday and literary experiences.

Reference Notes to Part II and Chapter Three

1 Jean-Paul Sartre, *L'Imaginaire* (Paris: Gallimard, 1948).
2 Maurice Merleau-Ponty, *Phénoménologie de la perception* (Paris: Gallimard, 1945).
3 Roman Ingarden, *Das literarische Kunstwerk* (Tübingen: Niemayer, 1960).
4 Hans Gadamer, *Wahrheit und Methode. Grundzüge einer philosophischen Hermeneutik* (Tübingen: Mohr, 1960).
5 E. H. Gombrich, *Art and Illusion. A Study in the Psychology of Pictorial Representation* (London: Phaidon, 1972).
6 Iser, *The Act of Reading*, p. 60.
7 Ibid.
8 Ibid., p. 179.
9 Ibid., p. 194.
10 Ibid., p. 182.
11 Ibid., p. 64.
12 Ibid., pp. 137-38.
13 James Joyce, *Ulysses* (London: The Bodley Head, 1960).
14 James Joyce, *Finnegans Wake* (London: Faber and Faber, 1957).
15 Graeme Gibson, *Five Legs* (Toronto: Anansi, 1979).
16 André Langevin, *L'Élan d'Amérique* (Montreal: Le Cercle du Livre de France, 1972).
17 Leonard Cohen, *Beautiful Losers* (New York: Bantam Books, 1976 [Viking Press, 1966]).
18 Hubert Aquin, *Trou de mémoire* (Montreal: Le Cercle du Livre de France, 1968).
19 A. M. Klein, *The Second Scroll* (Toronto: New Canadian Library, 1958 [Knopf, 1951]).
20 Hubert Aquin, *Prochain épisode* (Montreal: Le Cercle du Livre de France, 1965).
21 Cf. Tzvetan Todorov's definition of the fantastic in literature in his *Introduction à la littérature fantastique* (Paris: Seuil, 1970).
22 "Verweile doch! du bist so schön!" Goethe's *Faust*, Pt. I, l.1346.
23 Michael Gnarowski, ed., *Leonard Cohen: The Artist and His Critics* (Toronto: McGraw-Hill Ryerson, 1976).
24 Cf. Dennis Duffy, "Beautiful Beginners," in Gnarowski, pp. 29-32; George Woodcock, "The Song of the Sirens: Reflections on Leonard Cohen," ibid., pp. 158-67; Desmond Pacey, "The Phenomenon of Leonard Cohen," ibid., pp. 74-93; Douglas Barbour, "Down with History: Some Notes Toward an Understanding of *Beautiful Losers*," ibid., pp. 136-49.
25 Cf. Lawrence M. Bensky, "What Happened to Tekakwitha," in Gnarowski, pp. 136-49; John Wain, "Making it New," ibid., pp. 23-28.
26 Sheila Watson, *The Double Hook* (Toronto: McClelland and Stewart, 1959 [1954]).

Hans Holbein (c. 1497-1543): *The Ambassadors* (Jean de Dinteville
and Georges de Selve)
Reproduced courtesy of the National Gallery, London

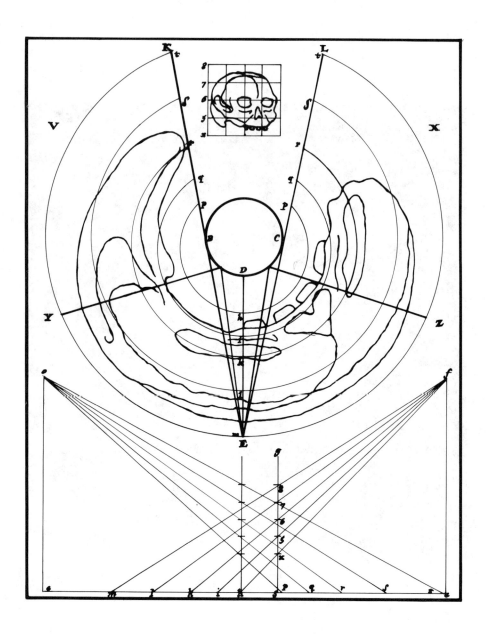

Père de Breuil: "Anamorphose du crâne pour un miroir cylindrique" (1649)
Courtesy NeWest Press

FOUR

Perspectival Segmentation, Anamorphosis and Isomorphism as Indeterminate Aspects in Hubert Aquin's *Trou de mémoire*

With *Trou de mémoire*, the metaliterary focus of the postmodern European, American and Latin-American novel was introduced into *québécois* fiction in one of its most self-conscious and complex forms. Hubert Aquin himself seems both to have recognized the technical breakthrough he achieved with *Trou de mémoire*, and to have anticipated that its hermetic structure would prove an almost insurmountable obstacle to a reading public accustomed to easily accessible novels of social realism. In an interview, he described *Prochain épisode*, his highly complicated first novel, as a *jeu d'enfant* compared with his second novel.[1] Nevertheless the persevering (and knowledgeable) reader is presented with abundant clues for the resolution of the indeterminacies, and the anamorphic structure itself is repeatedly referred to and "explicated" throughout the novel in a number of different contexts.

In spite of the fact that within ten years of the publication of *Trou de mémoire* several book-length studies, a number of theses, and a multitude of articles appeared on Aquin, the significance of his contribution to letters in Quebec and to the post-modernist genre as a whole will likely only begin to emerge with the publication of the critical edition of Aquin's works. The obvious parallels, for instance between Nabokov's

Reference notes for Chapter Four are found on pp. 119-20.

Pale Fire[2] and *Trou de mémoire*, persistently evoked in the latter novel, remained almost entirely unexplored by critics of *québécois* fiction until quite recently. Aquin's novels, including *Trou de mémoire*, seem to have had only a small reception in non-*québécois* or non-Canadian circles, even among critics of the post-modern novel. Relatively few articles devoted to Aquin have appeared in the non-*québécois* or non-Canadian literature compared, for example, to less demanding works such as Marie-Claire Blais's *Une Saison dans la vie d'Emmanuel* or other Canadian or *québécois* authors well-known abroad partly because of the fact that they publish outside Canada.

In examining the structures of indeterminacy in *Trou de mémoire* it is tempting to dwell on the striking effects created by the isomorphic superimposition of a sixteenth-century painting (which contains one of the most famous anamorphoses in the history of western art) on a modern narrative. These effects nevertheless cannot be described without referring to the norm underlying both works of art, namely the central perspective, which governs not only the representational technique of the artist but also the viewer's (or reader's) way of perceiving and grasping the represented object, or the text.

The central perspective, however, is precisely what *Trou de mémoire* seems to withhold from the reader, blurring or even cancelling the distinction between the experience of art as illusion and the representation of life as illusion, whose irreconcilability is so dramatically expressed by manipulation of the central perspective in Holbein's painting. For in *Trou de mémoire* the central perspective is not segmented into two mutually exclusive images, as in "The Ambassadors"; perspectival segmentation becomes an ongoing process resulting in a constant transformation of the "object" perceived. This perpetual segmentation thus constantly invokes and seemingly cancels the central perspective as norm, constituting the central blank of the novel.

Two quotations, taken from a study of anamorphosis as a representational technique and its visual effect, refer to the significance of the discovery of the central perspective in representational art. In a sense, these observations on perspective formulate the basic premises for understanding and interpreting *Trou de mémoire*.

> In addition to rationalizing the relationship between the depicted objects, the discovery of the central perspective creates a relationship between the viewer and the representation. An extreme example of this objectivization of the representation is to be found in the anamorphoses. The viewer is at first misled by a barely recognizable representation and is then directed to a spot determined by the formal construction of the picture. Even the etymological origin of the word [anamorphosis] indicates that the viewer himself must re-form [assemble] the image.[3]
>
> It is clear that deviation from the perspectival norms [as for instance in the anamorphoses] can only occur in a milieu in which the norms are commonly held.[4]

The extent to which viewers of painting and readers of fiction have become conditioned to the central perspective as a representational and perceptual norm becomes evident only when it is deliberately broken or consciously manipulated. In representational art, the anamorphosis as a form of such manipulation remains a curiosity, as is indicated by the subtitle of one of the best known of the modern studies of anamorphosis in art that have been undertaken so far.[5] In fiction, the concept of perspectivization has absorbed modern writers and critics alike since Henry James, but it has remained closely bound to the traditional notions of character and point of view.

In Hubert Aquin's *Trou de mémoire*, the function of the central perspective in graphic and fictional representation is not only exposed as analogous, but this analogy is revealed through a common element (the *figure cachée*) which represents one of the most extreme and esoteric representational forms. The most obvious basis for the correlation between the function of the central perspective in graphic and in fictional representation is that the novel describes itself as containing an anamorphosis, or *figure cachée*. To help the reader recognize it, the text provides two "examples," both of which turn out to be part of the novel's own *figure cachée*. Thus the two illustrations that stand at the beginning of this chapter may be seen to constitute central points of reference for *Trou de mémoire*. Père du Breuil's "Anamorphose du crâne pour un miroir cylindrique" (1649) appears as the graphic on the cover of the novel (extending over front and back). A description of Holbein's "The Ambassadors," with its anamorphic figure presented by one narrator, is recognized as a *texte à clé* or *texte codé* (p. 136) by another, and a third narrator explicitly formulates symbolic connections between individual elements of the painting and the novel ("Suite et fin," pp. 133-45).

In Holbein's famous portrait, the segmentation consists in the fact that the skull as an emblem of death is perceivable as such only from a certain point of vision, namely at a distance and from the left. Viewed from this angle, the skull dominates the picture. From all other points of view, however, the painting represents a highly conventional portrait of two historical figures masterfully executed according to the principles of illusionary art.

In his study entitled *Anamorphoses ou perspectives curieuses* Jurgis Baltrušaitis describes this striking double effect of "The Ambassadors" as follows:

Le "Mystère des deux Ambassadeurs" est en deux actes. . . .Le premier acte se joue lorsque le spectateur entre par la porte principale et se trouve, à une certaine distance, devant deux seigneurs, dressés comme sur une scène. Il est émerveillé par leur allure, par la somptuosité de l'apparat, par la réalité intense de la figuration. Un seul point troublant:

l'étrange corps aux pieds des personnages. Le visiteur avance pour voir les choses de près. Le caractère physique et matériel de la vision se trouve encore accru lorsqu'on s'en approche, mais l'objet n'en est que plus indéchiffrable. Déconcerté, le visiteur se retire par la porte gauche, la seule ouverte, et c'est le deuxième acte. En s'engageant dans le salon voisin, il lève la tête pour jeter un dernier regard sur le tableau, et c'est alors qu'il comprend tout: le rétrécissement visuel fait disparaître complètement la scène et apparaître la figure cachée. Au lieu de la splendeur humaine, il voit le crâne. Les personnages et tout leur attirail scientifique s'évanouissent et à leur place surgit le signe de la Fin. La pièce est terminée.[6]

The other illustration, Père du Breuil's "Anamorphose du crâne pour un miroir cylindrique," demonstrates the principle which makes possible the achievement of such a curious effect. The technique involves a deformation of the object by a fixed system of the lengthening of certain features and the foreshortening of others; its effect is determined by the multiplicity of perspectives from which the object can be viewed in the cylindrical mirror.

Considered retrospectively, i.e. after reading the novel, the cover design achieves its full significance. In a sort of anamorphosis of Du Breuil's "Anamorphose," the front cover is dominated by a shaded circle, identified in type by the title *Trou de mémoire* which appears in the widening space indicating the angle at which the object is to be viewed to be recognizable. On the back cover we find a system of diagonal (oblique) lines intersecting at regular intervals to indicate the virtual points of perspective, while a graphic schematization of the object itself—the *crâne*—is to be found underneath this network of intersecting lines of vision.

Without pressing the question of literary correlatives too far, it is possible to recognize in this complex cover graphic certain key features of the novel itself. For the illustration indicates the multiplicity of perspectives available for viewing a given object, the arbitrariness with which certain of these perspectives are selected and actualized, and the segmentation of perspectives which is necessary to perceive and grasp the object presented to view. The image of the cylindrical mirror thus constitutes at once an optical and symbolical model for the phenomenon of perspectivization, but also designates the reflexiveness of perceiving subject and object perceived. The hollow space, or that which is enclosed within or behind the *miroir cylindrique*, may be seen as a metaphor for the presence of an unnameable absence. It constitutes a symbolic allusion to *Trou de mémoire* as a mnemonic phenomenon, while it also invokes the cranial void implied by the representation of the skull as the object reflected in the mirror. Thus *Trou de mémoire*, in addition to designating a loss characterized by its unnameability, circumscribes the temporal and spatial categories which represent the perceptual norms of conscious experience.

Contingent to the isomorphism between Holbein's "Ambas-sadors" and the novel is a series of isomorphic and isochronic relation-ships which together constitute the fictional reality of the narrative as well as its alienation and cancellation. The relationship between Olympe Ghezzo-Quénum and Pierre X. Magnant, and between the "sisters" Joan and Rachel Ruskin are only the most obvious examples. The geography of the Swiss Alps and the Ivory Coast, the physical topography of Joan's body, the perfect crime and the work of art, pharmacology, sexuality and revolution, all designate themselves while pointing to their symbolic extensions and isomorphic counter-parts, and thence to the infinite number of points of their interconnec-tion.

A primary effect of withholding of the central perspective is to change the very nature of the reader's activity in the reading process. Unlike that in a traditional novel, reader involvement is not initiated by the familiar novelistic elements of plot and character, but by the read-er's own effort to learn "the truth"; the reading activity is bent on constituting, from the multiple options open throughout the novel, a "superior" perspective which would enable the reader to evaluate the relative validity of the contributions of Olympe, Magnant, the "editor" and RR in the novel that is being read. In this activity, which is motivated by the attempt to reconstitute a central perspective, the reader is handicapped not only by ignorance but by the irreconcilable contradictions of the various sections and the apparent arbitrariness of editorial selectivity and annotation.

If this quest of the reader for "truth" is initiated by the novel's denying recourse to the formal norms of traditional narrative dis-course, it is complicated by the negation of the familiar social and moral norms which make up the reader's ordinary everyday reality. The equation of sexuality with rape and masturbation, the description of pharmacologically induced self-narcosis as a desirable state, the invo-cation of violence as self-liberation, all represent to the reader a physi-cal and moral world which is both exotic and taboo.

The effect of this defamiliarization of the reader's social and liter-ary repertoire is heightened by the temporal and spatial disorientation created by the text. Where, for instance, is the reader to place the "Cahier noir" or RR's "Semi-Finale" chronologically; and how can Magnant be simultaneously in Montreal carrying out his homicidal intentions with regard to Joan and at the same time stalking RR in Lausanne? As in *Prochain épisode*, the reader's disorientation reaches its climax with the converging identities of the various *personae*, while this identicality is seen to allude to its own category of experience as belonging to the fantastic, the unreal.

But due precisely to the reader's own experience of the text, explanation of its "inconsistencies" on the basis of a schematization of reality has become unsatisfactory. With RR's complete contradiction of the fictional reality created by the text prior to her "Semi-Finale," the reader is confronted with both the virtuality of the textual reality itself, and also with that of his or her own interpretation. The habitual separation of the experience of reality and the experience of illusion is cancelled by the way reality and illusion respectively present themselves, and by the reader's increased awareness of the nature of their interaction.

The function of perspectival segmentation in *Trou de mémoire* is extremely radical in that it breaks even the vestiges of the consistency-building conventions to be found in English-Canadian novels like *Beautiful Losers* or *Five Legs*, or *québécois* novels like those written by Victor-Lévy Beaulieu or Jacques Rénaud (*Le Cassé*).

Instead of representing the multiple facets of a complex fictional reality, as in the conventional novel, or at least revealing the complementary nature of that which is felt to be realistic and that which if felt to be fantastic, as is still the case in *Beautiful Losers*, each perspectival segment in *Trou de mémoire* functions to disturb the hermeneutic performance of the reader in the segment which precedes it. Initially this disturbance is achieved by the apparent irrelevance of the sequence in which the segments occur, while ultimately the reader's consistency-conditioned imagination is taxed to the utmost by the flat contradiction of one segment by another.

Viewed by externally marked headings, or chapters, there are four separate perspectives presented throughout the novel, namely those of Olympe Ghezzo-Quénum, the African pharmacist and revolutionary; Pierre X. Magnant, his *québécois* counterpart whose perspective, though not "central," dominates the novel; the anonymous "editor" of Magnant's manuscripts; and RR, whom the reader takes to be Rachel Ruskin, Olympe's lover and the sister of Magnant's lover Joan.

Complicating these alternately foregrounded perspectives are copious footnotes, which constitute a context and a background, and thus a contrasting perspective, to whatever perspectival view is foregrounded. Furthermore, since they are appended to the pages of the text to which they refer, and so interrupt and even disrupt the reading of the text, the footnotes effect not only a temporal and linear discontinuity but also the simultaneous availability of two and sometimes three contrasting perspectives.

In the traditional novel the elements constituting the individual perspectival views combine to form a sort of code, the deciphering of which takes place as the reader assembles and groups the elements to form constantly enriched or broadened contexts for the particular passage being read. In *Trou de mémoire* there is also tangency between the individual elements of one section and those of another. Indeed, the reader finds a certain symmetry, suggesting a possible code, in the perspectival views presented through Olympe and Magnant, and in the "documents" presenting them. But this symmetry is cancelled by the capricious "revelations" of the "editor" and RR. It is the "editor's" and RR's interventions that disallow any schematization and so guarantee the readers' perpetual alteration of the code they use to decipher the "meaning" of the novel.

Nevertheless, like the individual and apparently heterogenic segments themselves, the elements presented through any given perspectival view are meant to be connected to those presented in other contexts. These connections are formed by the reader not only on the basis of certain differences or similarities in the way given elements appear through the various perspectival views, but also by the reader's recognition that each perspectival view itself represents only a mask of the respective narrator. The self-representation, in many segments overtly narcissistic, of any one given perspectival view *vis-à-vis* the others, involves revelation by strategies of dissimulation which increase the indeterminacies created by the perspectival segmentation itself.

In the tradition of the epistolary novel, to which it alludes, the letter from Olympe Ghezzo-Quénum to Pierre X. Magnant with which the novel opens provides a great deal of information about the receiver as well as about the sender. A host of features shared by the two men emerge: they practise the same profession, are both engaged in revolutionary activity, and both profess an ardent admiration for Bakunin and Thomas De Quincey.

While Olympe himself describes the similarities which let him and Magnant appear to the reader as *Doppelgänger*, his letter contains certain elements which make his invocation of his "twinship" with Magnant highly ambivalent. Thus, for instance, the excessive politeness, obsequiousness even, with which Olympe anticipates the effect his letter will have on Magnant reveals the potential manipulativeness of his rhetoric. In much the same vein Olympe manipulates the reader through his own (presumed) prejudices concerning black Africans, ironically undercutting the reader's conclusions as to the isomorphic relationship between the two figures by disqualifying them as irrational, and as being characteristic of tribal modes of thought.

Je sais que les Fons sont très enclins à survaloriser tout ce qui est occulte et à édifier interminablement des systèmes de correspondances entre les événements ou entre les hommes—systèmes absolument invérifiables qui finissent par tout expliquer. En cela, je reconnais que je procède mentalement comme ceux de ma race, et que j'ai tendance, trop souvent, à substituer à la raison un système séméiologique de remplacement. (p. 8)

It is this sense of Olympe's rhetorical manipulativeness that lets the reader recognize a connection between a talent Olympe has obviously cultivated and its political exploitation for the achievement of his revolutionary goals, and the nature of his practised profession. In its ability to control human response, language, especially in its political use, has an effect similar to the pharmaceutical narcotic, and ultimately results in an alteration or even abandonment of will. The suggested parallel between the effect of language as ideologically motivated rhetoric and the effect of a narcotic drug is strengthened by its implicit allusion to the famous Karl Marx image which declares religion to be the "opiate of the people." Given this ideological context, Olympe's description of his trips to Lagos to purchase "barbituriques 'made in England'" (p. 14) is politically evocative in equating the origin of the pain- and sensation-dulling, sleep- and forgetfulness-inducing, and so will-weakening drug with the origin of colonization as the paralysis of will of the conquered people.

A striking feature of Olympe's letter is that while at the beginning he seemed to have a certain purpose or goal in mind which he wanted to communicate to Magnant, his letter grows more and more personal and diffuse as it progresses.

In the end, the very intention of Olympe in addressing himself to Magnant remains ambiguous, for as Olympe reveals the two men are linked not only by their professions, revolutionary activity, and personal taste, but also by a mutual acquaintance, a white woman from Montreal whom Olympe has met in Lagos and with whom he has an intimate relationship. In the perception of the reader, the woman as racially and sexually "other," incarnating the experience of *altérité*, joins the first chapter's three other thematic complexes which are by definition also transformative agents, effecters of change, or of a state of *altérité*: language, revolution, and narcotics.

When the reader re-encounters Olympe, three-quarters of the way through the novel, he has difficulty evoking the author of the opening letter, for Olympe seems entirely changed. The stylistic resemblances between Magnant's *récit* and *cahier noir* and Olympe's *journal* are as striking as the fact that Olympe seems to be as obsessed with RR as Magnant is with Joan. With Olympe's journal, the isomorphism between the two couples becomes more and more explicit until they become almost totally superimposed figures.

This sense of duality and repetition is underlined by Olympe's reference to the transformation of his life as a consequence of his decision to leave Africa (pp. 148-49), which evokes a previous footnote (to Magnant's *récit*) alluding to the "'double passé' des pays africains" (p. 88). This allusion to the alteration of the collective identity of a people as an inevitable consequence of colonization, when connected with Olympe's changed life, lets his altered identity appear as an individual manifestation of a collective fate, forming yet another parallel to the individual fate of Magnant and that of the *Québécois* as a people.

Reporting RR's disappearance at a police station, Olympe, under questioning, finds that he has forgotten the name of his hotel, and that he is not carrying his passport. Both these circumstances invoke the loss of identity associated with loss of memory as a state caused by trauma. This association by the reader has a double effect. On the one hand, it re-evokes, and in a way illustrates, Magnant's description of this process in a conquered nation that develops collective cultural amnesia in the process of being "colonized." And though Olympe's "amnesia" does not require motivation (he is, after all, quite capable of describing the location and appearance of his hotel), the double circumstance of forgotten passport and forgotten hotel name externally confirms the unverifiability of an identity the reader has already begun to call into question.

It is in their respective relationships to RR that the merging identities of Magnant and Olympe begin to become a certainty for the reader. The fact that Olympe, in his journal, refers to Rachel as RR, strikes the reader as standing in curious contradiction to their intimate relationship. Also, the use of initials represents the anonymity behind which a second "editor" conceals her/himself. It is as if Olympe, in referring to RR, is referring to the fictional *persona* of the novel the reader is reading, rather than his lover. In other words, Olympe's reference to RR indicates his awareness of the text as text, and not as the only reality in which he dwells. This circumstance links him with both Magnant and the "editor."

A second element of Olympe's journal linking him with Magnant is RR's altered behaviour towards Olympe after the rape. Depressed and apathetic, she too seems to suffer from amnesia with regard to the circumstances of the rape. Desperate, she asks Olympe, who, for his part, is trying to learn the details from *her*, to recount the event and so liberate her from its traumatizing effects and her "amnesia." Unconsciously, in sleep, however, she seems to recall the rape with ecstatic emotion. Eventually, Olympe's obsession with the circumstances of the rape lets him construct a scene in which Magnant corners RR in a dark doorway, takes her to a dim, bare room, and rapes her on a sheetless mattress. The inherent plausibility of this scenario, together with Olympe's consistent evocation of the same scene, and RR's evident experience of the rape as pleasurable, contribute to the merging of Magnant and Olympe in the consciousness of the reader.

The ultimate ambiguity of the relationship between Olympe and Magnant is indicated in the inconsistent chronology. The dating of

Olympe's journal is irreconcilable with the date of his letter to Magnant and the events described in Magnant's *récit*. The "rape" of RR, or so the reader concludes, from the approximate chronology he is able to construct on the basis of Olympe's journal, coincides with Magnant's collective "rape" of his audience in the *discours* that plays such a central role in Magnant's own *récit*. Finally, Olympe's penetration of RR during her "narco-analyse," which is, in effect, a rape, seems to coincide chronologically with Magnant's murder of his lover Joan.

One effect of the dual perspective created by the ambiguous identities of Olympe and Magnant is to illustrate both the nature and inevitability of the processes initiated by the analogous events of sexual rape and colonial military conquest. Another is situated on the metaliterary level. By refusing to allow the reader to construct a consistent and unambiguous perspective in viewing its suggested relationships and described events, *Trou de mémoire* casts the reader in the role of author, confronted with the heterogeneous and contradictory realities of the quotidian and the imaginary. Furthermore, by exposing the logical irreconcilability of situations that the reader nevertheless perceives and experiences as "real" and equally valid, an impression created by the text's own strategies of illusion, the text reveals the restrictiveness of the empirical logic which normally determines the reader's perception of reality. As in Cohen, these communicatory strategies also restore the reader's faith in the intuitions and acts of imagination which an intellectually hypertrophied culture has relegated to the bottom of the perceptual norm hierarchy.

With the section entitled "Première partie du récit" the reader is immersed in Magnant's verbose description of his pharmacologically induced state of intoxication. In a *tour de force* of neologisms and superlatives, he describes his drug experience alternately as a never-ending orgasm, a state of possession, a sense of infallibility and "glory" culminating in his perception of himself as the sun.

This invocation of *mythos* is sustained in the "Suite" (chap. 3) of Magnant's *récit*. Having established altered consciousness as being, on the one hand, an effect of narcotics, and, on the other, of colonial conquest, thus analogically linking the two, the text describes the antithesis to the respective states, namely a drug acting as a counter-agent in the pharmacological context, and, in the socio-political context, revolution. Magnant describes the hiatus between these states, i.e. between conquest and revolution, in a Christian image in which, nevertheless, redemption is withheld: "Oui, le conquis s'est taillé une toute petite place entre la mort et la résurrection; il est mort et attend dans une espérance régressive et démodée un jour de Pâques qui ne viendra jamais" (p. 38).

It is in "Suite II" that the text shifts in focus from *mythos* to *logos*, from *faire* to *dire*. Magnant expresses the nature of the power of language, articulating its role in the creation of reality: "les mots que j'ai lancés au public m'ont enfanté. Je suis né à la révolution en prononçant les paroles sacramentales" (p. 46). Like Olympe's prophetic remark that "En nommant les choses souvent on les appelle," Magnant's words formulate the transformation of the virtual reality of fiction into the concrete reality of experience as being initiated by the act of communication and achieved by the reception and acknowledgment of that act.

Magnant evokes this relationship between action and language, or the dependence of action on its linguistic conception, not only in connection with Joan's murder, but in its collective context as the history of Quebec. The function of language as a dialectical system which ultimately brings about change (revolution) is illustrated by the image of the movement of a play to its *dénouement*. As Magnant describes it, the problem of the *Québécois* is that "Ils ne reconnaissent même pas le lieu dramatique et sont incapables de se rappeler le premier mot de la première ligne du drame visqueux qui, faute de commencer, ne finira jamais" (p. 56). The *Québécois*, then, are represented as unable to perform either the mnemonic or the linguistic act necessary to initiate a dialectic and thus to effect change.

It is this unilateral function of the act of speech as initiating both communication and action, which in turn results in an alteration of a given reality, that links it with the bizarre sexual incident described in "Suite III-A." Magnant's masturbation of Joan in London (against the fence surrounding Buckingham Palace) is described as a unilateral liberating gesture (p. 63) ending a state of mutual and self-alienation. Not only the details of the locale, but also Magnant's reference to an *évocation politique*, let the reader perceive the incident as an implied analogy to the political situation in Quebec, whose "gratification," too, will be created by a "unilateral" gesture engendering action and thence change. Like the speech act and the sexual act, the act of pharmacological intervention is also invoked as an illustration of the dialectic process necessary to effect change. In "Suite IV" Magnant says: "Mon activité politique, d'autre part, me prouve que j'incarne une image archétypale de pharmacien, car je rêve de provoquer des réactions dans un pays malade" (p. 65).

With the final part of Magnant's *récit*, introduced by the "editor" in the chapter entitled "L'Incident du Neptune," communication, sexuality, pharmacology and revolution as dialectical systems transforming a given reality are joined by a fifth category, namely that of art. It is at this point that the reader begins to perceive the implications and hence the motives underlying Magnant's murder of Joan: with all the finality of a work of art, her death represents the inalterability of her existence, allowing Magnant, as the executor of the murder ("work of art") to possess her eternally. Art, like murder, eliminates all virtuality;

the achievement, the realization of human action (art), transforms it into an immobile object whose ontological status can only be asserted by a perceiving subject. This view of murder as an imaginative creative act, which in its finality eliminates the virtuality and hence complexity of all human experience not contained in itself, is expressed by Magnant as resulting in a sense of loss: "Il ne me reste plus grand'chose, sinon d'avoir inventé, si l'on peut dire, la mort masquée de Joan" (p. 87). The act of murder, like the act of creation, abolishes its own virtuality, while the temporal hiatus between the conception and execution of these acts marks them off into separate events, one of which is a "repetition" of the other.

The aesthetic nature of this duplication—Magnant quotes Blanchot: "la répétition relève visiblement d'un art et cela équivaut, en fin de compte, à un style de la présence et implique une notion hautement consciente du temps parlé" (p. 78)—itself designates and is designated by the *"double passé"* in the isomorphic relationship between Magnant and Olympe. It also represents an allusion in the text to its own strategies of communication. For if the concepts of duality, repetition and isomorphism are indicated implicitly or explicitly in virtually every element of the text, their cumulative significance remains unformulated and hence indeterminate. It is the reader who assembles these individual elements, formulating their interaction into an interpretation and so "re-inventing" the work of art as it was conceived by its creator. The act of interpretation, then, represents a "repetition" of the creative act by eliminating the indeterminacy between text and meaning, thus completing the communicatory act initiated by the text.

Counterpointing the perspectives of Magnant and Olympe is the "editor," whose role in the opening chapter of the novel is extremely discreet: the excessively modest "editor's" footnotes have primarily a distancing effect.

In Magnant's narrative the reader perceives a subtle alteration in the *persona* of the "editor." In his first note, the "editor" informs the reader that he has arbitrarily "cut" Magnant's *récit*. Though he communicates this fact following the formulaic conventions of editorial style—"Je me suis permis de découper assez arbitrairement je le reconnais, le récit de Pierre X. Magnant" (p. 20)—the absence of any explanation of the basis on which he has proceeded detracts from the impression of editorial conscientiousness he has so far conveyed to the reader. As in the first chapter, the "editor" is responsible for a certain alienation between text and reader, for he draws the reader's attention to features of Magnant's manuscript that are neither perceivable nor verifiable by the reader.

In Chapter 3, or the "Suite" of Magnant's *récit*, the *persona* of the "editor" changes even more perceptibly. The perspicacity of his final footnote (p. 39) reveals a hermeneutic judgment of a different order from that which he has previously demonstrated. In fact, in the style and erudition he presents, he closely resembles Magnant himself. Furthermore, the apologetic editorial formulas give way to frank admissions of censorship. The reader's recognition of the gradual alteration of the "editor" and the role he plays in the text is confirmed in the subsequent section, "Suite II," which begins with an editorially unexplained and uncontexted sentence fragment. The conventional editorial functions initially presented are thus more and more overtly undermined.

On page 43 the reader finds a footnote written not by the "editor" but by someone who signs the initials RR, while the second footnote on the same page is signed as a "note de l'éditeur" and makes no reference whatsoever to the footnote which precedes it.

The introduction of what is apparently a second editor into the text has two effects. One is to baffle the reader as to who this second editor might be and why the original "editor," otherwise quick to point out and "explain" irregularities in the text, ignores RR. The second is to increase readers' awareness of their own manipulability by the superimposition of external perspectives on the text, for in view of contradictions between the "editors" (p. 49) readers recognize their dependence upon the authority of the text before them. Where one view is challenged by another seemingly holding the same authority, the readers themselves are at a loss, unless they are in a position to verify the views presented.

With "L'Incident du Neptune" the presentation of the "editor's" perspective is displaced from the footnotes to the text proper. Furthermore the observations of the "editor" concerning the historicity or reality versus the declared fictionality of Magnant's text have little in common with the pedantry and obtuseness he has manifested earlier.

The enigmatic reference to the relation between Magnant and the "editor" (p. 73), and the latter's observation that he is the only "dépositaire du manuscrit original" (p. 73) arouses the reader's suspicion that the "editor" might be a creation of the narrator Magnant, or vice versa. Certain scholarly references to psychopathological problems of identity, for instance to the "syndrome Jean-Jacques"[7] (p. 75), strengthen these suspicions.

The relation of the incident itself, on the authority of the Neptune's proprietor, Luigi, who is a mutual acquaintance of the "editor" and Magnant, increases the reader's sense of their possible identicalness. As a public "repetition" of the masturbation scene in London, described by Magnant himself, the incident demonstrates the theoretical observation of Magnant (quoting Blanchot) concerning the function of repetition in art. It thus combines Magnant's description of the scene in London with the editor's description of the "Neptune" episode into one narrative strand.

With the "Note de l'éditeur," which, however, constitutes the text itself, the "editor" openly casts doubt on whether Magnant is actually the author of what has gone before. Describing his own role as editor as a Brechtian mode of "distancing" (p. 101), he presents various arguments indicating that Magnant's text may not be authentic: Magnant's intimate familiarity with Africa as documented by his descriptions is suspect, for the "editor" assures us that he was never there (p. 102). In support of this argument the "editor" informs the reader that the "African" passage is the only typewritten one, and that it had been stored separately from the rest of the manuscript. The latter fact, of course, the reader is unable to verify. The former, however, is untrue, for the "editor" has previously indicated a different passage as being typewritten (pp. 24-25).

The reader, then, recognizes an implied connection between Olympe and Magnant on the basis of the intimate knowledge of African geography betrayed by the passage, suggesting that either it was written by someone other than Magnant (Olympe?), as the "editor" seems to suggest, or else is a result of a "rewrite" (by the "editor" himself? cf. p. 104).

The uncertainty generated by the increasingly ambiguous identities of the "editor," Magnant, and Olympe is increased with the second textual "Note de l'éditeur" (p. 121): the "editor's" use of "auteur" between quotation marks, his evident emotional involvement as he edits the text, and his image of being entombed in shifting sand (an evocation of the Sahara) indicate more and more explicitly the merging of the identities of Magnant and the "editor," culminating in the latter's declared sense of magic power strangely similar to the *délire hallucinatoire* he has ascribed to Magnant as author.

Even more evocatively, the section ends as a fragment and is annotated by RR, establishing a formal parallel in the relationship between text, author and editor of Magnant's *récit* and the corresponding elements of the "editor's" "note" which in fact constitutes the text itself.

In "Suite et Fin" the "editor's" voice speaks as such for the last time. Like his counterpart in *Pale Fire* and *The French Lieutenant's Woman*,[8] the "editor" as narrator announces an end which is not the end, since it is followed by two sections of Olympe's journal and a "Note Finale" by RR.

The "editor" also announces that he will present the reader with the truth, which, from the perspective of the "editor," lies in the "falseness" of RR and her writings. But as the reader has been made aware, precisely by the text itself, the "truth" cannot be identified by only one of the four designated perspectives, for the adoption of one perspective eliminates all the others. This feature, once recognized by the reader, links the text directly with the anamorphosis in the Holbein painting, which the "editor," in this section, "interprets," making the reader aware that the traditional norms that have hitherto dominated his or her literary experience are not valid for the present novel: "le spectateur du tableau de Holbein finit par regarder ce tableau selon d'autres critères que ceux qu'il a développés dans un musée" (p. 136). The sentence following this observation therefore becomes charged with irony for the reader: "Cette hypothèse me tue," for it is literally true in the sense that it abolishes both the "editor" and Magnant by upholding the validity of the perspective of RR, which denies their existence.

The intuitions of the reader concerning the ambiguous identities of the figures presenting the various perspectives seem to be confirmed in the self-doubt expressed by the "editor": "Ai-je donc un don de seconde vue? Suis-je moi-même en train de vivre une autre vie à force de récapituler les circonstances de la mort de Joan? Je ne sais trop; *mais ce que je sais ressemble de plus en plus à ce qu'on devine*" (p. 144, my italics). Thus beyond pointing to the implicit identicality of Magnant, the "editor" and Olympe, the passage may be seen to describe the perceptual process experienced by the readers themselves in the reading of the novel.

The chapter entitled "Semi-Finale," of which RR is the "author," constitutes the turning point of the novel in that it declares the invalidity of all that has preceded it in the text.

The "author" reveals: that she is female; that it is she who has written the entire text the reader has so far read, and that it is all fictitious; that Magnant therefore never existed and that she is no more RR than "Joan" is Joan.

This revelation creates an extremely complex set of "blanks" contingent to those produced by the other perspectives, not only because it calls them into question, but also because it requires motivation by the reader. The question the reader asks at this point in the narrative is not only who is who, and who did or wrote what, but to what purpose these illusory connections have been established.

Rather than reducing the indeterminacy of the text, RR's "enlightenment" of the reader increases it, for in negating the fictional separation of perspectives and identities presented in the novel by claiming to be the sole author, she is nevertheless obliged to refer to the figures and events described. By affirming their non-existence, she reinforces rather than abolishes the experience their respective "texts" constitute for the reader and so contributes to the reader's sense of their continuing presence, or fictional reality.

In casting herself as the sole author of the present novel, describing Joan, a stage designer specializing in *trompe-l'oeil* effects, as her homosexual lover, and thus "abolishing" Magnant, Olympe, and the "editor," RR creates a new fictional reality by exposing the strategies by which the previous "illusionary" reality was communicated to the reader. The description of "Joan's" illusion effects thus becomes recognizable to its readers as a kind of metaphor for the effects of the work of fiction, and so draws attention simultaneously to its fictional character and to the reality of the reader's experience of it.

Referring to her place of concealment in the *loge supérieure* and the theatrical "omniscience" it affords, RR lets the reader identify the perspective she represents as constituting, both literally and structurally, a *figure cachée*: "je me sens, ni plus ni moins, comme une effigie distordue qui, jamais regardée obliquement et selon le bon angle, reste infiniment une image défaite" (p. 129). Thus linked to the *figure cachée* in the Holbein painting she describes, RR is recognized by the reader to formulate the indeterminacy constituted by the anamorphosis as a narrative strategy of the entire novel.

RR's revelation of the "truth," however, is called into question in that it is apparently superseded by the "old" "editor," who comments upon her "text." With his appearance, he cancels the fictionality ascribed to him by RR who has informed the reader that she and she alone stands behind the various perspectives which have previously occurred.

The "Note Finale" itself cancels RR's previous claim to have invented all that preceded the "semi-Finale" in that RR admits that the passage in question was nothing but a *plaisanterie* (p. 202). While the first part of the "Note Finale," which represents the "editor's" perspective, confirms the reader's recognition that the "editor" and Magnant are identical, the second part, ostensibly written by RR, glibly résumés their respective deaths, her changed identity and her pregnancy from Magnant's rape.

The very glibness of RR's final declarations lets the reader view them with suspicion, for they do not seem to do justice to the complexity of the relations previously established between Joan and Magnant, Magnant and Olympe, and Olympe and RR. The validity of the information presented in the "Note Finale" is called into question by a chronological problem: the events alluded to. RR's rape by Magnant, for example, took place in 1966, as the reader recalls from Olympe's journal. Yet in the episode in Mullahy/Magnant's office, Olympe informs Mullahy/Magnant that "RR a été violée par Pierre X. Magnant il y a tout juste deux mois" (p. 194). The "present" of the office encounter, however, has already been identified as the summer of 1967 (p. 193).

As Patricia Smart has observed, these manifest inconsistencies of the "Note Finale" reveal the self-conscious artificiality of the novel.[9] The suggested identicality of Olympe and Magnant—indicated to the reader not only by the isomorphism between the two established throughout the novel but also by Olympe using the name of Magnant as an alias at the time of his suicide—contributes to this sense of *artificialité* and *littérarité*. It also points to the virtuality of any given perspective in the perceptual process which determines the experience of both reality and fiction.

In demonstrating the arbitrary nature of the segmentation of perspective achieved in the novel, RR's "Note Finale" reveals to the reader how the actualization of any one perspective relegates the other indicated perspectives to their original virtual status. The multiplicity of possible perspectives in their virtuality constitutes a *trou de mémoire*, which can only be filled when the previously actualized perspective is abandoned.

This principle of perspectivization which emerges as the reader recognizes the effect of the novel's strategies of segmentation may be invoked with respect to all the thematic elements presented in the novel. It reveals the significance of the term *trou de mémoire* as applied to the collective amnesia of a people who have been forced to adopt the cultural perspective predetermined by the nation that conquered them. At the same time the numerous references to the role of perspective in art as illusion, and particularly the effect of Holbein's anamorphosis in "The Ambassadors" in the novel, let readers recognize the nature of their own role in the aesthetic experience constituted by their reading of the novel.

Somewhat in the manner of the double ending in Fowles's *The French Lieutenant's Woman*, the novel reveals the aesthetic object perceived to be a product of the projections the readers themselves have formed as they adopt and then abandon perspectives following the "instructions" of the text. In *The French Lieutenant's Woman* the two endings are mutually irreconcilable. In *Trou de mémoire* the artificiality of the ending is irreconcilable with the illusion of reality created by the rest of the text. In Holbein's "Ambassadors," the perspective which allows recognition of the skull as *figure cachée* is irreconcilable with that which presents the realistic portrait of Jean de Dinteville and Georges de Selve.

The novel explicitly indicates isomorphism between Holbein's painting and the novel itself in the correspondences formulated by the "editor" in "Suite et Fin" (pp. 141 to 145): the two ambassadors correspond to the figures of Pierre X. Magnant and Joan; the Oriental tapestry uniting the two ambassadors has its equivalent in "la texture des mots ... dans ce livre" (p. 142); the enigmatic shape, the skull, at the feet of the ambassadors forms the "centre secret" of the painting just as "le meurtre de Joan est le socle sombre du roman" (p. 143).

Readers recognize a deeper resemblance between the painting and the novel once they have grasped the function of the novel's perspectival segmentation. Like the double perspective in the painting, the novel's foregrounding of one perspective results in the "blurring," elimination, or "loss" of that which was previously foregrounded. This phenomenon is expressed in the novel in that their mutual irreconcilability abolishes the figure presenting one of the perspectives, namely the one which is abandoned, nevertheless without destroying it: it remains virtually present in the form of memory, but it loses its function of representing a given reality. The "loss of memory" or, in the Holbein painting, the loss of sight of the subject of the portrait, results in the elimination of ambiguity, but also in the all-pervasiveness of the one perceived perspective. In "The Ambassadors" it is the representation of the skull, a symbol of death. In *Trou de mémoire* the final perspective ironically vanquishes this spectre by the fact that RR not only survives, but also shapes a future for herself and her child by changing her identity and bestowing one on her child. The ending therefore is ironic not only in its artificiality, but also in that it is not the figures of RR and her child that will prevail. Lurking (extra-textually) behind them is the "final" perspective of Holbein's painting, the "hidden and irreverent emblem of Death."[10]

As in all Aquin's works, *Trou de mémoire* is full of literary and historical allusions which specify the nature of the fictional world represented in the text.

Françoise Iqbal has analyzed at some length the pharmacological effects described in the novel in connection with the Dionysian elements in Nietzsche's works,[11] while Patricia Smart, in *Hubert Aquin, agent double*,[12] points out the degree to which both *Prochain épisode* and *Trou de mémoire* are ideologically determined by Frantz Fanon's *Les Damnés de la terre*[13] and Albert Memmi's *Portrait du colonisé*.[14]

The prominence of Magnant's multiple oblique Nietzschean references is exceeded only by his obsession with Sherlock Holmes and the perfect crime, while Thomas De Quincey (author of *Confessions of an English Opium Eater* and *On Murder Considered as One of the Fine Arts*)[15] and Bakunin form another allusive strand. Brief references to Stefan Zweig (p. 118) and Heinrich von Kleist (p. 151), both of whom committed suicide together with their partners under the extreme emotional pressure of a sense of exile and futility, illuminate yet another dimension of the text.

The author-narrator-editor complex and the copious footnotes evoke, as most obvious perhaps among the literary allusions, Nabokov's *Pale Fire*, which, like his *Laughter in the Dark*,[16] is explicitly alluded to in the text. But while the direct reference to Nabokov plays on the structural and thematic similarities of the two works, *Trou de mémoire* is also full of humorous allusions to *Pale Fire* which designate parallels and may also be seen as a sort of personal homage to the author. Thus Magnant's double name, Pierre Xavier, and the name he adopts in changing his identity, Charles Mullahy, constitutes a reference to Charles Xavier, the Zemblan alter-ego of the poem's author, John Shade.[17]

A more thematically significant allusion is to be found in the inventory of "Aunt Maud's room" as described by "John Shade" in Canto One of *Pale Fire*. It lists a number of elements which, as allegorical items visible in Holbein's painting, are exploded into the central metaphors of *Trou de mémoire*. The lines in question read as follows: "... the paperweight / Of convex glass enclosing a lagoon, / the verse book open at the Index (Moon / Moonrise, Moor, Moral), the forlorn guitar, / The human skull. ..."[18]

Though repeated allusions to itself as a *roman policier* occur in the novel, this generic allusion does not play the central role in *Trou de mémoire* that it does in Aquin's first novel, *Prochain épisode*, where it represents the governing communicatory strategy. In *Trou de mémoire* it is the narrative and perspectival segmentation, the isomorphism and isochronism between the individual segments and elements, and the isomorphic relationship between the text and Holbein's double portrait that create a high level of indeterminacy and so constitute the main narrative strategies of the novel.

The enormous demands its indeterminacies make on the reader place the novel in the modern esoteric tradition of Joyce, Beckett and Nabokov.

With its invocation of the fantastic and the metaliterary, *Trou de mémoire*, like *Beautiful Losers*, also contains the aesthetic playfulness with the reader that characterizes a number of more recent novels of other literatures, such as Gabriel García Márquez's *One Hundred Years of Solitude*,[19] Italo Calvino's *If on a Winter's Night a Traveller*,[20] and John Fowles's *The French Lieutenant's Woman*. Underlying these common features is a more and more explicitly formulated preoccupation of the authors in question with the kind of relationship created between text and reader as part of the communicatory process of literature. Aquin's description of this relationship as he presents it (from the writer's perspective) in his essay "La Disparition élocutoire du poète (Mallarmé)" sums up the position characterizing the authors of the auto-referential or "metaliterary" text:

> je suis préoccupé jusqu'à l'obsession par le lecteur. En écrivant, j'imagine que je me lis par les yeux de cet inconnu et je voudrais que son plaisir de lire mon texte ne soit pas uniforme, constant, prévisible en

quelque sorte, mais avec plusieurs seuils d'intensité, enrichissant, capable de le surprendre, voire de l'ébranler et difficile à prévoir. Quand j'écris, je pense au lecteur comme à la moitié de mon être, et j'éprouve le besoin de le trouver et de l'investir. Une écriture totale est celle qui est tout entière tournée vers la possible lecture qui en sera faite par le destinataire. Les recherches élocutoires de l'écrivain, ses figures, ses truquages, ses stratégies verbales sont autant d'éléments relationnels et non d'abord expressifs, car ces éléments reposent sur un rapport entre l'auteur et le lecteur.[21]

In the novels of Cohen and Aquin, "obsession with the reader" is manifest in the degree to which the participation of the reader as "cocréateur de l'oeuvre"[22] is demanded. As highly auto-referential novels, *Beautiful Losers* and *Trou de mémoire* require the reader to reciprocate the author's "obsession" with the reader and reader responses to the text. In inviting and even forcing the reader to participate in the "making" of a work whose effect is precisely the recognition of how the work is actualized by the reader, these texts demand an "obsession" with fiction of the same order as the "obsession" with the reader manifested in them.

Both *Beautiful Losers* and *Trou de mémoire* stand out in Canadian fiction not only because of their high indeterminacy (in this they have been equalled if not superseded by the more recent works of Kroetsch and Findley, Ducharme and Théoret, for example), but also because both novels have played a unique and possibly paradigmatic role in the formation of a Canadian post-modernist canon which is by no means unproblematic ideologically.

In the highly ideological controversy surrounding the concepts of postmodernism and the *avant-garde*, the respective frames of reference of both terms emerged very clearly in the positions taken by literary theorists and critics—and also writers—of various persuasions in the late sixties and early seventies. Typological studies undertaken since then[23] have to some extent depolemicized the debate, seeking to clarify the current usage of both terms by documenting their occurrence and fields of reference in previous writing and focusing mainly on the development of postmodernist fiction as a separate literary genre.

Aquin's work is likely to be of particular interest in connection with the emerging typologies, since it incorporates most of the elements considered characteristic of both generic terms and their subcategories. Thus, for instance, *Trou de mémoire* is both "violent" and "political" (features considered to be hallmarks of the *avant-garde*) as well as "ambiguous" and "auto-referential" (postmodern). It is, above all, highly intertextual and "metaliterary," actively engaging the reader in the political, revolutionary and aesthetic theorizations that underlie it.

Indeed, both *Beautiful Losers* and *Trou de mémoire* require a participation that actively involves the reader in the creative process itself, resulting in a flash of insight of the kind that Jean-Claude Margolin has described as the "practical equivalent of truth":

> C'est par [le] jeu d'écarts, de discordances et de projections obliques de la pensée ou de l'image, que peut s'opérer au moment favorable—le *kairos* des Grecs—le redressement ou la restructuration du sens qui, dans un éclair instantané, sera l'équivalent pratique de la vérité.[24]

Reference Notes to Chapter Four

1 Michèle Favreau, "Hubert Aquin, propos recueillis sans magnétophone," *La Presse,* avril 30, 1966, p. 11.

2 Vladimir Nabokov, *Pale Fire* (London: Weidenfeld and Nicolson, 1962).

3 J. Elffers, M. Schuyt and F. Leeman, *Anamorphosen. Ein Spiel mit der Wahrnehmung, dem Schein und der Wirklichkeit* (Köln: Dumont, 1981), p. 8; my translation. The original quotation reads: "Außer einer Rationalisierung der Beziehung zwischen den zur Schau gestellten Objekten, stellt die Erfindung der Zentralperspektive eine Beziehung zwischen dem Betrachter und der Darstellung her. Ein extremes Beispiel dieser Subjektivierung der Darstellung sind die Anamorphosen. Der Betrachter wird erst irregeführt durch eine kaum erkennbare Darstellung und danach zu einer Stelle dirigiert, die durch die formale Konstruktion der Darstellung bestimmt ist. Die etymologische Herkunft des Wortes weist schon darauf hin, daß der Betrachter selbst tätig sein und das Bild selbst zurückformen muß."

4 Ibid., p. 17; my translation. The original quotation reads: "Es ist deutlich, daß die Abweichung von der perspektivischen Norm nur in einem Milieu entstehen kann, in dem die Normen Gemeingut sind."

5 Jurgis Baltrušaitis, *Anamorphoses ou perspectives curieuses* (Paris: Olivier Perrin, 1955). On anamorphosis see also: Jean-Claude Margolin, "Aspects du surréalisme au XVIe siècle: Fonction allégorique et vision anamorphotique," *Bibliothèque d'Humanisme et Renaissance*, 39 (1977), pp. 503-30; Jeanine Parisier Plottel, "Anamorphosis in Painting and Literature," *Yearbook of Comparative and General Literature*, 28 (1979), pp. 100-09; Fernand Hallyn, "Anamorphose et allégorie," *Revue de Littérature Comparée*, 56, no. 3 (juillet-septembre 1982), pp. 319-30.

6 Baltrušaitis, *Anamorphoses ou perspectives curieuses*, p. 65.

7 This allusion to a *syndrome Jean-Jacques* would seem to refer to the "schizophrenic" autobiographical piece *Rousseau juge de Jean Jacques: Dialogues*, in *Jean-Jacques Rousseau: Oeuvres complètes*, vol. 1 (Paris: Gallimard, 1959), pp. 661-992; Rousseau's habit of referring to "Jean-Jacques" as "JJ" may also be the allusive source of Aquin's use of the initials RR.

8 John Fowles, *The French Lieutenant's Woman* (New York: New American Library, 1970).

9 Patricia Smart, *Hubert Aquin, agent double* (Montreal: Les Presses de l'Université de Montréal, 1973), p. 125.

10 Margolin, "Aspects du surréalisme au XVIe siècle: Fonction allégorique et vision anamorphotique," p. 506.

11 Françoise Maccabée Iqbal, *Hubert Aquin, romancier* (Quebec City: Les Presses de l'Université Laval, 1978), pp. 123-40.

12 Smart, *Hubert Aquin, agent double*, pp. 22, 74, 117.

13 Frantz Fanon, *Les Damnés de la terre* (Paris: F. Maspero, 1961).

14 Albert Memmi, *Portrait du colonisé* (Paris: Jean-Jacques Pauvert, 1966).

15 Thomas De Quincey, *Confessions of an English Opium Eater* (London: Routledge, 1867); *On Murder Considered as One of the Fine Arts*, in David Masson, ed., *The Collected Writings of Thomas De Quincey*, vol. 13 (London: A. and C. Black, 1896-1897).

16 Vladimir Nabokov, *Laughter in the Dark* (New Directions, 1960).

17 Nabokov, *Pale Fire*, p. 78.

18 Ibid., p. 36, l.92-96.

19 Gabriel García Márquez, *One Hundred Years of Solitude*, trans. from Spanish by Gregory Rabassa (Picador, 1978); originally published in Spanish under the title *Cien Años de Soledad* (Buenos Aires: Editorial Sudamericana, SA, 1967).

20 Italo Calvino, *If on a Winter's Night a Traveller*, trans. from Italian by William Weaver (Toronto: Lester and Orpen Dennys, 1981); originally published in Italian under the title *Si una notte d'inverno un viaggatore* (Torino: Giulio Einaudi, 1979).

21 Hubert Aquin, "La Disparition élocutoire du poète (Mallarmé)," in *Blocs erratiques* (Montreal: Les Éditions Quinze, 1977), pp. 263-64.

22 Ibid., p. 226.

23 In the context of Canadian literature I refer here to Janet M. Paterson, "Le Roman 'postmoderne': Mise au point et perspectives," *Canadian Review of Comparative Literature*, 13, no. 2 (June 1986), pp. 238-55; and Caroline Bayard, "Post-modernisme et avant-garde au Canada, 1960-1984," *Voix et images*, 10, no. 1 (1984), pp. 37-58.

24 Margolin, "Aspects du surréalisme," p. 530.

Part III

Patterns of Allusion

Traditionally, it was the invocation of the literary repertoire of forms and symbols that constituted the communicatory framework of poetry as a genre. In drama, too, the theatrical and literary effects of a work depended in large part upon the reader's (or theatre-goer's) familiarity with dramatic conventions. In contrast, the fictional world of the novel was constructed by allusions to elements of social and historical reality. Until the twentieth century, the mythological and symbolic features of the epic, if referred to at all, served mainly to designate individual aspects of archetypal patterns, the recognition of which did not usually determine the communicatory structure of the work.[1] The age of industrialism defined the communicatory intention of the novel more and more as that of social corrective, creating its own symbolic structures. In Canadian fiction, Frederick Philip Grove's *The Master of the Mill* [2] is a case in point.

In the twentieth century, the principle of deviation from a familiar pattern, the functional formula of all allusion (the deviation consisting in the occurrence of the familiar in an unfamiliar context), has resulted in a juxtaposition of generic features which in some works amounts almost to a reversal of the traditional rules of the respective genres. As Wolfgang Iser points out, twentieth-century poetry, particularly in the fifties and sixties, has tended to discard the literary repertoire, selecting its elements from the socio-cultural code of modern industrial society.[3] The modern novel, on the other hand, draws heavily from the literary repertoire, not only exploring thematic parallels, but also reaffirming the contemporary validity of epic and other generic conven-

---

Reference notes for Part III and Chapter Five are found on pp. 141-42.

tions, including whole mythological sequences. Joyce's *Ulysses* may be seen to represent a paradigm for this juxtaposition of epic myth and modern reality.

In novels in which allusion to previous literature determines the communicatory structure, as in *Ulysses*, the corrective intention of the work (namely the exposure of certain deficiencies in the socio-historical system constituting the fictional reality of the text) defers to the thematic relationships between text and model.[4] Whatever epithet one chooses for this type of literature—intertextuality,[5] *palimpseste*,[6] or parody[7]—the reading process is determined by the reader's attempt to relate the repertoires presented in the text and to motivate these relationships, and not by reader negation or affirmation of norms designated by the perspectival views of the characters. Attention is thus focused in large measure upon the readers' own perceptual and cognitive processes as they attempt to construct meaning in their reading of the text. It finds its formulation not in the proposal of an alternative to the possibilities designated by the text, but in an expanded awareness of the nature of these processes themselves.

The appearance of Canadian novels in which allusion to specific models determines the communicatory structure of the text is a fairly recent phenomenon. The Christian parallels evoked in some of the novels of Morley Callaghan function mainly as moral authority reinforcing the (socially unacceptable) perspectival views the reader is to affirm against the hypocritical attitudes of society, represented by characters whose views the reader is to negate. In Adele Wiseman's novels (*The Sacrifice*[8] and *Crackpot*[9]) and in W. O. Mitchell's *The Vanishing Point*[10] the Old Testament allusions lend symbolic extensions to some of the characters, but they do not constitute a second narrative framework juxtaposed with the fictional worlds represented in the novels. In a number of works the allusions invoked by the titles function only to sum up the central thematic problem, as in MacLennan's *Two Solitudes*, Robert Charbonneau's *Ils posséderont la terre*,[11] and Rudy Wiebe's *Peace Shall Destroy Many*.[12]

In Malcolm Lowry's *Under the Volcano*,[13] Leonard Cohen's *Beautiful Losers*, and Robertson Davies's trilogy (*Fifth Business*, *The Manticore*, *World of Wonders*), on the other hand, the allusive density results in the reader's perception of the complex psychological patterns underlying the motivations of the characters, all of whom take on symbolic features. But the communicatory effect of the novels lies in the metaphorical relationships between the elements of the novel and the elements alluded to, and not in the superimposition of two text systems which are in themselves whole and consistent.

Yet there are signs that this "palimpsest" genre is gaining importance in Canadian letters: Margaret Atwood's *The Handmaid's Tale*[14] conflates the Chaucer allusion and Orwell's dystopia. Timothy Findley explores the palimpsest in the Poundian leitmotiv of *Famous Last Words*[15] and subsequently in *Not Wanted on the Voyage*,[16] the tale of Noah told from the perspective of "Mrs. Noyes," Noah's wife. In the case of *Not Wanted on the Voyage*, however, one could argue that its aesthetic effect is derived from the strategies of discourse which result in the "magical realism" characterizing much of contemporary Latin-American fiction-writing, rather than from the thematic palimpsest itself.

Two earlier novels in which the superimposition determines the primary communicatory effect of the texts are A. M. Klein's *Second Scroll* and Hubert Aquin's *Prochain épisode*. As in *Ulysses*, the two novels bring the mythical elements of the literary repertoire into the fictional reality of the text, letting the reader ultimately perceive this reality as being determined by the literary pattern to which it alludes, while the source of this pattern itself is revealed as the individual human experience described in terms of a designated socio-historical reality.

Since M. W. Steinberg remarked in his introduction to the 1961 edition of Klein's *Second Scroll* that "indeed there is a wealth of meaningful allusion in Klein's writing,"[17] dozens of articles and a number of book-length studies have concerned themselves with the tracing of allusions and influences in the novel. But while the Klein scholar now possesses a wealth of reference material, as indispensable for studies of Klein's *oeuvre* as Stuart Gilbert's book on *Ulysses*[18] is to the student of Joyce, virtually all criticism of *The Second Scroll* has dealt with the cultural, historical, spiritual and so ultimately thematic elements, to the exclusion of the generic features through which they are communicated.

To a point, critical trends, like the texts to which they refer, themselves require interpretation. In the context of English-Canadian criticism, novels like *The Second Scroll*—another example would be Sheila Watson's *The Double Hook*—are often considered generically marginal not only because they happen to be the only novels written by their authors, but also because they fall outside the "mainstream" of what is usually considered to constitute the Canadian literary canon. Curiously, it is particularly the comparative Canadian approaches which have tended to depart not from the communicatory intention of the text, but from its socio-psychological genesis. In the case of Klein, the critics' persistent invocation of the thematic models of the novel, mainly the Pentateuch, has been at the expense of the novel's great generic paradigm, namely Joyce's *Ulysses*. Although individual Joycean allusions have been recognized and commented upon by critics of *The Second Scroll*, no referential context has emerged for identifying and demonstrating the structural and generic relationship between this novel and other Canadian novels, or novels of other literatures.

Hubert Aquin's *Prochain épisode* has also generated a large body of secondary writing. Like Klein's novel, it develops a complex system of allusion to its own generic deformation, particularly with regard to the "realism" principle which Aquin handles in a way reminiscent of Borges and Nabokov. Like Klein, Aquin also acknowledges his debt to Joyce. But as in the case of Klein, evidence for this debt is usually sought in the vague and ultimately unverifiable sphere of author influence, rather than in the text itself. Yet these patterns of generic allusion, which in both novels function as central narrative strategies, constitute a common denominator which can hardly be overlooked. In both novels, as in Joyce's, the problematization of both the systematic and historical features of literature itself, namely as a historical system of structures and conventions, is pointed to at least as explicitly as the thematic repertoire. It is this generic aspect which has been left largely unexplored.

Indirectly, Canadian critics' lack of formal interest may be seen to reflect a certain unawareness of the normative function of literary conventions and consequently of the essentially norm-breaking function of every work of art. If, as is proposed here, *The Second Scroll* and *Prochain épisode* in their thematic and generic allusiveness fit the modern definition of parody, i.e. parody in the ironic rather than comic or satiric sense, they indicate the necessity of measuring themselves against the texts to which they allude:

> Parody, it would seem, flourishes in societies of a certain cultural sophistication. This is due to its primarily formal, rather than social, intent and to the superimposition of texts . . . required of the [reader] as well as the [author].[19]

Each incident in *The Second Scroll* refers the reader to its mythological counterpart in the Pentateuch, while in *Prochain épisode* each plot element corresponds to the formula of the spy-story. But in both cases, the literary framework alluded to is both filled and expanded by literary and historical allusions not derived from the primary model. Their occurrence in the context of the model via the text creates relationships not existing before, exposing hitherto unrecognized features not only of the narrative elements of the texts, but also of the various allusions themselves. These newly recognized features expand the significance of both the model and the other allusions due to their simultaneous occurrence in the new context created by the novel. The novel's communicatory intention is in part fulfilled by the reader's recognition and motivation of these relationships. The selections from the literary repertoire thus serve to communicate the totality of the individual experiences represented in the novels due to the multiplicity of their manifestation in the various allusive contexts, while they also reveal the universal nature of these experiences by creating a composite paradigm for them.

The following studies of *The Second Scroll* and *Prochain épisode* explore the various forms of intertextuality that determine the effects of the two novels. Intertextuality is seen in both analyses as a form of indeterminacy, best described here not so much in the sense of the "silences" of the text, but in the Iserian sense of gaps or blanks prestructuring the reader's responses.

While both novels seem thematically to invoke almost the entire corpus of western thought and culture, it is the metaliterary, parodic play with narratological conventions—those of the epic in the case of Klein, those of the spy-novel in the case of Aquin—upon which the following readings of the two novels are focused.

FIVE

Epic Allusion as a Narrative Strategy in A. M. Klein's *Second Scroll*

The title of *The Second Scroll*, like that of *Ulysses*, explicitly designates the entire frame of reference of the text it alludes to and indicates that the novel is to be read in terms of this allusion. The reader brings all previous knowledge and experience of that frame of reference to bear in an attempt to understand and interpret the text. When Klein called his novel *The Second Scroll*, he established the fate of the people of Israel as his main theme and the biblical myth of the Pentateuch as a principal frame of reference in dealing with that theme. On the basis of this established relationship, the title evokes a certain association and anticipation which determines reader response to the text. Expectation built up in the reader is either fulfilled (when the text "corresponds" to the model) or frustrated (when the text "deviates" from the model). For neither *The Second Scroll* nor *Ulysses* offers character counterparts or plot correspondences in a one-to-one relationship. The significance of the allusions rests not on the similarities between text and model, but on the deviations of the text from the model. The reader sees the shared features, or the similarities between the two texts, as constituting a background against which the deviations are foregrounded to let the *Gestalt*, or the meaning intended by the text, appear to the reader.

The text may deviate from its model in various ways. The reader recognizes such deviations as omissions, additions, displacements, extensions or other deformations of the reality or "world" of the model; they may be seen as analogous to the selections the author

126

makes from his own reality as he perceives it in creating the reality or "world" of his text. The author's creation is thus the result of a deformation of his own world or reality, and that of his literary repertoire.

As in *Ulysses*, the epic features and allusions function as parody in the sense that they represent a deformation of some original epic reality. In *Ulysses*, Joyce's massive inflation often results in parody in the comic sense, or in caricature. In Klein this rarely happens. The epic features and allusions are usually introduced to ironically (not comically) expand the meaning.

Structurally the novel consists of five chapters whose titles correspond to the books of the Pentateuch, reinforcing the biblical frame of reference created by the title. The novel proper is followed by five glosses, named after the first five letters of the Hebrew alphabet, that constitute appendices to the five chapters: Gloss Aleph is appended to "Genesis," Gloss Beth to "Exodus," etc. Each gloss seems to designate and expand the salient feature of "its" chapter, so that the five glosses themselves represent not a miniature version of the novel, but a sort of "third scroll" or commentary on it.

The narrative itself unfolds in a double-stranded plot, the centres of which are the first-person narrator and his Uncle Melech, whose path the reader traces first in his letters to the narrator and his family, and subsequently in the narrator's efforts to find him. Throughout the novel the experiences of the two reveal a similarity indicated both by the narrator's aspirations to follow in the footsteps of his uncle, and by the parallel developments in their lives of which both remain unconscious. The reader never perceives these parallel experiences as being simultaneous due to the chronological and spatial distance established by the difference in age, on the one hand, and the uncertainty of Uncle Melech's whereabouts at any given time on the other, which, like his experiences, are communicated to the narrator (and hence to the reader) only in retrospect.

In "Genesis" the reader recognizes certain parallels to the model, suggested by the title of the chapter. At the same time the text presents a number of elements which cannot be accounted for in terms of this context. These deviations require motivation in order for the reader to determine their significance. The parallels are recognizable in three features shared by text and model: the beginning of the world represented by creation in the Book of Genesis coincides with the beginning or the "creation" of the world of the novel; the narrator's innocence (he is a child) is perceived as a parallel to the state of innocence of Adam and Eve, newly created; Uncle Melech's joining the Bolsheviks after turning away from Orthodox Judaism may be seen as a loss of innocence (through experience) with a subsequent fall from grace. The latter is explicitly and ironically expressed in the fact that Uncle Melech has "fallen from grace" in the eyes of the narrator's father, who henceforth forbids the mention of his name. The pogrom at Ratno, which led Uncle Melech to renounce his faith, may be seen as a re-enactment of the fall of man in view of this causality.

The deviations from the model consist in the transposition of the mythical pattern into the context of modern reality, in the displacement of the shared features of the biblical characters on to an entire family, and in the event leading to the fall as well as the communication of that event, which is mediated by both the letter and the messengers. Each of these deviant features modifies the reader's initial anticipation in the way text and model are to be related. The transposition of ancient myth into modern reality seems to eliminate the supernatural features and hence the possibility of divine intervention. The displacement of the features of the biblical figures results in a constellation of characters which has no counterpart in the myth.

Yet because of the chapter titles and the suggested similarities, the reader anticipates a development of the plot along the lines of the myth. The anticipated events of the Jewish migration, the theme of the Pentateuch, are to be related to the characters of the novel, who form a youth-family-mentor pattern within a specific society, a pattern familiar to the reader from the *Bildungsroman*, but also from the ancient epics. A number of literary patterns thus converge in the image of the anticipated journey ("Exodus"), which is a double symbol of quest and life-experience shared by all the literary forms invoked, expanding the reader's anticipation beyond an extended biblical parallel to the sequences designated by them.

The reader's recognition of the epic as a generic model for what is to be communicated in the novel is reinforced by two epic conventions Klein has taken over more or less intact from ancient models. Uncle Melech's "fall" (his joining the Bolsheviks) is communicated to the narrator by a messenger report, familiar to the reader not only from classical literature, but also from Renaissance drama, where it is used to solve staging problems as well as to avoid breaking decorum. The communicatory function of the epic messenger corresponds to that of the Jewish prophets, strengthening the relationships the reader has determined between classical epic and biblical myth: the letter brought by the two strangers, as a tangible object of reality, establishes the credibility and authenticity of their message. But the invocation of the messenger's report as a means of maintaining decorum also suggests that what happened (the event they describe) was too dreadful for the narrator himself to express (although of course the events are related to the reader through the voice of the narrator). On the other hand, the classical idea of the messenger bringing news from the divine world to the world of the mortals is present in the "foreignness" of the two strangers; with their "strange" appearance they seem to represent figures from another world, and as such they wear an aura of mystery which both awes and entices, though their message is one of dread.

Another convention Klein uses without deformation is the heroic catalogue. In Uncle Melech's letter, the names of the victims of Ratno, each one "blocked out, as if laid in little coffins" (p. 21), are listed as though familiar, indeed legendary, and associated with epithets as in the classical epics.

> The marked-out blocks on the letter . . . were the names of those who were no longer among the living: the old rabbi, Rabbi Heshel; Israel Meyer, the shochet, slaughtered with his own knife; our cousin Aryeh Leib, Yentel Baila's son; both daughters of Braina, the potter's daughter; and others. (p. 21)[20]

Klein uses the heroic catalogue again in "Deuteronomy," when he lists the names of refugees among whom the narrator searches for Uncle Melech, and when he lists the representatives from the Israeli settlements who come to Uncle Melech's funeral. Although these lists remind the reader primarily of the genealogies of the Old Testament, recognition of the epic convention in this defamiliarized context causes the reader to associate the names with heroic attributes. Although the attributes themselves are missing, in contrast to the epithets of those who died, the people whose names appear take on heroic stature. The very lack of an epithet reveals the tragic irony of the context, for the heroism of the refugees and representatives of the settlements, Klein seems to imply, lies in the fact that they have survived.

Klein's use of epic conventions is rarely as obvious as in the case of the messenger report and the heroic catalogue. In the second chapter, "Exodus," the non-biblical allusions manifest themselves thematically, in terms of the journey as quest and experience, converging with the fairly literal though highly ironic transposition of the Jewish exodus of the Pentateuch into the modern context. But the part of Uncle Melech's letter from Bari describing his waiting to go to Israel contains an echo of the epic catalogue used in "Genesis," only this time the items enumerated are not names of victims, but an inventory of vessels whose names ring with hope.

> Already there come to this harbour the rescuing ships of the Israeli navy. I stand here on the shore and watch them as they take on their passengers. Clarion names they bear, these ships: *Negba* — to the south! *Kedma* — to the east! *Atzmouth* — independence! (p. 36)

The situational resemblance between Uncle Melech's longing to leave for Israel and the Greeks in their ships at Troy, longing to return home, reinforces the relationship the reader has perceived between the two texts, while the suggested parallel lets the reader perceive the voyage to Israel (which Uncle Melech has never seen) as a homecoming, a return.

As in "Genesis," the deviations from the model fulfil a communicatory function beyond the development of the plot. "Exodus," in which the narrator and Uncle Melech are, each without the knowledge of the other, preparing to go to Israel, closely parallels the Book of Exodus, the experience of the Jews in captivity being expressed in terms of the massacre at Kamenets. The departure of the Israelites from Egypt has its counterpart in the departure of the narrator and Uncle Melech. The fact that the two leave for Israel from two different points, however, diverging from both the Pentateuch and the *Odyssey*, suggests the dispersion of the Jews and seems to negate their existence as a people.

The transposition of the Books of Genesis and Exodus into the modern age, with an individual replacing not only the human paradigms of Adam and Eve but also an entire society, reveals characteristic features of the modern age itself. In taking on the features of individuals, both the narrator and Uncle Melech demonstrate the isolation of the individual within society as well as the individual's alienation from it. In the biblical context, Uncle Melech may be seen as an extension of Moses, but he is a Moses without a people, and only the narrator, drawn to him by some sort of metaphysical rather than familial bond, follows him to the promised land.

In "Leviticus," which finds the narrator in Italy, anxiously pursuing his uncle who he fears has been converted to Roman Catholicism, there is a more basic deformation of the model. The biblical Leviticus deals mainly with Jewish rules and customs, and so Klein's "Leviticus," in which deviation from the Jewish faith and customs is the main theme, appropriately deviates from its model.[21]

"Numbers," in which the narrator follows his uncle to Casablanca, like "Leviticus" shows a less obvious relationship between text and model than is the case in the first two chapters. A large part of the Book of Numbers is devoted to a cataloguing of the tribes of Israel. The theme of Klein's "Numbers" thus refers obliquely but unmistakably to the Book of Numbers in Uncle Melech's desire "to be with his Sephardic brothers, the lost half of Jewry" (p. 55), and in the narrator's sense of "forgotten kinship" with the Arab singer in the café in Casablanca.

In "Deuteronomy" the reader perceives the deformation of the biblical myth in that unlike Moses, the narrator and Uncle Melech actually reach Israel, or the promised land. However, the promised land has been only partly reconquered, and so, in a way, Uncle Melech's death near the border may be seen to parallel that of Moses.

The circumstances of Uncle Melech's death, like the events in "Genesis" and "Exodus," represent a transposition of symbolic biblical features into the modern context. Uncle Melech's having gasoline poured over him may be seen as an ironic allusion to the "anointment with oil," or the notion of being chosen by God, an idea also suggested by his name Melech (= king) Davidson, or son of David. In an ironic way, Uncle Melech fulfils the Messianic prerequisites. The burning of his body may be seen as an ironic displacement of the story of the burning bush[22] as well as an allusion to the Christian Pentecost myth. But his place of death, near Safed, also associates his burning with the fire signals announcing a new month, or marking cyclical time. Furthermore, Safed is the place where the "miracle," the Israeli war of liberation, was "realized" in 1948. Thus the Moses allusion and the reference to Safed result in the simultaneous expression of prophecy and fulfilment.[23]

Structurally, the reader perceives a close parallel to the Pentateuch in the shared features of the two texts. But it is the inevitable ironic tension between the projected structure of the Pentateuch and the events of the novel which determines the reader's response to the allusions.

First, it creates the distance between text and model which is necessary to maintain the reader's credulity. It disallows the reader's mere equation of the individual and the paradigmatic, since the shared elements remain solidly situated in their respective worlds of biblical myth and fictional reality: the relationships between the two, never explicitly expressed in the text, are formulated by the reader and so assume their validity.

As in Joyce, irony is also recognized by the reader in the allusive inflation of improbable incidents for comic effect, or in the metaphorical designation of an allusive relationship, exposing features of an event whose symbolic significance would otherwise remain unrecognized. In both cases, the effect upon the reader is determined by the unexpectedness of the allusion. In "Leviticus," the allusion to John the Baptist is wholly out of proportion to the episode in which it is invoked, banalizing the context to the level of comic parody: the narrator, being marched through Rome by Settano and his friends, is suddenly forced to look into a shop window in order not to attract the attention of passing policemen. In the window is a "large empty silver platter," and the narrator observes that his "own head, level with the tray, seemed to be mirrored as lying upon it" (p. 49).

The metaphorical allusion to the manifestation of God's presence during the migrations of the Israelites, on the other hand, lends the European holocaust symbolic significance in that the allusion designates it as a sign: the narrator describes the fate of the Jews during the war in terms of a "great smoke ... billowing over the Jews of Europe—their cloud by day, their pillar of fire by night" (p. 26).

There is an irony of a different order in the fact that the story is told by a first-person narrator. The notion of the artist as an *alter deus*, creator of an *altera natura*, takes on special significance for the reader due to the subject of the novel. The Bible, itself considered to be the word of God, is implicitly superseded by the word of man. The novel is not the statement of "truth" possessed by the narrator, as the Bible is, but rather an account of his search for it and its ultimate revelation. The revelation, however, comes about not through the manifestation of the divine, but through the real author behind the narrator. The reader thus recognizes an ironic (implied) equation between the real author, the creator of the fictional reality of the novel, and the divine creator of the world.

In the five glosses appended to the novel, the reader recognizes a double allusion which, on the one hand, points to the Jewish frame of reference in that the glosses represent a sort of third scroll constituting a parallel not only to the novel, but also to the Talmud. On the other hand the relationships between the various structural units of the novel may be recognized as an artistic convention, in which the work in some way becomes represented, in miniature, in one of its parts.[24]

Klein's use of this self-allusiveness, in which each unit refers the reader to its counterpart in another structural and historical system, reveals a series of categories in terms of which the novel is to be read. Since each element defines the Jewish situation both in historical and contemporary terms, and at the same time indicates its relationship to a system outside that in which it occurs, the structural systems describe a pattern which may be compared to a series of concentric circles, resulting in a sense of the cumulativeness of all previous human existence within the individual.

The reader's recognition of non-biblical allusions is determined in large part by the themes they share with the events of the Pentateuch. The journey, the promised land, loss of faith and loss of innocence, rebirth and metamorphosis, death and resurrection are universal themes which occur in some form throughout literary history, from the classical epic to *Ulysses*.

The journey as a symbol of life and as quest is perhaps the most prominent epic feature of *The Second Scroll*. On the "literal" level, the narrator's journey has the goal of finding and translating the new Israeli poetry. But this goal becomes more and more bound up with finding Uncle Melech. The two, as simultaneous objects of the narrator's quest, become closely identified with one another. The significance of Uncle Melech, like the source of the poetry the narrator is after, begins to grow once both are recognized as epic archetypes. It is not difficult to recognize the narrator's quest as a Telemachian one, and the search for Uncle Melech representing the narrator's quest for his spiritual origins. The "poetry" represents the "hidden treasure," or that key which will unlock the secrets of the universe.[25] Thus equated with Uncle Melech, these two goals turn out to represent two different aspects of the same thing: Uncle Melech incarnates all of Jewish history and represents the collective Jewish identity, hence also the narrator's spiritual as well as genealogical origin. The Israeli poetry turns out to be the voice of that collective Jewish identity, and of its history: it is language itself.

As Telemachus sets out in search of Odysseus, the narrator makes his travel experiences in the wake of Uncle Melech. The arrival of the narrator and Uncle Melech in the promised land of the Pentateuch, in Israel, is, in a sense, a homecoming. Yet the deviations from the allusion point up the uniqueness and at the same time the universality of both the Jewish and the Greek experiences. Odysseus return to Ithaca after wandering abroad for ten years. In the case of Uncle Melech and the narrator, however, as for the other Jews, the homeland of Israel had been inaccessible or even non-existent for centuries. The Homeric allusion thus serves to intensify the emotional impact of a "return" after not merely ten years, but literally centuries.

The frustrations and setbacks experienced by the narrator in Italy ("Leviticus") may be seen in terms of the Aeolos episode in the *Odyssey*, where Odysseus, within sight of Ithaca, is driven away from the coast by the "winds" given him by Aeolos. This allusion is underlined as it is superseded by the Aeolos episode in Joyce, where the theme of "almost" attaining one's goal is developed to the point where almost every feature in the chapter points towards this elusiveness and frustration. Furthermore, the "winds" of change blowing through Myles Crawford's newspaper office can be seen as being related to the various changes of faith undergone by Uncle Melech. The "Leviticus" chapter is closer to Joyce than to Homer not because the events come about "naturally" and not "supernaturally," but because of the multiplicity of the "almost" events witnessed by the reader, for which Odysseus's almost-reaching Ithaca is the paradigm.

In "Leviticus" the narrator has *just missed* Uncle Melech in Bari and again in Rome; Uncle Melech has *almost* been converted to Roman Catholicism. The narrator, in his encounter with Settano, *almost* loses Uncle Melech's letter and *almost* gets seriously involved in a political incident.

The experiences described in all three texts may be interpreted in terms of what Stephen Dedalus calls "almosting it," or the elusiveness of a sense of the meaning of life. In Homer, one of the implications of the Aeolos episode seems to be that the essence of life is to be found in the experiences and adventures encountered on the journey rather than the destination itself, an implication also designated by the amount of attention Homer gives to Odysseus's travel experiences *vis-à-vis* the actual arrival in Ithaca. Bloom's experiences in Joyce's Aeolos chapter seem to radically negate any teleological aspects from Bloom's point of view, while the reader is able to organize Bloom's experiences, in any given context, so that they become meaningful. In Klein's "Leviticus" the reader is locked solidly in a teleological context, a context established by the historical significance of Rome, both as the seat of modern Christianity and as the state that destroyed Jerusalem. In that both Uncle Melech's and the narrator's journeys represent the individual's retracing or reliving the whole of Jewish history, the "Leviticus" chapter, in contrast to both Homer and Joyce, demonstrates a teleological view while it exploits the very features of the other two texts which seem to negate such a view.

The journey of Uncle Melech and the narrator, which the reader has identified as a homecoming, is also a journey into the unknown. In this sense it allegorically represents life itself and alludes, through the various experiences made by the narrator, to the universality of human experience expressed through the metaphor of a journey in Dante's *Commedia* or Goethe's *Faust*.

It is this dimension of the unknown which dominates Klein's Casablanca chapter ("Numbers"). The narrator decides to go to Casablanca almost in spite of himself. He is at first seduced by the exotic beauty of the city which lulls and lures him like the sirens and those two seductive enchantresses of the *Odyssey*, Circe and Calypso. In fact Klein alludes explicitly to one of them, and expresses the narrator's fascination, the irresistibility with which he is drawn into this strange and magic world.

> As upon some Circean strand magical with voices, I could have halted my travels there [in Casablanca]; indeed, it was music, a singing that issued like silken coloured thread from the door of a café hard by the Hôtel des Ambassadeurs, where I had just registered for my initial Arabian night, that first snared me, enchanted me to enter, and there held me entangled in the nostalgia of its distant Oriental evocations. (pp. 56-57)

The narrator's visit to the *mellah* of Casablanca, which may be seen as a microcosmic Jewish universe, is an extension and expansion of the journey theme, and can be related to a number of epic situations.

The narrator himself compares his visit to the *mellah* to a journey back in time. He is entering a world different from his own not only culturally, as is the case with Casablanca itself, but historically. This juxtaposition of spatial and temporal elements has the effects of underlining the diachronic nature of the Jewish experience already suggested by the parallel between the lives of modern individuals and the events of the Pentateuch.

> We parked off the boulevard and proceeded on foot. We entered, we slid into the mellah; literally: for the narrow lane which gaped through the gateway at the clean world was thick with offal and slime and the oozing of manifold sun-stirred putrescences; metaphorically: for in a moment we knew that the twentieth century (with all its modern conveniences) had forsaken us, and we were descending into the sixteenth, the fifteenth, twelfth, eleventh centuries. . . . (p. 62)

Like Dante and Odysseus, who visit the realm of the dead, the narrator needs a guide to visit the *mellah*. Secondly, the entrance to the *mellah* has to be negotiated—the gate is too narrow to permit passage by car. This particular feature can be seen as corresponding to the various obstacles encountered in the epics before the visitors can gain access to the underworld. The elimination of the car may also be seen as a sign of the *mellah* dwellers' isolation from modern civilization (thus strengthening the illusion that the narrator has left his contemporaneity behind to enter the Middle Ages), but also suggests the impossibility of such material things in a place which is, symbolically, not a "place" in the geographical sense, but rather a condition of the soul. The reference to the "clean world" outside the *mellah* thus attaches moral values to the two worlds being contrasted.

The poverty and the suffering witnessed by the narrator in the *mellah* point quite obviously to Dante's *Inferno*, which, in fact, is explicitly referred to.

> As we made our way with difficulty through the congested lanes, avoiding a body here, evading a donkey there, we were everywhere beset— by hands! Wherever we turned—hands! I was reminded of those drawings illustrative of Dante's *Inferno* in which the despair of its denizens is shown rising from the depths in a digitation and frenzy of hands, hands snatching at straw, at air, at hands. (p. 63)

The epic allusions to visits to the underworld let the reader perceive the *mellah* as a place of the dead, a site of evil, and a place of punishment for the Jewish society that inhabits it. Linking this notion with that of the *mellah* representing medieval Jewish existence, the rebirth of Israel, as described in *The Second Scroll*, must indeed be viewed as the "miracle," the fulfilment of prophecy, not only as a collective resurrection from the dead (of the Jews as a people) but also as a form of redemption from eternal punishment. Israel as the alternative to the *mellah* metaphorically represents Dante's *Paradiso*. The medieval Christian universe, with its conception of hell and its didactic notion of the way to deliverance, is here invoked by the reference to Dante not only for the sake of creating another temporal dimension but also as a pathos-laden *j'accuse* directed at the very roots of that Christian society which created the *mellah*. Furthermore, in using Dante as model here, Klein also opposes two Christian societies within the history of Christendom itself, the other being the Renaissance Christianity represented by Michelangelo, which proves so seductive (for the "wrong" reasons) to Uncle Melech in Rome ("Leviticus").

It is in "Numbers" that the reader encounters another epic convention, namely the story within the story. In the title of the "most seriously received and most loudly applauded" story told by the Arab in the café, the reader recognizes one of the most significant themes of the novel, the theme of metamorphosis: the Arab tells the "Tale of the Ethiopian who Did Change His Skin." This protean allusion fits the elusiveness and constantly changing image of Uncle Melech as it fits the various assimilations undergone by the Jews into European societies. This allusion is reinforced by another reference to the protean nature of Uncle Melech in the incident of the photograph. Although it is Uncle Melech who is represented in the picture, it is a multiple exposure, and so his true image is concealed in the very multiplicity of its appearance.

The conclusion of "Numbers," the narrator's departure from Casablanca, remains consistent with the epic frame of reference. Like Odysseus, who recognizes the dangerous wiles of Circe and ultimately resists the charms of Calypso, the narrator leaves the city which had at first seduced him with its exotic beauty, for after his experience in the *mellah* he now regards its very seductiveness as obscene, its art as hollow.

The theme of the journey, which in Klein's novel turns out to be both a homecoming and a journey into the unknown, diverges from the promised land theme as it occurs both in Homer and Joyce. Israel, the narrator's destination, differs from both Ithaca and 7, Eccles Street not only in that it is not the geographic point of departure, but also in that it seems to represent an ideal, the realization of Jewish prophecy. In terms of the Bible, it may be seen as a realization of the vision set before Adam and the fulfilment of the prophecy God gave to Moses. But as the reader has already recognized, the promised land or its allegorical counterpart, ultimate fulfilment, is characterized by its very elusiveness.

Thus the narrator's arrival in Israel does not in itself represent the attainment of the promised land. For as the Homeric allusion suggests, the narrator's arrival is not so much an arrival at an unknown destination as it is a return. The promised land is not something to be discovered but something to be recognized and returned to. The object of the quest is the familiar. The promised land is "reached" not when the narrator arrives in Israel, but when he recognizes that he has found what he has been looking for in the everyday life of the people, in their creation of their own "world," the symbolic act of which is, as in biblical Genesis, "naming," or the rebirth of Hebrew as a language of everyday discourse:

> the creative activity, archetypal, all-embracing, that hitherto I had sought in vain, at last manifested itself. . . . In the streets, in the shops, everywhere about me. I had looked, but had not seen. It was there all the time—the fashioning folk, anonymous and unobserved, creating word by word, phrase by phrase, the total work that when completed would stand as epic revealed! (p. 84)

This moment of "profound insight," in view of the epic contexts designated, may be seen as both biblical revelation and Joycean epiphany, evoking Joyce's famous "Welcome, O life! I go to encounter for the millionth time the reality of experience and to forge in the smithy of my soul the uncreated conscience of my race."[26] Klein sustains this state of revelation reached in "Deuteronomy" to extend through the narrator's learning of Uncle Melech's death to the funeral at which the narrator, as the lone family representative, intones the *kaddish*. The journey, as an allegory of life, appropriately ends in death, and this death marks the end of the novel itself. But the journey also ends in this state of revelation, which is the recognition of the "miracle," that life force, that existence of race or collective identity which transcends the individual. In a sense, this transcendence is effected through the communicability of experience, through poetry, through "epic revealed," as Klein puts it. Thus in *The Second Scroll*, in the allusion to the "miracle," the text comments ironically upon itself, and, appropriately enough, alludes to literature to do so:

> the phenomenon was being made everywhere explicit. The fixed epithet wherewith I might designate Israel's poetry, the poetry of the recaptured time, was now evident. The password was heard everywhere—the miracle!
> I had found the key image. (p. 87)

"Fixed epithet" describes formulaic language. The "password" suggests the symbolic, the secret sign, the metaphor that is language, or "naming." Just as, in the epic context, Odysseus's taunt to Polyphemus that his name is "nobody" is both a disguising and a revelation of the truth, it is through the "miracle" of language which simultaneously conceals (in that it consists of signs) and reveals (in that these signs can be interpreted) that humans experience the divine, with which language shares this feature of simultaneous revelation and concealment.

The principle of simultaneous revelation and concealment as a feature of language becomes not only a key *image*, but also the governing dialectic of the novel, retrospectively recognizable to the reader as the principle designated in the epigraph Klein chose for the novel, from Milton's *Areopagitica*.

> ... And ask a Talmudist
> what ails the modesty
> of his marginal Keri
> that Moses and all the prophets
> cannot persuade him
> to pronounce the textual Chetiv ...

Klein himself interpreted these lines as signifying that the "*Chetiv*—that is the written—is not often identical with the *Keri*—that which is read."[27] Although one can understand the passage as focusing upon the difference between the written and the spoken word (as Edel, Gotlieb and Steinberg do), it can also be seen as the invocation of language itself, namely as metaphor, in the substitution of *Keri* for *Chetiv*. The *Chetiv* as that which is written, and the *Keri* as that which is read, may thus be seen to designate text and interpretation, and so to refer to the unformulated intentions of the novel itself, actualized by the reader in his reading of the text, but never identical with it. In the novel itself this principle is recognizable in the incident of the photograph, for instance, and in Michelangelo's depiction of the face of God, as described in Uncle Melech's letter:

> where Michelangelo for the first and only time dared to show (and not show) *the face of God*, here Uncle Melech chose as the place finally to assert his adherence to the creed. In a single circular sentence, without beginning or end, he described God coming to the rescue of His chosen. It was a sentence in which I distinguished, between commas, in parentheses, and in outspoken statement, all the thirteen credos of Maimonides. (p. 52)

Klein's use of a dialectic which resolves itself in the "eternal circle" reveals the opposition between the Christian and the Jewish view. His treatment of the themes of loss of faith and loss of innocence may be seen as an implied allusion to Milton's *Paradise Lost* as well as to the events of Genesis. Klein seems to be addressing himself to Christian dialectics as presented by Milton in his poem, and opposing this to the Jewish view of the universe. In Milton, the story of mankind consists of a before and after, the event marking this sort of linear time being the fall of Adam and Eve. In Klein, this thinking is opposed by a cyclical view of time and history. The fall of man is re-enacted in the pogrom at Ratno. It is significant that the narrator learns of the pogrom at Simchas

Torah, a festival commemorating the "eternal circle," the "beginning anew," the joining of the last verses of Deuteronomy and the first of Genesis. Although Klein and Milton allude to the same events, the implications they see in them differ.

An example of such an opposing view is the effect Michelangelo's ceiling has on Uncle Melech. The visit to the Sistine Chapel, cannily suggested by Monsignor Piersanti in the certainty that it will prove the decisive factor in favour of Uncle Melech's conversion, in fact has exactly the opposite effect. Uncle Melech relates the depictions to events of his own age and to past events in Jewish history. The irony of Uncle Melech's visit to the Sistine Chapel lies in the fact that he is "saved" (in the sense that he does not lose but gains in his faith) by a Christian interpretation of the history of his people. Thus a Christian interpretation, the product of an ultra-Christian society (Italian renaissance) gives him the experience of "rebirth" (a Christian theme) into his own faith (Judaism). Uncle Melech, in his letter, expresses this through the metaphors he uses (the corridor leading to the chapel is seen as an umbilical cord, the penetration of the chapel itself is compared to an infant pressing its way into a "new" world), and hails Michelangelo almost as a Jewish prophet.

> In vain did Buonarotti seek to confine himself to the hermeneutics of his age; the Spirit intruded and lo! on that ceiling appeared the narrative of things to come, which came indeed, and behold above me the parable of my days. (p. 106)

Uncle Melech sees the ceiling not only as a "paean to the human form divine, a great psalter psalmodizing the beauty and vigour and worth of the races of mankind" (p. 105), but also as a depiction of "the shedding of life for the sons of Belial vanity's temptation" (p. 107). Interpreted in terms of the Jewish fate, then, the pogrom at Ratno, the massacre at Kamenets, become a collective manifestation of guilt which, like the fall, represents humankind's perpetual and ultimate assertion of its freedom.

The fall from grace theme is ironically anticipated in the attitude the narrator's parents take toward Uncle Melech. His loss of faith and embracing Communism in the wake of the events at Ratno results in the narrator's father forbidding his name to be mentioned. This fact invites allegorical interpretation, since historically in Judaism the name of God was considered too sacred to pronounce. Thus Klein, in referring to the pogrom at Ratno by speaking of those "perished for the Sanctification of the Name," ironically and seemingly inadvertently confers divine status upon the Jewish renegade.

Uncle Melech is, however, reconverted to the Jewish faith after his experience in Stalinist Russia. He becomes a Zionist. But he "errs" again by almost allowing himself to be converted by Monsignor Pier-santi. The "fall" is thus seen in Klein not so much in the sense of original sin, but as an integral part of the human condition. As in *Faust*, redemption comes because of the questing nature of humanity, which necessarily leads to error, and not in spite of it.

The numinous extensions of Uncle Melech are recognized by the reader in connection with the photograph and the pronouncing of his name, the meaning of his name, his rebirth into his faith and his protean metamorphoses. Furthermore, he incarnates the Christian myth of death and resurrection in his survival at Kamenets, where he literally "rises from the dead." His death in Israel, where tombs are "not tombs but antechambers to new life," is not final.

It is in the figure of Uncle Melech with all his numinous extensions that the various allusive strands come together. In the designated allusive contexts, Uncle Melech wears the biblical features of Christ, the medieval features of Dante, and, in the mysteriousness of his manifestation, features of God himself. The reader has also recognized him as an Odysseus, a leading figure of his society, yet so representa-tive of it that he fuses with it completely, becoming at the same time nobody and everyman. The ontogenetic notions suggested by the figure of Uncle Melech are expanded beyond the mythical allusions themselves by the use of certain images, mainly protean ones like the incident of the photograph. At his most explicit, Klein lets Uncle Melech express his sense of identity with the Jewish race and the events constituting its history in the letter describing the European tragedy (p. 30).

Melech's learning as a Talmudic scholar, his experiences in exile, and finally his death within sight of holy Jewish land not yet conquered by Israel clearly establishes Moses as the main model. But his name suggests that he is also a Messianic figure. The *Ilui* teaching the bearded sages in the temple, and his compassionate brotherhood with the pariahs in the *mellah*, associate Uncle Melech with the life and teachings of Christ.

Uncle Melech may thus be seen through the allusions to wear transcendental features. But the same allusions reveal that he is very much a human being. He is, like Odysseus, a leader in his society and, to its members, an almost legendary figure. Unlike his Homeric model, however, he lacks the heroic epithet, a lack which may be seen to designate the multiplicity of allusive features he wears. At the same time he has weaknesses, and his "erring" in faith as well as in space, his being driven by forces beyond his control or even awareness, suggests not only the "erring" of Odysseus but also the banal contem-porary, the groping everyman that is Leopold Bloom, a similarity underlining the double temporal dimension which is implicit in Klein's subject.

To recognize the epic features of Klein's novel is, in a sense, to agree with what may well be a critical consensus expressed by Desmond Pacey, who designates the place of *The Second Scroll* as being situated in "the corpus of Klein's poetry."[28] Georg Lukács says:

> The novel is the epic of an age in which the extensive totality of life is no longer directly given, in which the immanence of meaning in life has become a problem, yet which still thinks in terms of totality.[29]

Insofar as *The Second Scroll* attempts to solve this problem of the "immanence of meaning in life," and to restore its "extensive totality," the novel may be considered a Jewish epic of the modern age.

It seems clear that neither the invocation of epic conventions nor the self-allusiveness of the text to its own communicatory structures represents merely the conspiratorial wink of the author to the informed reader. Such "inside" allusions are rather to be found in the Jewish elements and have been convincingly identified in a number of studies. The generic allusions themselves perform communicatory functions, and their recognition by the reader determines the effect of the novel. For the insight and expanded awareness gained by the narrator can only be perceived by the reader if the latter recognizes the perceptual processes which brought it about. In this sense the experience of the narrator is shared by the reader, and their perceptual roles may be seen as being analogous.

The reader's recognition of the allusions themselves and of their functional significance presupposes points of tangency between the text at hand and the reader's own experience. Since the reader's own previous experience is constantly invoked by the allusions, yet "defamiliarized" by the new context in which they occur, the reading of the novel brings about a re-structuring of reader experience to accommodate the unfamiliar features designated in it. It is this "restructuring" of the reader's own experience which constitutes reader response to the text. Since it is the literary repertoire of the reader that the text refers to, in its presentation of apparently banal realities, it makes readers aware of their literary experience as a universal code in terms of which their extra-literary experience can be perceived.

Reference Notes to Part III and Chapter Five

1 Cf. George Lukács's discussion of the epic and the novel in his *Theory of the Novel* (Boston: MIT Press, 1971).

2 Frederick Philip Grove, *The Master of the Mill* (Toronto: New Canadian Library, 1960 [1941]).

3 Iser, *The Act of Reading*, p. 79.

4 Cf. Iser's discussion of various *Ulysses* episodes in *The Implied Reader*, chaps. 7 and 8 (pp. 179-233).

5 Cf. Julia Kristeva, *Sèméiôtiké* (Paris: Seuil, 1969).

6 Cf. Gérard Genette, *Palimpsestes. La littérature au second degré* (Paris: Seuil, 1982).

7 Cf. Linda Hutcheon, *A Theory of Parody. The Teachings of Twentieth-Century Art Forms* (New York and London: Methuen, 1985).

8 Adele Wiseman, *The Sacrifice* (Toronto: Macmillan, 1956).

9 Adele Wiseman, *Crackpot* (Toronto: McClelland and Stewart, 1974).

10 W. O. Mitchell, *The Vanishing Point* (Toronto: Macmillan, 1973).

11 Robert Charbonneau, *Ils posséderont la terre* (Montreal: Éditions de l'Arbre, 1941).

12 Ruby Wiebe, *Peace Shall Destroy Many* (Toronto: McClelland and Stewart, 1962).

13 Malcolm Lowry, *Under the Volcano* (London: Penguin, 1963 [1941]).

14 Margaret Atwood, *The Handmaid's Tale* (Toronto: McClelland and Stewart, 1985).

15 Timothy Findley, *Famous Last Words* (Toronto: Clarke Irwin, 1981).

16 Timothy Findley, *Not Wanted on the Voyage* (Toronto: Viking, 1984).

17 M. W. Steinberg in his introduction to *The Second Scroll*, p. vii.

18 Stuart Gilbert, *James Joyce's Ulysses* (New York: Vintage Books, 1955).

19 Linda Hutcheon, "Parody Without Ridicule: Observations on Modern Literary Parody," in *Canadian Review of Comparative Literature*, 5, no. 2 (Spring 1978), p. 211.

20 Phyllis Gotlieb has traced the sources of some of these names as well as of the 36 which appear in the lists in "Deuteronomy" in "Hassidic Influences in the Work of A. M. Klein," in Seymour Mayne, ed., *The A. M. Klein Symposium* (Ottawa: University of Ottawa Press, 1975), p. 55. In the same volume Leon Edel points out the significance of the number 36 as alluding to the ". . . 36 names of the secret saints of the Cabbala . . . each of which is a synonym in various languages of humility, piety, subjection, wandering." In "Marginal *Keri* and Textual *Chetiv*: The Mystic Novel of A. M. Klein," p. 27.

21 This kind of mimetic play is to be found throughout Klein's work, not only in the way the "form" designates the "content," but in his use of language as well.

22 Cf. Exodus, 3:2.

23 Phyllis Gotlieb has identified Buber's *Tales of Rabbi Nachmann* as an allusive source for the experiences of both the narrator and Uncle Melech ("Hassidic Influences in the Work of A. M. Klein," pp. 52-54). Her observations are particularly illuminating in our context in connection with the reference to Safed: "Melech Davidson, like Rabbi Nachmann, dies on the Sabbath eve after Tish B'Av, the anniversary of the Destruction of the Temple. His nephew in Safed, mourning his death, feels that his martyrdom has opened up a redemption for the lost of his race. This conception of redemption by metempsychosis, or *gilgul* (wheel) is a Kabbalistic one, principally expounded by the Safed mystic Chaim Vital" (p. 54).

24 The description of Achilles's shield in the *Iliad* (Bk. XVIII) where the shield represents a microcosmic view of the Greek world as it appears in Homer is one of the famous epic examples.

Phyllis Gotlieb offers another interesting interpretation of the function of the glosses: "I do not believe the glosses are meant to be commentaries, like the Talmud's, but rather Haftorath, the sections of other scriptures that are included with the weekly Torah portion because of some particular suitability" (in "Hassidic Influences in the Work of A. M. Klein," p. 61).

25 The search for the holy grail in the medieval epic or for the blue flower in German romanticism are two obvious manifestations of the hidden-treasure myth.

26 James Joyce, *A Portrait of the Artist as a Young Man* (London: The Bodley Head, 1952), p. 288.

27 Leon Edel, "Marginal *Keri* and Textual *Chetiv*: The Mystic Novel of A. M. Klein," in Seymour Mayne, ed., *The A. M. Klein Symposium* (Ottawa: The University of Ottawa Press, 1975), p. 15.

28 Desmond Pacey, "A. M. Klein," in *Ten Canadian Poets* (Toronto: Ryerson, 1958), pp. 254-92.

29 Lukács, *Theory of the Novel*, p. 56.

SIX

Generic Parody as a Communicatory Strategy in Hubert Aquin's *Prochain épisode*

C'était un roman à lire; ou mieux, un drame à jouer, et dans lequel il avait son rôle. Une bien belle chose est le métier d'espion, quand on le fait pour son compte et au profit d'une passion. ... Alors, ne faut-il pas avoir une âme multiple? n'est-ce pas vivre de mille passions, de mille sentiments ensemble?[1]

[C]'est en supposant tout, en choisissant les conjectures les plus probables que les juges, les espions, les amants et les observateurs devinent la vérité qui les intéresse.[2]

Either of these passages from Balzac's *Histoire des Treize* might stand as a fitting epigraph to *Prochain épisode*. Readers of Aquin's novel, who are repeatedly referred to the adventures of the *Treize* (as well as to the biography of their author), may recognize in Balzac's prologue a hermeneutic formula describing the roles of text and reader in the reading of the novel. If the narrator/hero of *Prochain épisode*, whose changing identity makes him at least as elusive as the counter-revolutionary spy he is after, possesses *une âme multiple*, he never represents a single point of view which, in its exclusion of all the other points of view which he also represents, could be adopted by the reader. In the

---

Reference notes for Chapter Six are found on pp. 170-72.

reading process, the activity of the reader becomes analogous to that of the spy, and the knowledge or truth discovered by interpreting the elements of the novel is, like that of the spy interpreting his observations, predetermined by that which the reader seeks.

Disoriented not only by the irreconcilability of the multiple points of view designated by the narrator/hero, but also by the multiple significance of the allusions to be related to them, the object of the reader's quest remains a mystery from beginning to end, the nature of which can be speculated upon, but the validity of which the reader can never verify.

As Patricia Smart points out in her study of Aquin, "La vraie progression dans le roman est de l'ordre de la perception."[3] The conflicting realities presented to the reader defy any attempt to separate them into the familiar categories of truth, fiction or fantasy. Although its effect depends upon the reader's recognition of allusive patterns and their relevance to the narrative, *Prochain épisode* offers no fixed system of allusive equivalents.

The apparently clear distinction between two narrative frames, one constituted by fictional reality, the other by an imaginary spy-story, is self-contradictory even in its invocation. The narrator is in a psychiatric institution in Montreal awaiting his trial and apparently writing a diary. An extended metaphor describes his reflections as an endless dive.

> Cuba coule en flammes au milieu du lac Léman pendant que je descends au fond des choses. Encaissé dans mes phrases, je glisse, fantôme, dans les eaux névrosées du fleuve et je découvre, dans ma dérive, le dessous des surfaces et l'image renversée des Alpes. (p. 7)

This apparently metaphorical invocation of Lake Geneva coincides with the setting of the spy-story he plans to write, the outline of which appears as a formula in which all the elements are inflated to the point of comic parody.

There will be a revolutionary agent called Hamidou in it, camouflaged as a special envoy from Senegal, and perhaps a secret agent called Wolof.[4] The story will turn on episodes involving CIA and MI5 agents. The streets of Lausanne will be full of smiling and sinister Chinese, casting conspiratorial glances at Hamidou as they pass by. Everyone he deals with will inevitably be killed. There will be numerous attempts to assassinate Hamidou, anonymous telephone calls, and daggers planted in the door of his hotel room.

The reader's response to this facile formula is determined by its context. The enigmatic reference to the Cuban revolution, the date of the narrator's trial, and the setting of Lake Geneva cause the reader to infer a relationship between the spy-story yet to be written and the narrator's experience. These references are drawn from different allusive repertoires and associated with different kinds of reality. The Cuban revolution, an historical reference, and Lake Geneva, a geographical one, seem to designate objective realities, verifiable by the reader. Though the narrator's imprisonment is unverifiable and his state of mind subjective, three factors, namely the present tense of the narrative, the diary form and the implication that the verifiable references constitute part of the narrator's experience induce the reader to perceive these elements as "real," in contrast to the implausible spy-story, which, the narrator declares, is purely imaginary.

The reader's expectations are thus simultaneously taken in two different directions. On the one hand, the reader anticipates a fairly predictable sequence of events by the narrator's declared intention to write a spy-story. The genre demands that the hero survive the episode; that he accomplish his mission unscathed, preferably with the involvement of an attractive female who is either on the side of the hero or a sexual bait used by the other side to trap the hero; that he be working for the "right" side.[5] At the same time the reader knows that the narrator, who has already been associated with the story he is writing, is in prison for revolutionary activities in Quebec, awaiting his trial. The demands of the genre conflict with the narrator's experience, which the reader anticipates to be the basis of the spy-story. The reader's expectations are geared to a resolution of this conflict, which would explain the narrator's presumable failure and yet satisfy the generic rules of the spy-story.

These conflicting expectations are not only modified by the mutual allusiveness of the two narrative frames, but also complicated by other allusions which can be seen to refer equally to both contexts. The ideological background of the spy-story, designated by the hero's mission on behalf of the Quebec revolution, is underlined by references relating it to Third World movements, such as Cuba and Senegal, and in associations evoked by the setting. The revolution of faith (the Calvinist Reformation) and political liberations invoking not only the history of Switzerland, but also its traditional role as a place of refuge, exile and intrigue, link it with the great socio-political revolutions of Europe, the French and the Russian. The allusive linking of Quebec with the Third World lets the reader perceive the Quebec revolution as the overthrow of an exploitive colonial power system, while the suggested historical context of the European revolutions lets it appear as a self-liberation from social injustice. But the very allusions designating events resulting from successful action (and so pointing to the hero's triumph in the spy-story) also evoke the background of these events, and reveal the individual failures which constitute a collective victory, thus reflecting the situation of the narrator.[6]

The inevitability of these revolutionary patterns is communicated through the implications of the allusions themselves. First, the historical breadth of the revolutionary patterns alluded to gives the reader a sense of their universality. Secondly, various features of the allusions overlap, often anachronistically, as in the references to Caesar's conquest of the Helvetians and the Punic Wars, which point not only to historical paradigms but also, in the context of the novel, suggest parallels to the British conquest of New France. At the same time Caesar's fall (and the presumed suicide of the last of the family of Scipio, the Roman hero of the Punic Wars) inevitably also evoked in the Roman allusions, strengthens the notion that triumph of a cause is brought about at the expense of those who achieved it. The reference to the battle at Uxellodunum[7] by H. de Heutz, the hero's enemy, whose engraving of General Wolfe dying on the Plains of Abraham is much admired by the hero, reinforces the implied parallel between the two empires (and the humiliation of the states they conquered), as well as presenting yet another example of human sacrifice for the victory of a cause.

The reader's sense of the inevitability of this pattern of cause and effect is derived not only from the multiplicity of events evoked, but also from the historical ideologies that brought them about. Both the Calvinist doctrine of predestination and the Marxist view of history point to the futility of individual human effort to effect change. At the same time both systems posit individual will as a prerequisite for spiritual and revolutionary salvation respectively. Thus the narrator's plunge into the fast-running waters of the Rhône can be seen as an ambiguous manifestation of will, while it may also be recognized as a protean image signalling a metamorphosis. Each time the narrator "dives" into the lake, his identity changes, a transformation indicated in the text by the narrator's abandoning his spy-story and continuing his journal. The name of H. de Heutz, or de Heute, meaning "of today," is curiously related to these "metamorphoses." Since it designates the present, the narrator's repeated "dives" into the past of his memories, which also represent metamorphoses, suggest a constant evasion of the present. The hero's finally missing H. de Heutz, having once recognized their identicality, thus represents not only the failure of his revolutionary mission, but also irrevocable self-alienation. The passing of the "ultimatum" of twenty-four hours (the rendezvous with K) without revolutionary action suggests its future impossibility, for in two different respects H. de Heutz is no longer "himself," since he has "dissolved" in his multiple identities, among them that of the narrator/hero, and because of the irretrievable "passing" or disappearance of "today" (von Heute).

A number of the historical associations evoked by the setting overlap with literary ones, multiplying the points of contingency between text and allusion. In the context of the novel, Byron is alluded to not only as the poet who celebrated Bonnivard,the revolutionary narrator/hero and the patriot of Geneva, but also as a revolutionary in his own right, like the narrator (and also like their respective heroes). Geneva as the birthplace of Rousseau evokes not only the *Contrat Social*, the allusive counterpart to the revolutionary ideology of the narrator/hero, but also his *Confessions*, revealing, like the narrator's journal, the anguish of a tortured soul. Furthermore, both texts played a seminal role in the two great revolutions of the age, the *Contrat Social* influencing the French Revolution as a social model, the *Confessions* engendering the Romantic revolution which later swept Europe.

Similarly, the confrontation at Coppet designates the dual roles of Mme de Staël and Benjamin Constant, whose literary salon fame was derived partially from their considerable political activities during the *empire*. Constant's once famous pamphlet, *De l'esprit de conquête et de l'usurpation*[8] represents a formulation of the narrator/hero's motivation to revolution, superseding the more obvious literary parallel.[9]

These allusions, many of them recognizable from the beginning of the novel through the reader's associations with the setting, evoke a sense of the cumulativeness of human experience within the individual due to the number of features he shares with figures of the past. The historical patterns indicated by the revolutionary allusions let the reader perceive the revolution of the narrator in terms of these patterns, the will to revolution constituting a futile but necessary instrument in the achievement of history.

The Swiss setting itself is perceived, through the allusions with which it is evoked, as a microcosmic universe, in which the polarities of political positions, emotional and rational imperatives, metaphorical and literal associations are ironically reconciled in the realities of its existence. An ambivalent place of refuge and exile, shared by revolutionary and anti-revolutionary alike, it harboured not only revolutionary failures like Bakunin but also White Russian *émigrés*. It brought forth the excesses of the Romantic revolution in Rousseau and the "voice of reason" in Voltaire. It was always a place of discreet financial and political transaction as well as a base for illegal or semi-legal intrigue and revolutionary activity behind a solid façade of prosperous and respectable bourgeoisie. Finally, the Swiss national industry, watch-making, symbolizes the mechanistic conception of history as following a predetermined course. The timepiece, as a symbol of time itself, unites the collective memory expressed in history with the personal memory of the individual, both aspects of which are represented in the narrator/hero's possession of the popular tourist *souvenir*, the Swiss watch.

The problematization of time effected by the allusions and metaphors of the journal determines the problematization of the narrator's identity created by the juxtaposition of journal and spy-story. Associations made by the readers are brought into play with each attempt to relate the two, which first involves recognition of their respective communicatory intentions, and so an attempt to separate them. But this effort is constantly undermined by the structural ambiguity of the text; just when the readers seem to have identified Lake Geneva and its evocations as an extended metaphor to express the narrator's state of mind, the references become totally ambiguous. The narrator and hero of the spy-story merge in the abrupt switch from the narrator's imagined presence in Lausanne as the setting of his story in one sentence to his actual presence there, as the hero, in the next:

> J'inspecte les remous, je surveille tout ce qui se passe ici; j'écoute aux portes du Lausanne Palace et je me méfie des Alpes. L'autre soir à Vevey, je me suis arrêté pour prendre une chope de bière au Café Vaudois. (p. 11)

In the café a calendar of events announcing a lecture on Roman history catches his eye.

The lack of transition between the narrator/hero reading the lecture announcement in a café at Vevey and the narrator in his institution cell in Montreal constitutes a structural gap in the linearity of the spy-story. From the perspective of the narrator, the scene in the café in Vevey is the opening incident of an unfurling spy plot. Since the incident does not coincide with the end of the novel chapter (but presumably with the end of the spy-story chapter) the reader, who has been induced to read the spy-story as part of the novel and not as a story within the novel, is now forced to call the previous interpretation of the café incident into question. The nature of its reality, whether the beginning of an imaginary spy-story or the narrator's own experience, eludes the reader, who is further mystified by the significance of the allusion to Balzac's *Histoire des Treize*. Though the narrator professes to be moved by his identification as a revolutionary with the conspirators, the reader recognizes the (unformulated) identification of the narrator/author with Balzac. In retrospect, the Balzac allusion is expanded in the opening incident of the spy-story: the lecture notice the hero comes across by chance may be seen as a structural counterpart to the letter to Ferragus discovered by coincidence by Maulincour. The response of the reader recognizing this similarity is to anticipate that in the spy-story (and hence in the novel) the announcement will turn out to have a similar importance. The Balzac allusion thus is more than situational. In the juxtaposition proposed by the allusion of writing, reading and reflection on the one hand and revolutionary action described in it on the other, the narrative becomes self-allusive. For the narrator's identification with Balzac lets the reader recognize the same juxtaposition of action and inaction in the present novel. It is to be found in the narrator writing his spy-story and in the narrator/hero acting as a revolutionary and writing his diary. Writing becomes the only activity possible for the imprisoned revolutionary, and so bears witness to his impotence. Words thus become a surrogate of action used by the narrator to preserve his revolutionary energy.

> Je me jette de la poudre de mots plein les yeux. ... Je farcis la page de hachis mental, j'en mets à faire craquer la syntaxe, je mitraille le papier nu, c'est tout juste si je n'écris pas des deux mains pour moins penser. (p. 14)

In the second chapter, the reader is plunged into the spy-story with the same uncertainty as to its reality as manifested before. For the hero's activity is prefaced by a remark of the diary narrator:

> Entre le 26 juillet et le 4 août 1792, à mi-chemin entre deux libérations et tandis que je m'introduis, enrobé d'alliage léger, dans un roman qui s'écrit à Lausanne, je cherche avidement un homme qui est sorti du Lausanne Palace après avoir serré la main de Hamidou Diop. (p. 19)[10]

The man he is looking for has disappeared in a Mercedes 300SL. For some reason ("Quelque chose me dit ...") this encounter causes the hero to suspect Hamidou of being a double agent. Unable to follow the man in the 300SL, the hero wanders about the streets of Lausanne, ending up in a cinema on the Place Benjamin Constant to see an old film, *Orfeu Negro*.[11] Back at his hotel, he finds a cryptogram, written on blue paper, which he is unable to decipher.

From here on, the spy-story takes on readily identifiable features of the genre which alternate with references to the narrator's imprisonment and psychic state, and flashbacks revealing scenes with his lover. These sequences perform a number of communicatory functions. First, the constant interruptions of the spy-story by associations evoked in it let the reader perceive an intimate relationship between the narrator's experience and his story. Secondly, they imitate the interruption of the reading of a novel, which is usually done in several sittings, and therefore reinforce the reader's illusion that the diary represents "reality" or "truth," and that the spy-story is imaginary. Thirdly, the circular movement of the sequence diary-spy-story-flashback disorients the reader, who can no longer identify its starting-point or the "beginning" of the sequence: does the writing of the imaginary spy-story set off associations which bring back memories of his lover and his past life, causing the two to converge? Is his spy-story merely the story of his own past experience as an agent? Or does his past experience, transformed in the act of remembering, fall retrospectively into spy-story formulas?

The reader's sense that the story has ceased to be determined by the will of the narrator is confirmed by the narrator himself (pp. 89-90). This feature of his writing coincides with the mechanistic conceptions of history invoked by the implicit allusions of the setting, and so seem to illustrate their validity.

The reader's gradual recognition of the relationships between the narrator's literal imprisonment and his "lack of control" over the story he is writing reveals additional aspects of certain metaphors which have occurred near the beginning of the novel.

Thus the narrator's metaphorical plunge into the Rhône may be seen, in the context established by the reader, as an abandonment of will. The symbolical functions of the flowing river as designating time, past and future, and memory, but also forgetfulness and a death-wish—"Je m'ophélise dans le Rhône" (p. 22)—are expanded by the reader, who attempts to relate the image to the other elements of the novel. The plunge in search of his *cadavre* transforms his previously intransitive act ("je descends") into a transitive one ("je plonge … à la recherche de mon cadavre"), evoking another cluster of ambiguities, for *cadavre* in this context is at least three ways ambiguous. In connection with submersion as a metaphor for memory, *cadavre* may be seen as a symbol of the past the narrator is invoking. On the other hand, when related to the spy-story he is planning, *cadavre* may be interpreted as its inevitable corpse. The *cadavre* as a reflected image of the narrator and his plunge beneath the surface of the water in search for it evoke narcissistic associations. But whereas in the Narcissus myth the hubris consists in the act following aesthetic recognition, which leads to death or metamorphosis, the element of beauty is here replaced by death itself, which, due to its function in the allusion, becomes equated with beauty. Since this reflection of death gives rise to what the narrator is writing (the object of his self-exploration having been designated as *cadavre*), the juxtaposition of the Narcissus elements lets the reader perceive the writing of the novel as a narcissistic act of aesthetic fulfilment as well as the expression of a death-wish designated by the metaphor itself.

In a subsequent chapter, the details of the Lausanne setting suggest the genre-specific *exotisme* which forms the background of the spy-story,[12] and the dialogue with K fits the spy-story formula: the hero's mission is defined, and it contains all the features demanded by the genre: a description of the enemy agent, his aliases, his car, the nature of his counter-revolutionary activities. The limitation of time is also respected: H. de Heutz has to be eliminated within twenty-four hours, which is when the hero and K agree to meet. It is in the dialogue between K and the hero that the reader's memory is challenged in the same way as in the reading of a spy-story. Both the Mercedes 300SL and H. de Heutz have occurred before in the text, not as actual realities but as virtual ones, namely while the narrator is describing the elements of his spy-story, but before it actually "begins." The information provided in the dialogue has a contradictory effect on the reader. The obvious following of spy-story formula suggests an omniscient narrator who follows a preconceived outline of characters and events, reinforcing the declared non-identicality of hero and narrator. On the other hand the points of tangency previously recognized between hero and narrator, spy-story and diary, and the reader's attempt to motivate these elements and so make sense of what is being read as a novel, result in a questioning of the validity of all the types of reality represented: that of the spy-story, that of the diary, and that of the novel as a whole. The habitual clear distinction between real and imaginary, truth and fiction is called into question by the reader's own attempt to interpret the text.

The hero's pursuit of H. de Heutz takes on parodistic features in the density of the generic features presented. In the chase after his enemy, the hero encounters numerous obstacles, all of which he overcomes, yet always just missing his prey. The tip-off from a hotel waiter, bought with Swiss francs, the detailed description of the chase itself, H. de Heutz's whereabouts and his alleged motive seem stripped of all communicatory value except for that which they would have in a "real" spy-story, namely to create suspense, motivate the plot, and increase the credibility of the text by the precision of references in keeping with what the reader anticipates on the basis of previous information. The language, too, takes on a parodistic character due to its use of spy-story clichés and aggressive images—"le temps travaillait contre moi," "j'ai pressé l'accélérateur de ma Volvo jusqu'à faire gondoler la feuille d'acier sous mes pieds!" (p. 45).

The persistent equation of narrator and hero counteracts the reader's attempt to separate the two narrative strands in order to be able to determine their relationship. The parodistic consistency with which the spy-story formula is invoked alienates the plot from the fictional reality of the journal, yet the connection between narrator and hero is invoked with equal persistence. The text thus simultaneously confirms and negates the validity of the relationships it suggests, constantly frustrating the reader's attempts to build up a consistent pattern of meaning. Since the narrator adopts the perspective of the hero, and the narrative perspective is the only one available, readers are forced to identify with it. At the same time they are not able to define the nature of the obviously close connection between hero and narrator and so are unable to motivate the double frame. The recognition of the significance of the double narrative is therefore anticipated with the same suspense as the *dénouement* of the spy-story, so that in creating reader mystification the text proposes a riddle which contains, at least in part, its own answer. It is situated in the reader's perception of this similarity of effect.

In the same way, the ambiguity of the narrator/hero's identity is alluded to by the spy-story plot, in which the agents' aliases make multiple identities a plausible phenomenon.

In the spy-story the hero finds that his victim has eluded him at the first point of encounter, Château d'Oex, having changed his identity. It is now no longer a Swiss banker he is after, but a Belgian historian, whose hobby-horse, as a Roman specialist, is Scipio *l'Africain*.[13] The hero, too, feigns a different identity, namely that of an authority on the Punic Wars, which, however, he also seems to be: "Dieu m'est témoin que j'ai été tout surpris d'apprendre, par ce subterfuge, la présence en Suisse d'un collègue qui connaissait Scipion l'Africain comme le fond de sa main" (p. 48). In both cases the transformation of identity seems to be complete. At the same time the strategies of dissimulation of both the hero and his intended victim reveal an astonishing similarity between pursuer and pursued.

The about-turn and subsequent race are similarly recognizable features of the genre, as is the reference to time, often used in suspense stories to lend them something of the documentary, of the official report, in addition to contributing to the reader's suspense. But the reference to time is also self-allusive in the context of the novel: "Ma montre-bracelet, de fabrication suisse, indiquait dix heures et douze minutes" (p. 50).

At the historical society meeting where the hero has hoped to find H. de Heutz, he misses him again, and, to his surprise, discovers that it was he who gave the lecture he had decided to hear on "César et les Helvètes," which he missed due to his chase of, precisely, the conférencier. The scene which follows at the Café du Globe, where the hero overhears a conversation about Balzac while he is waiting for H. de Heutz to appear, mixes a number of elements from the various sub-repertoires already designated by the text.

In the hero's resulting fantasies about Balzac the reader recognizes certain features of the narrator's relationship to his hero. Balzac's alleged sexual impotence and the narrator's revolutionary impotence are equated by the shared element of displacement, bestowing their inability to act on their fictitious heroes. Although the reader is no closer to discerning the "reality" of the narrator's hero, the Balzac reference points to the significance of the act of writing as an escape from one's own failure or inability: it proposes fiction as an alternative to life. This theory seems valid for the narrator, who slips so completely into the role of his hero, yet it is contradicted precisely by the reader's sense that the spy-story is, down to the smallest detail, constituted by the actual experience of the narrator. The reader's habitual questioning of fiction versus truth is thus transformed in the anticipation that they will reveal themselves to be, at least in the present novel, one and the same.

Situational parallels to the *Histoire des Treize*, particularly to *Ferragus*, become recognizable due to the context pre-established by the references to Balzac in the café. Like Maulincour's idle pursuit of Mme Jules, which involves him in a conspiracy over which he has no control and of which he ultimately becomes a victim (for reasons he is entirely unaware of), the hero's pursuit of H. de Heutz leads him into the midst of an intrigue of which he is not sure that he is the intended object.

As the hero observes H. de Heutz leaving the café, he follows. He suddenly realizes that H. de Heutz is with a woman. During his pursuit, first by car, then on foot, the woman suddenly disappears while H. de Heutz proceeds, almost running, towards Carouge. The reference to the "ancien refuge des révolutionnaires russes," where H. de Heutz leads him against his will, so to speak, re-evokes the historical allusions with which the novel opened, while its allusion to Russian revolutionaries invokes Marxism as a teleological theory, an invocation ironically alluded to in the hero's necessity to follow. It suggests that he is no longer free by equating his subjectedness to history with the fact that his actions are determined by H. de Heutz. Lack of freedom, first suggested by the narrator's literal captivity, then by his consciousness of the collective captivity of Quebec, thirdly by the unarticulated restraints imposed by his writing, and finally by his story's following a pre-established literary pattern, is recognized by the reader as one of the central themes of the novel. Furthermore, in recognizing the restriction of the reader's own role in following the apparently contradictory "instructions" of the text, the reader perceives the consequent "lack of freedom" as a point of tangency between the reader (in the act of reading) and what is expressed in the text. The reader's role in fulfilling the communicatory intention of the text may be seen as analogous to the role of the revolutionary hero in achieving the revolution. Similarly, the Balzac allusion describes an act (which in its banality denotes the virtual aspects of any act and hence also the act of reading) as the involuntary yielding up of precisely that freedom manifested by the act itself. Since it also encompasses the multiple identities of Ferragus (and the hidden identity of Mme Jules), the allusion creates a number of points of contingency which go beyond the situational parallel of Maulincour's experience in a dubious *quartier* of Paris and the hero's adventure in Carouge. The multiple identities of Balzac's heroes thus lend their various extensions to the characters in the novel, not only increasing their functional ambiguity, but also disorienting the reader as to which features of the various allusions are to be invoked with respect to the different characters.

The Carouge incident ends with the hero's being attacked from behind. The following chapter opens with the hero in a château overlooking the lake, facing an interrogator who is, presumably, H. de Heutz. There is thus a gap in the plot of the spy-story corresponding to the gap in consciousness of the hero, both of which remain uncompensated for by the narrator. This gap itself may be seen as a Balzac allusion, namely to a character's being spirited away into an unfamiliar and exotic setting, the *enlèvement* being always so conducted that the character in question has no possibility of retracing the path which led him there.[14]

In the hero's assessment of his situation, as he regains consciousness in the château, K is increasingly implicated in the mind of the reader as playing a decisive role in the hero's misadventures. The château overlooking the lake calls to mind a previous dialogue between K and the hero, in which they envision living in a villa on the lake near Lausanne. The hero's reference to their night at the hôtel d'Angleterre (also on the lake), followed by his realization that he has been disarmed, constitutes a sexual dimension re-evoking the Balzac discussion in the café, with its effect of equating sexual and revolutionary impotence. This psychologistic interpretation induced by the sequence in which the associations are evoked is underlined by the double significance of the position of the hero's interrogator. He is sitting with his back to the window, against the light. This element is motivated by interrogation procedures as they occur in detective and spy-stories to increase the captive's vulnerability, but it is also a psychoanalytic technique, in which the analyst remains in obscurity to encourage the patient to drop his defences.[15] These situational associations induced in the reader are expanded to include yet another element in the symbolic equation of sex and weapon, namely language, and hence constitute another self-allusion of the text. As in the Balzac episode, discourse is recognized as a surrogate of action as well as of sex. "Il me fallait ... puisque je n'avais plus d'arme à dégainer, vider mon chargeur dialectique sur cet inconnu dressé entre le jour et moi" (p. 58).

While the situation fits perfectly the spy-story formula, the double framework is constantly evoked by the ambiguity of reference of each utterance to the two contexts: "Je parle, mais qu'est-ce que je dis au juste? C'est illogique. Mon improvisation oblique dans le genre allusif" (p. 60). There is, in the scene which follows, constant invocation of this duality through the form of discourse as well as through the elements to which it refers. It thus becomes recognizable to the reader as the governing dialectic of the novel, which the reader recognizes in retrospect (in what has been read) and prospectively, in terms of anticipation.

The re-appearance of the cryptogram, produced by H. de Heutz, seems to temporarily suspend the reader's inter-textual and extra-textual associations and to revert to the spy-story formula, designated by a stock situation and dialogue. H. de Heutz presents the cryptogram with the inevitable comment: "Et ça, c'est une lettre d'amour peut-être?" (p. 63).

The hero reflects that ironically enough the cryptogram is probably a joke on the part of his friend Hamidou. The hero's falling victim to a harmless joke which has no connection with his true conspiratorial intentions (of which his adversary is ignorant) constitutes another spy-story cliché, to which the hero responds, appropriately enough in this parodistic context, with a series of comic-strip blurbs: "décidément, j'étais surcuit comme un steak de Salisbury, définitivement perdu, Kaputt, versich" (p. 63).

Subsequently, the hero manages to turn the tables and reverse the situation. But with H. de Heutz safely locked in the trunk of his own car, the hero is at a loss as to what action he should take. He reflects upon his hesitancy to kill H. de Heutz.[16] This hesitation is at first comic, then grotesque, and finally tragic in its effect. It is at first comic due to the spy-story context, in which H. de Heutz is reduced to a disposal problem. At the same time the ensuing passage in the journal, with its allusions to suicide, evoke Hamlet's famous monologue, not only owing to the present context, but also to an image which has occurred previously in the text ("Je m'ophélise dans le Rhône").

With this double hesitation, that of the hero to kill H. de Heutz and that of the revolution which does not take place, the two narrative frames approach each other more and more explicitly. The mutual motivation of journal and spy-story also becomes increasingly evident to the reader.

The spy-story is interrupted at the moment when the hero inserts the key into the lock of the trunk to let H. de Heutz out. This technique of cutting a narrative when the reader's suspense is at its height is typical of the segmentation of the detective or spy-story, where it is used either in the way the chapters are segmented or in the way a multi-stranded narrative describing simultaneous events changes perspective. Here, however, the cut seems to be structurally unmotivated. The narrator interrupts his story to evoke a Quebec landscape and his dreams of buying a house near La Nation, in the back-country of the Outaouais River, to live there peacefully with K.

The reader's attempt to interpret this seemingly incongruous interruption of the spy-story results in a grouping of this reference to an idyllic place of refuge for himself and K with previous references describing such a place of retreat. It re-evokes the villa on the lake and so H. de Heutz's château, both of which represent similar contexts. Thus the fictional reality of H. de Heutz's château which occurred in the spy-story becomes equated with the virtual possibilities represented by the narrator/hero's villa on Lake Geneva, also referred to in the spy-story, and the house he dreams of owning at La Nation, described in the journal, strengthening the reader's sense of identification between the narrator/hero and H. de Heutz, the owner of the château. Since the château (where he was imprisoned) represents a refuge such as he describes, it becomes associated with the objects of his longing, his *pays* and his lover, K. Standing between him and the fulfilment of his visions is H. de Heutz, whose imprisonment in the trunk of his car is prolonged, in a way, due to the narrator's own imprisonment:

> Je ne peux pas briser les cerceaux qui m'ensèrent, pour aller vers cette maison qui nous attend sur la route sinueuse qui va de Papineauville à La Nation, pour aller vers toi mon amour et vers les quelques journées d'amour que je rêve encore de vivre. Mais comment me déprendre de cette situation? Impossible.
> Comment me défaire de H. de Heutz? (p. 79)

This rhetorical parallel indicates the increasing explicitness with which narrator, hero and H. de Heutz are seen to merge. The reader perceives this converging in the almost simultaneous references to their respective imprisonments, the narrator in his institution cell, the hero caught in his plot, and H. de Heutz locked in the trunk of his own car.

Simultaneously designating the unexpected turns taken by spy-stories and the merging of apparently irreconcilable identities, H. de Heutz comes up with still another identity, namely that of a Belgian agent called Marc de Saugy. This alias turns out to represent an exact counterpart of the role assumed by the hero in the château: "de Saugy" serves the hero the identical story the hero had fabricated earlier in the château, and precisely because of this audacity, the hero almost believes him. As in the case of the hero, the reader cannot with certainty exclude the possibility that there is an element of truth in the story, since the only available perspective is that of the narrator/hero, whose own lack of knowledge makes him unreliable. The striking symmetry of roles and situations is underlined by the reader's perception of the hero's characterization of H. de Heutz as an involuntary and ironic self-characterization:

> Cet homme possède un don diabolique pour falsifier la vraisemblance; si je n'étais pas sur mes gardes, il m'aurait à coup sûr et pourrait me convaincre qu'il est mon frère, que nous étions nés pour nous rencontrer et pour nous comprendre. (p. 85)

Should any one of the aliases be authentic, a possibility the reader is unable to exclude, the reader's entire interpretation of the spy-story and therefore of the novel would be invalid. It is with a sense of the possible distortion of his or her own reasoning and perceptions that the reader proceeds from the beginning of the episode at Coppet.

A further feature complicating the problem of identity is the fact that both men seem quite prepared to die. This reaction on both their parts can be interpreted as a bluff to play for time, a recourse to contrary suggestion. At the same time the narrator's repeated allusion to suicide and his near-identity with the hero induces the reader to see in this challenge more than a strategic bluff, making the resemblance between the hero and H. de Heutz all the more striking and baffling. The hero is fascinated and attracted by his adversary's inexplicable performance. In his mystification he muses: "À qui ai-je affaire au juste? À l'ombre métempsychée de Ferragus?" Ferragus/Balzac thus becomes the common denominator of all three men, hero, narrator and H. de Heutz, and with the reference to metempsychosis the reader recognizes an allusion to a relationship in which the term plays a central role, namely that between the two Joycean heroes Stephen Dedalus and Leopold Bloom. This oblique allusion to *Ulysses* constitutes a frame of reference in terms of which the nature of the identification between hero and H. de Heutz is illuminated, while the connection, as in *Ulysses* itself, remains unformulated. In indicating a possible code by which to decipher the baffling elements of the novel, and yet withholding the meaning itself, the text designates its own structure as a sort of riddle or puzzle, the satisfactory solution of which is always relative, since it is contingent upon the perceptual performance of the reader. Yet it is precisely the reader's habitual perceptual performance which is challenged by the text, since it exposes its one-dimensionality and hence distortiveness.

With the spy-story suspended in mid-air and H. de Heutz weeping before the hero who confronts him with his own weapon, the narrator articulates the nature of his own imprisonment, confirming the reader's interpretations of previous allusions as manifestations of a predetermined sequence of events. The narrator refers to his literal imprisonment but also to his figurative imprisonment in his memories, in the inevitability of history as it follows its predetermined course, and in his inability to break out of the pre-established patterns of literature. Consequently, he perceives each act as a new manifestation of his lack of freedom, a consciousness which paralyzes his will to act.

J'hésite à commettre un acte de plus; je ne sais plus comment agir soudain. Je sens bien que le prochain virage est dangereux et que je risque tout à m'avouer le sujet de mon hésitation. (p. 91)

In the parallel structure of journal and spy-story, the narrator's hesitation to write (and so create) coincides with the hero's hesitation to kill (and so destroy). The two instances of hesitation, in their merging of narrator and hero and hero and victim, are mutually motivating and so one act cancels the other, making both impossible. The transcendant motivation is the narrator's *will* to write, the enactment of which is its own motivation.

> [S]i je suis subitement privé de ma raison d'écrire parce que je perçois mon livre à venir comme prédit et marqué d'avance, ... je n'en cesse pas pour autant de vouloir écrire, c'est donc que l'écriture ne devient pas inutile du seul fait que je la départis de sa fonction d'originalité et que justement cette fonction génétique ne la résume pas. (p. 92)

Writing as an act of will and at the same time an historical act becomes the manifestation of the affirmation of self-existence, and so a revolutionary act. Since his writing is both a manifestation of self and a constant revolutionary act, the end of the novel will be extra-textual.

> Ce livre est le geste inlassablement recommencé d'un patriote qui attend, dans le vide intemporel, l'occasion de reprendre les armes. ... Il est tourné globalement vers une conclusion qu'il ne contiendra pas puisqu'elle suivra, hors texte, le point final que j'apposerai au bas de la dernière page. (p. 93)

The double frame recognized by the reader throughout the novel is only seemingly cancelled in this self-exegesis. For what is to follow, *hors texte*, is not only the revolution, the liberation of the hero and the liberation of humankind, but the reception of the novel in history, the establishing of its place in a historical sequence. Furthermore, in view of the inconclusiveness of the text, this sentence may be seen as a reference to the reader's own response to the text. In this sense the reader "concludes" the novel, but the reader's conclusion is only valid to the extent that it incorporates the elements of the text, and processes them according to the coded instructions contained in it. Thus the extra-textual conclusion may be seen as a reference to the effect of the text on the reader, brought about by the interaction between text and reader, both of which, however, are historically predetermined, the text by its historical and literary repertoire, the reader by previous experience.

This hermeneutic dialectic, in which the reader's expectations and recognitions become indistinguishable from the intentionality of the text, structurally resembles the revolutionary dialectic described in the novel. Its circularity is suggested by the metaphorical invocation of the literal sense of the word revolution—"j'ai vu une dizaine de révolutions tourner à l'échec"—and by referring the reader back to the historical associations evoked by the setting at the very beginning of the novel.

> ... la révolution de Genève de 1781, celle des Provinces-Unies des Pays-Bas en 1787, celle des Pays-Bas Autrichiens et de Liège. ... J'ai frémi aux mille suicides de Tchernychevski et au romantisme insurrectionnel de Mazzini. Ces grands frères dans le désespoir et l'attentat sont à peine moins présents en moi que les patriotes, mes frères inconnus, qui m'attendent dans le secret et l'impatience. Me reconnaîtront-ils? (p. 96)

In the same journal entry, a new dimension of the curious relationship between the hero and H. de Heutz emerges. In a phrase sandwiched between references to landmarks around Lake Geneva, the narrator alludes to "ce chalet que j'ai rêvé d'acheter à Evolène dans la haute vallée de Hérens" (p. 97). This reference to the chalet described by H. de Heutz (alias Marc de Saugy) in his improbable narrative identifies the narrator, hero and H. de Heutz with all his aliases as one and the same, yet in the narrator's story the reader retains the image of H. de Heutz and the hero in a position of confrontation in the bois de Coppet. In an attempt at consistency-building the reader is thus induced to attempt to reconcile the seemingly irreconcilable, to formulate the range of possible explanations of this identicality by referring to the givens of the text, and to the reader's own habitual experience of life, but also of literature.

When the spy-story is taken up again following the journal entry invoking the chalet at Evolène and hence indicating the convergence of the identities of H. de Heutz and the hero/narrator, it is to describe how H. de Heutz gains the upper hand. In retrospect it seems the hero has been watched from the château as he leaves with H. de Heutz, and followed.

The hero refers to the events at the château as resembling a scene in a film: "tout s'est déroulé comme au cinéma avec une facilité louche" (p. 99). This reference to the film describes the reader's own response to the spy-story, and re-invokes the mechanistic conception of history already identified in the allusions. The film image points up the reader's gullibility in accepting the sequence described by the text, for the text induces the reader to direct attention exclusively to what will happen next, to what the hero will do next. There is no premonition of danger, no ominous detail. It is only in retrospect that the hero realizes he has been watched, and that he has taken no precautions: "Si j'avais eu juste la force de me retourner vivement, j'aurais aperçu deux yeux braqués sur moi, derrière une des fenêtres de la face nord du château" (p. 100).

On the other hand the reference to the departure from the château as a film scene suggests a preconceived sequence of events whose virtual existence can only be actualized in fragmented form at a given moment in time, while its description as a facile movie formula re-invokes the inevitability of the spy-story pattern. Instead of breaking the illusion of reality, however, the reference to the formula lends credibility to the events, since it is made by the narrator/hero who experienced them.

By revealing to the reader that the entire preceding sequence was unforeseen by the hero while it seems to have been carefully planned by H. de Heutz, the text at once deflates the notion of historical deter-mination by presenting H. de Heutz as the planner, all the while affirming its validity by positing H. de Heutz as a historical agent. For H. de Heutz could only plan thus by predicting the hero's actions, presupposing a close and familiar relationship through identification. H. de Heutz himself becomes associated with the metaphysical will determining history: "je ne faisais que lui obéir docilement sans même qu'il ait à préciser ses ordres. J'étais devenu son médium" (p. 100). H. de Heutz's omniscience is underlined by the shadowy figure of the hero's observer, known to H. de Heutz but not to the hero. This strengthens the reader's identification with the hero, for unlike in the spy-film, where, typically, a long shot of an empty room or a flapping curtain, a following car unperceived by the hero, or an inconspicuous neighbour at a bar communicate to the viewer a knowledge not shared by the hero, the hero's distress at the retrospective consciousness of an unknown presence observing his every move is shared by the reader. This identification is strengthened by the narrator/hero's reconstruc-tion of the event from the perspective of this unknown enemy.

The shift to the narrator's situation involves a contradiction of the same order as the allusion to the chalet at Evolène. The narrator reflects on the story of despair he has told to his interrogator, but with H. de Heutz's variant:

> [J]'étais face à mon ennemi numéro un, découragé de mesurer les erreurs qui m'avaient conduit à cet échec, incapable d'imaginer autre chose, pour meubler les vides de la conversation, que cette histoire de dépres-sion nerveuse : deux enfants, femme abandonnée, fuite, mes ambitions lamentables de vols de banque et ma résolution finale d'utiliser mon Colt spécial à bon escient en me flambant la cervelle dans un terrain vague de Carouge. (p. 103)

The reference to the Carouge as the chosen place of suicide lets the reader perceive the hero and H. de Heutz as identical, while the sub-sequent reference to H. de Heutz facing him in the bois de Coppet annuls this identicality. It is while H. de Heutz tells his story, weep-ing, that the unknown presence of the accomplice manifests itself. "C'est à ce moment précis que j'ai aperçu un signe!" (p. 104). The *moment précis* can only refer to H. de Heutz's story, obviously longer than a *moment*. The reader is therefore induced to seek the momentary perception of the hero, which can only refer to the sentence fragments designating the identicality of the hero and H. de Heutz: the *moment précis* may be seen to describe the reader's own perception of the merging of identities of two men confronting each other in the bois de Coppet.

The sign perceived by the hero is undeterminable. It seems to have been an intuition on his part rather than a fleeting perception. The hero perceived something, then fled. It is not clear exactly what he perceived, in what the sign consisted: H. de Heutz's smile recognizing the arrival of his accomplice; the sound of a motor, tires on pavement, a blond woman whom the hero, while not sure that it was a woman, or that she was blond, associates with H. de Heutz's companion as he pursued him in Geneva. His own doubts of his perceptions, and his description of them, elicit a number of responses from the reader. The uncertainty of the hero's perceptions could stem from the simultaneity of a number of stimuli and the momentariness of their manifestation. It could also be due to the absence of any sign at all, an equally plausible explanation in view of the hero's stressful situation: a case of nerves. This latter explanation would cast doubt on the incident in Carouge, in which the blond woman dimly associated by the reader with K could also have been imaginary. Thus the reader's responses are directed in a number of different directions at once. Previous interpretations and associations become at once more plausible and yet less certain.

The hero flees in H. de Heutz's blue Opel to Coppet, where, in the relief of his escape, he has an enormous lunch at the Auberge des Emigrés. This scene and the ones following it at Coppet restore the old spy-story frame. All metaphysical connections seem to be eliminated in the text itself, while they persist in the mind of the reader. The events themselves are thus always doubly motivated, by the plot of the spy-story on the one hand, and in the reader's awareness of their allusive significance on the other.

The hero's sense of well-being after his meal makes his stroll in Coppet and browsing in a bookstore plausible, while each element of his apparently coincidental and casual experience is recognized to be self-allusive by the reader. The *Guide Bleu* of Switzerland does not include the map the hero is looking for in its description of Coppet, but a lengthy exposition about the Necker family and Mme de Staël, and a reference to her being placed under surveillance in her own château. Asked about H. de Heutz's book on Caesar and the Helvetians, the bookseller recognizes the name, but cannot place it or find it in his shop. Finally, out of politeness, the hero buys the first book he happens upon: it is Graham Greene's *Our Man in Havana*.

The implausibility of all these chance points of tangency with the hero refers the reader to the spy-story's neat puzzle pattern, in which every piece fits. Yet each element of the episode is so well-motivated that the illusion of reality is maintained. The hero's opening the *Guide Bleu* at Coppet (which is, after all, where he finds himself) is as consistent with the situation as the didactic guide's long excursus on Mme de Staël, which turns out to be of allusive relevance to the hero. The shopkeeper's reaction to the hero's reference to H. de Heutz's book confirms its existence, while his inability to place it corresponds to the elusiveness of its author. Finally, the hero's haphazard choice of Greene's spy-novel, highly probable in view of the popularity of the book, represents a double allusion to previous references to the Cuban revolution and to the spy-story itself. The reader's recognition of the spy-story formula's plausibility, created by the consistent motivation of the events, calls into question the habitual separation of the obviously fictitious and the obviously "real." As in Greene's novel, life resembles fiction at least as much as fiction resembles life.

Leaving the bookstore, the hero hails a taxi to take him back to the bois de Coppet, apparently acting on an impulse formed by his experience in the bookshop. While this act parodies the proverbial return to the scene of the crime and so represents a formulaic motivation of the spy-story, its very implausibility is a strategic advantage to the hero and so represents a plausible motivation for the reader. Furthermore, the hero, speeding back to Echandens in H. de Heutz's car, in possession of his keys and (false) identity papers, represents a situational reversal which is at the same time recognizable as a reversal of roles, the pursuer becoming the pursued, and so effects a circular rather than a linear movement of the plot. The outcome of the episode remains unpredictable.

In the hero's leisurely inspection of the château and the objects it contains, the text becomes more and more obviously self-allusive. The hero's seduction by the château which finds its ultimate expression in the statement: "C'est ici vraiment que j'aimerais habiter" (p. 124) refers the reader to a number of previous allusions to the home of his longing: the villa he and K dream of possessing somewhere on the lake; the narrator's vision of a peaceful retreat at La Nation in Quebec; and finally the chalet at Evolène H. de Heutz (alias de Saugy) talks about. This sense of "home" the hero feels in H. de Heutz's château thus represents another facet of their shared identities, of the same order as the improbable stories they tell each other. The hero's comment on H. de Heutz's story, upon which he reflects as he senses the harmony between himself and his surroundings, lets the reader perceive his comment as a summing up of the suggested identicality of the hero and H. de Heutz, and indeed of the narrative strategies of the entire novel, encompassing the various responses of the reader as well as the ambiguous narrative perspective:

> Dire que H. de Heutz demeure ici! Son histoire d'enfants abandonnés à Liège n'est qu'une imposture d'occasion, une sorte de monologue pris au hasard à partir de la premiére trame donnée (la mienne, en l'occurrence) et poussé jusqu'au bout de l'invraisemblable par mesure de vraisemblance, car, une fois engagé dans son inextricable épopée, comment pouvait-il changer d'intrigue ou de personnage sans m'armer résolument contre lui? (p. 124)

In the hero's summing up of the situation the reader's recognition of the reversal of roles is underlined while its implications are expanded: the change in identity suggested by the hero's possession of H. de Heutz's car, papers and keys is made complete by the hero's taking over H. de Heutz's previous role. "H. de Heutz me cherche, moi je l'attends" (p. 127).

At the same time the hero's strategy represents an innovation of the spy-story formula. Although it is a case of the tables being once more turned, the hero's disguise is not one of dissimulation but one of recognition, revelation, a backward replay, so to speak, of what has gone before. His disguise as killer is that of his victim. The reversal of roles, the shared tastes, the duplication of strategic reasoning let the two identities overlap more and more in the perception of the reader. This recognition lets the reader interpret the hero's admiration of the two warriors symmetrically facing each other on an antique chest as a confirmation of the reader's interpretation of the roles of the two adversaries, while H. de Heutz's engraving of the death of General Wolfe underlines the symmetry of the roles of the two men. The hero, whose revolution has as goal the "reversal" of the conquest, is faced with an adversary whose historical orientation seems to be the precise counterpart: the duality manifesting itself in each feature of the novel becomes, in this scene, manifestly only another aspect of the same phenomenon. The hero's emotion at the setting in which H. de Heutz is at home reveals to him the possibility of a fulfilment he has never known. This personal fulfilment is given a collective dimension in the reader's association of the hero with his cause, namely that of Quebec.

> H. de Heutz vit dans un univers second qui ne m'a jamais été accessible, tandis que je poursuis mon exil cahotique dans des hôtels que je n'habite jamais. A travers la croisée de la porte-fenêtre, le paysage surabondant s'étale jusqu'aux parois brumeuses de la France, de l'autre côté du lac. Ah, vraiment je veux vivre ici, dans cette retraite empreinte de douceur et où s'exprime un vouloir-vivre antique qui ne s'est pas perdu. (p. 128)[17]

In the description of the bookplate (*ex-libris*) the hero finds in a book on Caesar's civil wars, the reader can recognize, in miniature, the hermeneutic riddle of the novel itself. For the bookplate is so elaborate that it is indecipherable. The hero at first seems to recognize Arab letters, then the initials of the owner (who is, however, not named in the text). The hero relates the book to the H. de Heutz of the Caesar lecture in Geneva, and the bookplate to the inhabitant of the château. Yet with each additional piece of information the identity of the man he is after, or rather who is now after him, becomes less certain. This mystification may be seen as paralleling that experienced by the reader: the elements he or she recognizes are constantly being deformed by the way they are connected to other elements and events. Each additional piece of information only complicates the pattern perceived by the reader, since it brings about constant changes in its constellation.

The fact that the bookplate is indecipherable links it with Hamidou's note, the cryptogram the hero finds at the hotel. The hero at first perceives it as consisting of Arab letters, strengthening the connection made by the reader. These relationships point to a connection between Hamidou and H. de Heutz, seeming to confirm a previous conclusion held by the reader (due to the 300SL in which Hamidou's partner disappears after their encounter at the Lausanne Palace).

However, the hero assures the reader that in fact the bookplate bears the initials of its owner. This perceptual juxtaposition is significant for the reader as it communicates the unreliability of the perspective, but an unreliability which offers the reader several possibilities of interpretation.

One is that the hero was for some reason (for instance due to his connection with Hamidou) predisposed to see Arab letters in the ex-libris, but was then able to correct his deficient vision to recognize it for what it "objectively" represents, namely H. de Heutz's monogram.

Another is that his readiness to attribute the book to H. de Heutz lets him "recognize" a sign which, in reality, is not there.

Finally, the ex-libris could be a *trompe-l'oeil*, letting its viewer perceive both signs (Arab and monogram) but never at the same time.

These possibilities of interpretation, all equally valid in view of the unverifiability of the ex-libris by the reader and the unreliability of the narrator/hero, illustrate the multiplicity of interpretations open to the reader of the novel. For the graphic technique of the ex-libris may be seen as a miniature representing the structural technique of the novel.

This strategy is referred to by the hero himself as he describes H. de Heutz. He presents as a certainty the fact that all information accessible through H. de Heutz is double-coded, and hence totally unaccessible and meaningless (unless, presumably, one knows both codes) (p. 135).

During his endless wait for H. de Heutz at the château, the hero suddenly realizes that his watch has stopped, and that there is no clock in the château. His resulting temporal disorientation involves the possibility that he may miss K, whom he is to meet at 6:30 p.m. on the terrace of the hôtel d'Angleterre at Lausanne.

The absence of "time" in the château has numerous levels of significance. The fact that the narrator's own watch has stopped (its reliability has previously been implied by reference to its Swiss fabrication) communicates a sense of time standing still. In the already established context of time as history, the elimination of any unit to measure time suggests the elimination of history, letting the hero's self-imposed confinement in the château take on features of the infinite. The validity of this impression is confirmed by the hero's sense of panic at his situation when he discovers that there is no way for him to tell the time.

This panic and sense of imprisonment associates the hero once again with the narrator in his cell, and, as in previous episodes, the reader cannot tell whether the narrator's panic is due to the point arrived at in his story or due to a quickened awareness of his isolation in his cell, which he then attributes to his hero. The reference to having been devoured by the revolution suggests his disappearance ("La révolution m'a mangé") in the enormous "body" of the revolution of which he forms an invisible, anonymous and passive part. The allusive significance of the phrase, however, encompasses Büchner's play *Dantons Tod* in its entirety.

The invocation of *Dantons Tod*[18] results in the reader's awareness of a series of parallels which underline the inevitability of the revolutionary historical pattern described by both texts. At the same time the dissimilarities between the two contexts, particularly the two heroes' revolutionary motivations and the circumstances of their respective failures, mutually reveal virtual dimensions of each other which are actualized only in their interrelationship.

Danton's revolultionary motivation is revealed as a desire to expose the discrepancy between *Schein* and *Wirklichkeit*, in order to establish the truth.[19] In *Prochain épisode* the reader has recognized the communicatory intention of the text as precisely the opposite, namely to induce the reader to perceive *Schein* and *Wirklichkeit* as a dynamic reversible schema of cause and effect. In both cases, the chosen generic forms negate the hypotheses underlying the two texts. Danton's negation of illusion is presented in the form of an illusion, the play. The narrator's negation of the separation of imaginary or remembered experience and the reality of experience is presented in the form of fiction. The principle of negation as the source of revolutionary energy is thus recognizable not only in the negation of a historical system, but also as a principle underlying communication.

The explicit invocation of Büchner's play results in the reader's retrospective recognition of previous implicit allusions to it. The narrator's metaphorical dive into the Rhône and its extended aquatic images may be seen as expanding the context of St. Just's equation of historical and natural processes. His famous image, comparing the revolution to a fast-flowing river which washes up its corpses at every bend,[20] is invoked not only by the narrator's plunge (thus simultaneously designated as his submersion in revolutionary history as well as his own memory and subconscious), but also by the object of his quest, his own *cadavre*.

The fact that the explicit allusion to *Dantons Tod* occurs as the hero waits for H. de Heutz to appear suggests another similarity between the two revolutionaries. Like Danton, whose resignation and refusal to speak publicly in his defence (until it is too late) seems to derive from lack of communication, isolation and guilt, the hero feels the impossibility of accomplishing his mission. The seemingly interminable wait for H. de Heutz to appear saps his energy and strength. But unlike Danton, who invokes the future of history as the ultimate posthumous justification of his revolutionary role, the hero invokes the heroic failures of the past. In an allusion to his *frères anciens de St. Eustache*[21] the historical dilemma of Quebec is evoked and equated with that of the hero/narrator: "Je suis un peuple défait qui marche en désordre dans les rues qui passent en-dessous de notre couche" (p. 139).

The sense of time passing, with no event to mark it, is thus perceived as a failure of history (as event) to accomplish itself but also as a case of history (as time) passing the designated event without its having taken place, leaving the reader, like the narrator/hero, with a sense of an irrevocable passing of the goal itself.

The wait for H. de Heutz is perceived as paralleling the wait for the revolution: "Et si H. de Heutz ne revenait pas? Et si la révolution ne venait jamais bouleverser nos existences?" (p. 141). Furthermore, the reference to the revolution can be seen to apply to the narrator as well as the hero, and so the different repertoires are evoked as though they referred to a single reality.

The hero's sense of failure as he recapitulates the events in the bois de Coppet, and his sketching of an alternative course of action are summed up in the sentences: "J'ai perdu le fil de mon histoire, et me voici rendu au milieu d'un chapitre que je ne sais plus comment finir" (p. 142). Like the reference to the revolution which does not take place, the sentence simultaneously refers to the hero and to the narrator. The narrator/hero's sense of having reached a dead end coincides with the reader's feeling that the identities of the two adversaries have somehow merged. This interpretation is reinforced by the hero's repetition of the allusion to the chalet at Evolène, which originated in the story of H. de Heutz while he was at the hero's mercy.

When H. de Heutz finally arrives, the hero glimpses a grey 300SL with Zurich licence-plates, letting the reader identify H. de Heutz both as the man who met Hamidou at the outset of the story, and as the man described by K as the Zurich banker called van Ryndt. This time, the change in identity suggested by the use of the Mercedes is brought about by the hero who, in taking possession of the blue Opel, has "robbed" H. de Heutz of his identity. This feature, in combination with the hero's precautions and minutely planned strategies, leads the reader to anticipate the success of his mission. Without catching so much as a glimpse of H. de Heutz himself, the hero hears him making a telephone call. The conversation with his wife or lover, with whom he arranges a meeting at 6:30 on the terrace of the hôtel d'Angleterre, seems to confirm the previous interpretations of the reader that the blond woman associated with H. de Heutz is K. This recognition poses a series of new problems, since it casts K in the role of double agent and makes it impossible to tell which side she is really working for. In attempting to motivate K's action, the reader recalls the conversation between K and the hero at their meeting in Lausanne. K's remarks, recalled in the context of her conversation with H. de Heutz, indicate the plausibility of a double conspiracy involving H. de Heutz and the hero motivated by a personal crisis K has undergone.[22]

The audible side of the dialogue on the telephone also poses other mysteries: H. de Heutz seems to be referring to the hero, yet insists that he does not know him, has never seen him, and, furthermore, the other man (presumably the hero) does not know him, either (p. 149).

The entire complex of possible interpretations as to the identity of H. de Heutz and the hero is thus re-evoked. Even the reference to the children (H. de Heutz says: "Maintenant, dis-moi : où sont les enfants?") does not eliminate the ambiguities of their respective identities, for the reader knows nothing of their past. The reader is therefore no closer to solving the mystery in spite of this new information.

The segmentation of the story at this point, constituting a gap between H. de Heutz's telephone call and the hero wandering about in Lausanne, having missed K, increases the reader's suspense to find out how the confrontation at the château ended and what K's true role has been in the hero's and H. de Heutz's pursuit of one another. Instead of supplying the answers, the text dwells on the hero's desperation at having missed K.

In the midst of his mourning for K, the hero states outright that he did not kill H. de Heutz and does not even know if he has hit him. He returns to the hotel terrace, hoping to see if H. de Heutz has come to his rendezvous and also to see his blond accomplice, but his search is in vain. Not finding either of the two, the hero goes to the reception desk, where the clerk, immediately recognizing him, gives him a message which underlines all the ambiguities previously evoked in the text. The message mentions that K's leader has received an "unexpected visitor" that afternoon, and that all activities have therefore been cancelled. It suggests he return to Montreal, and, in a postscript, extends greetings from Hamidou.

The message contains a number of clues which make the various possibilities the reader has construed so far all the more puzzling and irreconcilable. The message is written on blue paper, like Hamidou's cryptogram. This together with the postscript referring to Hamidou seems to attribute a role to him which the reader is unable to interpret or motivate, though Hamidou has been associated with both the hero's and the enemy's side. The message also re-evokes the telephone conversation between H. de Heutz and his accomplice, who seems to be K, letting the reader perceive the message as possibly being coded: "n'oublie surtout pas la couleur du papier et le code, tu comprends? Tu trouveras cela dans le récit de la bataille d'Uxellodunum par Stoffel, page 218" (p. 149).

Since the Hamidou reference also connects Hamidou and K, the reader's mistrust of Hamidou is extended to K herself, whose role in the affair has already been recognized as dubious. The reader's linking the *patron*'s unexpected visitor with the hero, and hence H. de Heutz with the *patron*, offers three possibilities of interpretation. Either H. de Heutz is really on the hero's side, and the entire episode is a mistake, or K is a double agent really working for the enemy (represented by H. de Heutz), or K herself has been the victim of a plot to precipitate the incident, behind which could be either the counter-revolutionary enemy or the revolutionaries themselves. In any of these three possible interpretations, the only motive of either side in sending the hero on this mission would seem to be his elimination. Since the text presents no clue by which the reader could motivate this, the only explanation would be the conjecture that for some reason the hero is no longer useful for the revolution, or has become too dangerous for the enemy. If, however, as has already been suggested, the entire episode is a hallucination of the narrator/hero, in which he himself plays two opposing roles, the motivation can only lie in the communicatory effect of the complex allusive patterns already presented.

In the spy-story, the hero follows K's instructions and returns to Montreal. Against the rules of his organization the hero arranges a meeting with M, who informs him that their cell has been broken up by an anti-terrorist squad and that their money has been confiscated. Before meeting M, he buys a pocket watch in an antique store.

The incident of the watch-purchase, kaleidoscope-like, rearranges the familiar elements of the repertoire of the novel into a new pattern. It symbolically suggests the hero's assumption of another identity, that of the deceased owner whose initials are engraved on it:

"Finalement, j'ai avisé une montre de poche, en or terni mais finement ciselé au chiffre d'un mort anonyme" (p. 162). The qualities associated with its origins may be seen to allude not only to the object itself, but also to its symbolic functions as previously designated in the text. "Le boîtier, fait en Angleterre, contenait un mouvement suisse qui tournait avec une régularité éternelle" (p. 162).

The synecdochal relationship between the watch mechanism and the multiple temporal dimensions of the novel, subsumed in the term *mouvement*, designates the contraction of historical experience into its smallest unit, the almost imperceptible movement of time as well as the individual moment, whose prolongation is a repetition of itself. Since the features of time implied by the description of the watch are easily linked with previous allusions to time in different contexts, particularly to the "absence" of time in the château, they describe the reduction of the hero's temporal perspective to the immediacy of the following moment. "Je disposai les aiguilles à l'heure juste. Il était exactement onze heures quarante-cinq minutes. Mon temps était venu" (p. 162).

What follows, or the *prochain épisode*, is the final episode of the novel.

In the final chapter, in which the narrator reflects on how his capture came about, the clues point more and more towards a betrayal of the hero/narrator, always with the possibility of a mistaken identity, namely that of H. de Heutz. Instead of moving towards a resolution, the problems multiply, namely with the possibility that the message from K was a fake, a trap, not written by K at all.

The ending offers no answers to the puzzles of the novel except for the reference to the *prochain épisode*. In the future tense, the narrator/hero describes the accomplishment of his mission, his reunion with K, and the achievement of the revolution itself. This will be, he says, the end of the novel, beneath which he will write, in capital letters, the word FIN.

Unlike the events of the novel and the allusions referring to them, the ending of the novel lies in its extra-textual futurity and not, as in the text, in the fact that certain designated possibilities of interpretation require actualization by the reader. The incommunicability of the future act, except as a statement of intention or prediction, involves the reader only in that he or she can affirm or negate its validity. The reader's disposition to do so is determined by the cumulative effect of the text, which expressly equates the concrete reality of experience with the virtual reality of fiction. If, then, the narrator lays his writing aside at the end of the novel to achieve the revolutionary mission proposed in it, the reader recognizes this act as being, in a sense, brought about by the text, which represents the communication of revolutionary experience.

Perceived in terms of a schema of cause and effect, the relationships between the categories proposed by the text—fiction and reality, historicity and futurity—these elements are seen to be reflexive in function and circular in pattern due to their mutual negation. The principle of permanent "revolution" is thus represented as the governing principle of human thought and experience.

In evoking the reader's response to an event it does not contain, the novel represents the interdependence between text and reader as a reflexive relationship, of the same order as those between the concrete and virtual realities presented in the text. For reader response depends upon the reader's interests and predispositions, which, in turn, are determined by the repertoire constituted by all previous experience. The alteration of the reader's predispositions is due to the constant enlarging of the reader's repertoire through experience, of which the reading of the novel itself represents an item.

Since the text makes the reader negate certain features of previously-made experience and so anticipate the future with the resulting alteration of awareness, the "success" of the novel may be measured in terms of the degree to which it has "revolutionized" the consciousness of the reader. In this sense, the fulfilment of the communicatory intention of the text may be seen as an ironic indication of the achievement of the revolutionary goal described in it.

Reference Notes to Chapter Six

1 Honoré de Balzac, *Histoire des Treize* (*Oeuvres complètes* [Paris: 1874]), p. 30.

2 Ibid., p. 36.

3 Patricia Smart, *Hubert Aquin, agent double* (Montreal: Les Presses de l'Université de Montréal, 1973), p. 25.

4 The Wolof were the first tribe in Senegal to come into contact with French civilization.

5 These elements are described by Tzvetan Todorov in "Typologie du roman policier," in his *Poétique de la prose* (Paris: Seuil, 1971).

6 Danton and Bakunin fell victim to the events they themselves had brought about. Bonnivard died in prison for trying to liberate Geneva from Savoy, while Lord Byron, having immortalized Bonnivard's fate, himself died as a consequence of his attempt to aid in the liberation of Greece. The allusions to revolutionary events also expose the betrayal of the visions which gave rise to them. Calvinism, having liberated the individual from his spiritual dependence on the Church, cancelled all spiritual freedom with its doctrine of predestination. The Russian revolution, in the name of freedom and equality, created one of the most oppressive political regimes in history.

7 At Uxellodanum, where the last battle of the Gallic campaign took place, Caesar exercised excessive brutality in order to discourage subsequent revolts. (Cf. Julius Caesar, *The Conquest of Gaul*, trans. by S. A. Handford [Pelican Books, 1963], pp. 225-58.)

8 Benjamin Constant, "De l'esprit de conquête et de l'usurpation," in *Cours de politique constitutionelle* (Paris: Librairies de Guillaumin, 1861), pp. 135-282.

9 The reference to Mme de Staël and the Necker family has a more complex allusive significance: Joseph Necker, son of a Geneva clockmaker, owner of the Château de Coppet and later finance minister of Louis XVI, was the indirect cause of the unrest

preceding the French revolution. His exposure of the court budget led to his dismissal, which, in turn, provoked the formation of the first constituant assembly. His daughter, Mme de Staël, was exiled from Paris due to the influence of her liberal attitudes and was, for a time, placed under surveillance in her own château at Coppet. The parallels between the narrator and his lover K and the relationship between Mme de Staël and Constant are thus not the only focus of the allusion. As in the case of Constant, the reader finds the most significant feature alluded to in the least obvious element of the suggested parallel. Turning to Mme de Staël's own writing, the reader finds a discussion of the role of fiction in revealing historical truth. (Cf. Mme de Staël, "De la littérature," in *Oeuvres complètes* [Geneva: Slatkine Reprints, 1967].)

10 On the 26th of July in Cuba "a symbolic gesture of defiance had been made by a group of 165 youths who assaulted the Moricada Barracks in Santiago. The few who were not killed were imprisoned. . . . As a result of this, Castro gave a speech at his trial, later published as *History Will Absolve Me."* (Martin C. Needler, *Political Systems of Latin America* [Cincinnati: Van Nostrand and Reinhold, 1970], p. 211ff.) On August *10*, 1792 the Tuileries were taken and the monarchy was overthrown. August 4, *1789*, the National Assembly voted to abolish the feudal system and privileges in a document the king then refused to sign.

11 Marcel Camus's film version of the Orpheus and Eurydice myth, set at the Mardi Gras of Rio de Janeiro.

12 Cf. Todorov, "Typologie du roman policier."

13 Scipio Publius Cornelius Africanus is described as a "brilliant commander" who was removed from power by his political opponents in Rome. He died in bitterness after withdrawing from Rome to Laternum. "Though essentially a man of action, he was also something of a mystic in whom contemporary legend saw the favoured of Jupiter Capitolanus as well as a spiritual descendant of Alexander the Great." His adopted grandson conquered and destroyed Carthage. He and a circle of his friends were largely responsible for the establishment of the new Greco-Roman education, *humanitas*. (Sources: *Encyclopedia Britannica, Brockhaus Enzyklopädie*.)

14 Cf. particularly *La fille aux yeux d'or*.

15 André Berthiaume's analysis of this passage seems to me unconvincing: "H. de Heutz s'interpose donc entre le héros et le lac, où sombre l'interné. Cette fois, c'est H. de Heutz qui est plus près du lac et qui subit son influence dissolvante. De Heutz sert de paravent au héros, il le protège du lac" (p. 142). From "Le thème de l'hésitation dans *Prochain épisode,"Liberté*, 15, no. 1 (janvier-fevrier 1973), pp. 135-48.

16 Berthiaume suggests several motivations for the hero's hesitation in the article quoted above. The most important seems to me to be that the hero, like the narrator, is an intellectual rather than an *homme d'action*, and that his intellectual reflectiveness as well as his emotional sensitivity is what lets him sense the "identicality" between himself and H. de Heutz, paralyzing his will to revolutionary action (i.e. to kill H. de Heutz). Berthiaume also discusses the function of structural, temporal and spatial hiatus in *Prochain épisode*, relating these elements to the hero's hesitancy to act (cf. p. 139).

17 "Quand Cicéron disait: *pro quâ patriâ mori, et cui nos totos dedere, et in quâ nostra omnia ponere, et quasi consecrare debemus*, c'est que la patrie contenait tout ce qu'un homme avait de plus cher. Perdre sa patrie, c'était perdre sa femme, ses enfants, ses amis, toutes ses affections, et presque toute communication et toute jouissance sociale: l'époque de ce patriotisme est passée. Ce que nous aimons dans la patrie, comme dans la liberté, c'est la propriété de nos biens, la sécurité, la possibilité du repos, de l'activité, de la gloire, de milles genres de bonheur. Le mot de patrie rappelle à notre pensée plutôt la réunion de ces biens que l'idée topographique d'un pays particulier. Lorsqu'on nous les enlève chez nous, nous les allons chercher au dehors." Footnote, pp. 254-55, in Benjamin Constant's "De l'esprit de conquête et de l'usurpation."

18 "... die Revolution ist wie Saturn, sie frißt ihre eignen Kinder." Georg Büchner, *Dantons Tod. Gesammelte Werke* (München: Goldmann, n.d., I, 5).

19 Asked by Camille why he has begun the revolutionary struggle only to abandon it, Danton answers: "Die Leute waren mir zuwider. Ich konnte dergleichen gespreizte Catonen nie ansehen, ohne ihnen einen Tritt zu geben. Mein Naturell ist einmal so." *Dantons Tod*, I, 1.

20 Cf. *Dantons Tod*, II, 7.

21 A fierce battle during the 1837 rebellion at St. Eustache, northwest of Montreal (cf. J. A. Lower, *Canada: An Outline History* [Toronto: Ryerson, 1966], p. 94).

22 During their meeting in Lausanne, K says to the narrator: "Tu sais, depuis que j'ai obtenu ma séparation, je vois les choses plus froidement qu'avant. A vrai dire, j'ai changé ma philosophie d'existence, en faisant de la mienne un gâchis ... ." Subsequently she specifies: "Je crois que j'ai fait une grande dépression: j'ai pris quelques médicaments à l'occasion, mais je ne me suis jamais fait traiter. Maintenant, c'est fini. Comment me trouves-tu?" (p. 40).

Afterword

The foregoing chapters reveal the multiplicity of narrative patterns that have developed in Canadian fiction since the Second World War. While the path that has been traced from MacLennan's hierarchic and symmetrical perspectival system to Aquin's metafiction can hardly be seen as a straight evolutionary line, this overview reveals the development of certain narratological trends whose historical significance requires interpretation in the light of their cultural context.

Perhaps the most striking finding in this regard is the occurrence in the English-Canadian novel of the forties and fifties of communicatory strategies that have long been abandoned in "serious" novels of other literatures, such as oppositional perspectival structures, lack of narrative ambiguity, relatively little problematization of the characters and the views they represent, and generally high textual determinacy. In the light of the typology described by Iser, against the background of which the novels in question (Hugh MacLennan's *Two Solitudes*, Ernest Buckler's *The Mountain and the Valley*, and Ethel Wilson's *Swamp Angel*) have been analyzed, these features seem historically revealing, for in the history of the novel they may be seen to be characteristic of the eighteenth century. In western literatures today these communicatory elements can be found almost exclusively in didactic, propagandistic or trivial forms of fiction. The English-Canadian novels under discussion, however, cannot be seen as belonging to any of these sub-genres.[1]

An explanation of the occurrence of these structural "anachronisms" must hence be sought elsewhere.

One factor that undoubtedly played an important role in forming the literary canon of the forties and fifties was the programmatic nationalist position that characterized the mainstream of English-

Reference notes for the Afterword are found on p. 178.

Canadian letters of the period. Indeed, this position, which focused on the socio-cultural particularities of the Canadian situation, persists in some quarters to this day. Canadian critical writing abounds with articles in which these particularities form the central interest, and in which the role of Canadian nationalism in canon formation is often a contentious issue.[2] These studies reveal the absence in Canadian society of an established cultural consensus. Hence the tendency, in the writing that reveals a nationalistic bias, to view literature as a didactic medium with a programmatic function. The occurrence in a number of novels of the forties and fifties, and even in some later ones, of oppositional perspectival structures represents the positive-negative polarization inherent in this view, dramatizing it in fiction.

It is interesting that these programmatic and didactic aspects can hardly be observed in the post-war fiction of Quebec. It seems that the predominance of a firmly established cultural consensus, resulting from both a common social and ethnic history and geographic concentration, has created a sense of collective cultural identity further accentuated by the separatism issue. Thus in the *québécois* novel few instances of oppositional perspectival arrangements and the features associated with them are to be found. Those which do come to mind, for example Lionel Groulx's *L'Appel de la race* (1922)[3] and Jean-Charles Harvey's *Les Demi-Civilisés* (1924),[4] seem to be solely didactic and polemical in their communicatory intention. Furthermore, they appeared well before 1945, and so considerably predate the English-Canadian novels that have been discussed in this context.

Indeed, analysis of the narrative strategies that come into play in Canadian and *québécois* novels seems to reveal a considerable divergence (rather than the similarities observed by a number of English-Canadian critics) between the two literatures, in both the social and literary repertoires alluded to. The *québécois* novel seems to be more radical in its violation of novelistic conventions and also in its negation of the predominant social norms, and there is a marked tendency to equate the artistic *avant-garde* with a generally emancipatory movement. In the English-Canadian novel, such general tendencies are difficult to identify or speculate upon. Certainly it seems that in English Canada, where there has been no cohesive political movement which would subsume the period under discussion, the political aspect is markedly less dominant. If one were to postulate an emerging literary tradition, it is not likely that it would be one common to the two socio-political groups representing English and French Canada.

The inevitably posed question, whether or not a recognizably Canadian novelistic tradition is emerging, is further complicated by the efforts of certain writers and critics, mainly English-Canadian, deliberately to create such a tradition. In a surprisingly large number of novels one finds an implicitly or explicitly expressed ideological need for a national culture based on an indigenous tradition (i.e. one that would distinguish itself from the American and European), an anchor-point that would legitimize the country's literary production by providing a readily recognizable, nationally acknowledged framework of cultural tradition in terms of which the individual work might be interpreted. Such programmatic consensus-seeking involves close control of the appropriate reader responses, and this would explain the occurrence of the communicatory strategies discussed earlier.

Whereas an empirical study would be necessary to determine the attitudes of both readers and writers, a number of critics have explicitly taken the nationalist position concerning the function of literature in a developing society. The didactic goal is usually formulated as the reader's "knowing oneself," or "finding one's cultural identity," and the programmatic function of the literature itself is seen as defining or even creating that identity.

That these programmatic elements may determine the intended effect of the MacLennan, Buckler and Wilson novels, and a number of other works not discussed in this study, can be supported, if only indirectly, from both the authorial and critical sides. In *Two Solitudes*, the narrator refers to Canada as a "land so near the frontier that in most of it everything was black and white, uncomplicated" (p. 203). Paul Tallard, the hero, reflecting on the Canadian background for his novel, seems to suggest that in a developing society literature takes on a quasi-didactic function:

> Canada was a country that no one knew . . . because it used the English and French languages, a Canadian book would have to take its place in the English and French traditions. Both traditions were so mature they had become almost decadent, while Canada herself was still raw. As Paul considered the matter, he realized that his readers' ignorance of the essential Canadian clashes and values presented him with a unique problem. The background would have to be created from scratch if his story was to become intelligible. He could afford to take nothing for granted. He would have to build the stage and props for his play, and then write the play itself. (p. 365)

In thematic criticism, there is an unmistakable tendency to favour writers to whom the critics attribute a primary concern with "Canadian identity." This is illustrated by John Moss's *Patterns of Isolation*,[5] which discusses all three novelists mentioned above. While MacLennan, Wilson and Buckler fare well, Robertson Davies's satirical Salterton trilogy indicates, for Moss, "the embarrassment of Robertson Davies at being born a Canadian."[6] Morley Callaghan is unfavourably compared with MacLennan, seemingly because, as Moss sees it, Callaghan is "never to be accused of being too much a Canadian spokesman."[7]

Margaret Atwood's *Survival* presents a similar evaluative bias. Wilson's novel is only briefly mentioned, but in a context supporting the argument of *Survival*.[8] While Buckler and MacLennan are repeatedly invoked to illustrate Atwood's hypothesis that the theme of survival is a characteristically Canadian feature,[9] Robertson Davies, for instance, does not appear at all, and Callaghan only twice in passing.[10]

The kind of bias implied in Moss's and Atwood's position (and also in that of Ronald Sutherland as set forth in *Second Image* and *The New Hero*) may be motivated, as Margot Northey suggests, by "growing feelings of nationalism and the desire for a recognizable cultural identity."[11] Anthony Dawson refers to "the desire currently felt in Canadian academic circles for great works," a desire derived "not only from literary and quasi-literary considerations but from unacknowledged ideological needs as well."[12] Dawson also observes that "If we look at the actual canon, we can see too that these ideological pressures are linked to a conservative ethos, manifested not only in the existence of the canon itself but also in the form and content (narrative structure and overt morality) of the canonized texts."[13]

It seems that in English Canada the amount of critical attention given to thematic elements in the past, derived, according to critics like Northey and Dawson, from certain ideological needs, has unquestionably played an important role in the formation of the literary canon. The current swing of the pendulum to more formalistic analysis, due not only to general critical trends but also to the appearance of works resisting thematic interpretation, may well result in its retrospective redefinition.

In recent Quebec novels (Yolande Villemaire, Nicole Brossard and France Théoret) the increasing preoccupation with feminism permits a closer critical parallel with the feminist writing that has emerged in English Canada (Margaret Atwood, Alice Munro, Margaret Laurence), at least thematically. Formally, however, English-Canadian feminist fiction writers remain committed to a realistic treatment of their subjects, while their French-Canadian counterparts continue to explore more radical narrative possibilities of the novel genre.

In the past few years, increased literary production in the postmodernist genre seems to be channelling in the same direction what, around mid-century, were highly divergent trends in the two literatures. Recent novels by Kroetsch and Findley mark a continuation and radicalization of the postmodernist exploration of these authors themselves, as well as that undertaken earlier by writers like Klein, Cohen and Godfrey. The work of these writers, together with that of novelists like Godbout, Aquin and Ducharme, may be seen to form the nucleus of a Canadian literary postmodernism whose "national cultural identity" consists, paradoxically, in the implicit negation of the relevance of this concept to itself. If, as Linda Hutcheon contends, the parody, auto-referentiality and intertextuality characterizing postmodernist works indeed signal the mastery, incorporation and transcendence of previous literary codes,[14] the emergence of postmodernist writing in Canada must be viewed as a collective act of cultural emancipation, perhaps even the fulfilment of the "unacknowledged ideological needs" alluded to by Dawson.

The acceleration of the cultural process in Canada—the movement from social realism to postmodernism having taken place within approximately two decades—met with considerable resistance on the part of readers.[15] While reader resistance to postmodernist fiction is a phenomenon that is not restricted to Canada, a certain critical reluctance to canonize this sort of writing has broadened the inevitable historical gap between production and reception of the works in question.

Although postmodernist fiction can hardly be seen as a *consequence* of the text theorization that now constitutes the focal point of much contemporary literary study,[16] it eminently lends itself to a theoretical analysis whose object and frame of reference, in seeking to determine the role and function of literature in society, is ultimately anthropological (not to say ideological) as well as aesthetic. But as long as postmodernist writing continues to be viewed (when measured against traditional literary values) as a manifestation of loss, as "absence" (of "content," of "social relevance"), its significance as a reaction to a given historical situation will remain unacknowledged.

Like the incorporation of any new trend into the cultural mainstream, the process of canonization involves modifying the status of certain norms and values to accommodate others. This process of historical transcendence is inevitably perceived in some quarters as "loss" and "absence." And like all forms of incorporating change, this process represents the assimilation of new cultural elements, a learning experience which itself may be perceived as loss.

In a literature whose evolution, until the emergence of its first postmodernist works, trailed behind its historical contemporaneity, it is perhaps inevitable that the sense of loss accompanying the rise of a form perceived by many to be a manifestation of the lateness of a cultural epoch is particularly acute. But like the literary work itself, the canon is a carrier of meaning in and beyond the culture that produces it. It is the ultimate task of the critic to account for and to interpret the significance of both in the nonfictional reality in which they are rooted.

Reference Notes to Afterword

1 The stereotyped conventions of these three types of fiction inevitably result in a certain similarity of effect, which is clearly not the case with the novels in question. Furthermore, the didactic novel represents an affirmation of a given system, while in the novels examined here a plurality of alternatives is presented to oppose the indicated fictional reality. The same argument may be invoked with regard to the trivial romance, which reinforces the wishful fantasies induced by societal values by affirming their validity in fiction.

2 The following are only a few of the many critical books and essays that reflect this position: T. D. Maclulich, "Our Place on the Map: The Canadian Tradition in Fiction," *University of Toronto Quarterly*, 52, no. 2 (Winter 1982-83), pp. 191-208; Chantal Zabus, "A Calibanic Tempest in Anglophone and Francophone New World Writing," *Canadian Literature*, 104 (Spring 1985), pp. 35-50; Geert Lernout, "Twenty-Five Years of Solitude," *Canadian Literature*, 104 (Spring 1985), pp. 52-64; Antoine Sirois, "Littérature et Nationalisme," *Journal of Canadian Studies*, 9, no. 4 (November 1976), pp. 54-56; James Foley, ed., *The Search for Identity* (Toronto: Macmillan of Canada, 1976).

3 Lionel Groulx, *L'Appel de la race* (Montreal: Fides, 1956 [1922]).

4 Jean-Charles Harvey, *Les Demi-Civilisés* (Montreal: Les Editions de l'Homme, 1962 [1934]).

5 John Moss, *Patterns of Isolation* (Toronto: McClelland and Stewart, 1974).

6 Ibid., p. 56.

7 Ibid., p. 218.

8 Atwood, *Survival*, p. 199.

9 Ibid., pp. 186-87, 137-38, 141.

10 Ibid., pp. 150-51.

11 Northey, *The Haunted Wilderness*, p. 3.

12 Anthony Dawson, "Davies: His Critics and the Canadian Canon," *Canadian Literature*, 92 (Spring 1982), p. 158.

13 Ibid.

14 Hutcheon, "Parody Without Ridicule," pp. 201-11.

15 See Robert Kroetsch, "A Canadian Issue," *Boundary 2*, 3, no. 1 (Fall 1974), pp. 1-2.

16 For an overview of the role of text theory in Canadian criticism, see E. D. Blodgett, "European Theory and Canadian Criticism," *Zeitschrift der Gesellschaft für Kanada-Studien*, 6. Jahrgang/Nr. 2, Band 11 (Spring 1986), pp. 5-15.

Selected Bibliography*

Adams, Robert Martin. "What Was Modernism?" *The Hudson Review*, 31 (1978), 19-33.

Alain, M. "Recherches psycho-sociologiques sur les habitudes de lecture au Canada." *Association Canadienne Bibliographique de Langue Française*, 18 (septembre 1972), 191-97.

Alter, Robert. *Partial Magic: The Novel as a Self-Conscious Genre*. Berkeley: University of California Press, 1975.

Altieri, Charles. "The Hermeneutics of Literary Indeterminacy: A Dissent from the New Orthodoxy." *New Literary History*, 10, no. 1 (1978), 71-100.

_____ . "An Idea and Ideal of a Literary Canon." *Critical Inquiry*, 10, no. 1 (September 1983), 37-60.

Anderegg, Johannes. *Fiktion und Kommunikation*. Göttingen: Vandenhoek und Ruprecht, 1973.

Aquin, Hubert. *Prochain épisode*. Montréal: Le Cercle du Livre de France, 1965.

_____ . *Trou de mémoire*. Montréal: Le Cercle du Livre de France, 1968.

_____ . "Considérations sur la forme romanesque d'*Ulysse*, de James Joyce." Dans *L'Oeuvre littéraire et ses significations*. Ed. P. Pagé et R. Legris. Montréal: Les Presses de l'Université du Québec, 1970, pp. 53-66.

_____ . "La Disparition élocutoire du poète (Mallarmé)." *Blocs erratiques*. Montréal: Les Éditions Quinze, 1977, pp. 263-67.

Atwood, Margaret. *The Edible Woman*. Toronto: New Canadian Library, 1973 [1969].

_____ . *Surfacing*. Toronto: McClelland and Stewart, 1972.

_____ . *Survival: A Thematic Guide to Canadian Literature*. Toronto: Anansi, 1972.

_____ . *Second Words: Selected Critical Prose*. Toronto: Anansi, 1982.

_____ . *The Handmaid's Tale*. Toronto: McClelland and Stewart, 1985.

Aury, Dominique. "Vive le Canada." *La Nouvelle Revue française*, 28, no. 168 (décembre 1966), 1066-70.

---

* Where applicable, the original date of publication is given in square brackets for Canadian and *québécois* texts. In the case of other items the dates of the editions consulted are provided.

Austen, John L. *How to Do Things with Words*. Oxford: Oxford University Press, 1962.

Bakhtin, Mikhail. *Esthétique et théorie du roman*. Trans. Daria Olivier. Paris: Gallimard, 1978.

Baltrušaitis, Jurgis. *Anamorphoses ou perspectives curieuses*. Paris: Olivier Perrin, 1955.

Balzac, Honoré de. *Histoire des Treize*. Oeuvres Complètes. Paris, 1874.

Barbour, Douglas. "Down with History: Some Notes Toward an Understanding of *Beautiful Losers*. In *Leonard Cohen: The Artist and His Critics*. Edited by Michael Gnarowski. Toronto: McGraw-Hill Ryerson, 1976, pp. 136-49.

Bayard, Caroline. "Postmodernisme et avant-garde au Canada, 1960-1984." *Voix et images*, 10, no. 1 (1984), 37-58.

Beaulieu, Victor-Lévy. *Un Rêve québécois*. Montréal: Éditions du Jour, 1972.

Bensky, Lawrence M. "What Happened to Tekakwitha." In *Leonard Cohen: The Artist and His Critics*. Edited by Michael Gnarowski. Toronto: McGraw-Hill Ryerson, 1976, pp. 27-28.

Benstock, Shari. "At the Margin of Discourse: Footnotes in the Fictional Text." *PMLA* 98 (1983), 204-25.

Berger, Yves. "Zola au Canada." *Le Nouvel Observateur*, no. 77 (4 au 10 mai, 1966), 31.

Berthiaume, André. "Le thème de l'hésitation dans *Prochain épisode*." *Liberté*, 15, no. 1 (janvier-février 1973), 135-48.

Bjerring, Nancy. "Deep in the Old Man's Puzzle" [re Robertson Davies]. *Canadian Literature*, 62 (Autumn 1974), 49-60.

Blais, Marie-Claire. *Une Saison dans la vie d'Emmanuel*. Paris: Grasset, 1966 [1965].

_____ . *Les Manuscrits de Pauline Archange*. Montréal: Éditions du Jour, 1968.

Blodgett, E. D. "Canadian as Comparative Literature." *Canadian Review of Comparative Literature*, 6, no. 2 (Spring 1979), 127-30.

_____ . *Configuration: Essays on the Canadian Imagination*. Toronto: Essays on Canadian Writing Press, 1982.

_____ . "European Theory and Canadian Criticism." *Zeitschrift der Gesellschaft für Kanada-Studien*, 6. Jahrgang, Nr. 2, Band 11 (Spring 1986), 5-15.

Bond, David J. *The Temptation of Despair: A Study of the Québec Novelist André Langevin*. Toronto: York Press, 1982.

Booth, Wayne C. *The Rhetoric of Fiction*. Chicago: The University of Chicago Press, 1961.

Borduas, Paul-Emile. *Refus Global*. Saint-Hilaire, Quebec: Mithra-Mythe, 1948.

Borges, Jorge Luis. *Labyrinths*. Edited by Donald A. Yates and James E. Irby. New York: New Directions, 1962, 1964.

Bourauoi, Hedi. *The Canadian Alternative*. Toronto: Essays on Canadian Writing Press, 1980.

Bowering, George. *The Mask in Place: Essays on Fiction in North America*. Winnipeg: Turnstone Press, 1983.

Brochu, André and Gilles Marcotte. *La Littérature et le reste*. Montréal: Les Éditions Quinze, 1980.

Brown, Russell. "Critic, Culture, Text: Beyond Thematics." *Essays in Canadian Writing*, no. 11 (Summer 1978), pp. 155-83.

Brûlé, Michel. "Introduction à l'univers de Marie-Claire Blais." *Revue de l'Institut de sociologie de Bruxelles*, fascicule 3 (1969), pp. 503-13.

Büchner, Georg. *Dantons Tod*. In *Gesammelte Werke*. Munich: Goldman, n.d.

Buck, Günther. "Literarischer Kanon und Geschichtlichkeit (Zur Logik des literarishen Paradigmenwechsels)." *Deutsche Vierteljahresschrift*, 57, no. 3 (1983), 351-65.

Buckeye, Robert. "*Nouveau roman* Made Easy." *Canadian Literature*, 31 (Winter 1967), 67-69.

Buckler, Ernest. *The Mountain and the Valley*. Toronto: New Canadian Library, 1969 [1952].

Caesar, Julius. *The Conquest of Gaul*. Trans. S. A. Handford. New York: Pelican Books, 1963.

Callaghan, Morley. *Such Is My Beloved*. Toronto: New Canadian Library, 1957 [1934].

Calvino, Italo. *If on a winter's night a traveller*. Trans. William Weaver. Toronto: International Fiction List, 1981; originally published in Italy under the title *Se una notte d'inverno un viaggatore*. Torino: Einaudi, 1979.

Cameron, Barry, and Michael Dixon. "Mandatory Subversive Manifesto: Canadian Criticism vs. Literary Criticism." *Studies in Canadian Literature*, 2, no. 2, (1977), 137-45.

Cameron, Donald. *Conversations with Canadian Novelists*, Part 2. Toronto: Macmillan, 1973.

Cameron, Elspeth, ed. *Hugh Maclennan*. Toronto: University of Toronto Press, 1982.

Camus, Albert. *L'Étranger*. Paris: Gallimard, 1942.

Cappon, Paul, ed. *Our Own House: Social Perspectives on Canadian Literature*. Toronto: McClelland and Stewart, 1978.

Chadbourne, Richard, and Hallvard Dahlie, eds. *The New Land: Studies in a Literary Theme*. Waterloo, Ontario: Wilfrid Laurier University Press, 1978.

Chapman, Marilyn. "Female Archetypes in *Fifth Business*." *Canadian Literature*, no. 80 (Spring 1979), 131-38.

Charbonneau, Robert. *Ils posséderont la terre*. Montréal: Éditions de l'Arbre, 1941.

Chessex, Jacques. "Marie-Claire Blais: *Une Saison dans la vie d'Emmanuel*." *La Nouvelle Revue française*, 14, no. 168 (décembre 1966), 1093-94.

Christ, Carol P. "Margaret Atwood: The Surfacing of Women's Spiritual Quest and Vision." *Signs*, 2, no. 2 (Winter 1976), 316-30.

Clark, Richard C. "Bibliographical Spectrum and Review Article: Is there a Canadian Literature?" *Review of National Literatures*, 7 (1976), 133-64.

Cohen, Leonard. *Beautiful Losers*. New York: Bantam Books, 1976 [1966].

Constant, Benjamin. *De l'esprit de conquête et de l'usurpation*. Paris: Librairies de Guillaumin, 1861.

Cude, Wilfred. "Miracle and Art in *Fifth Business*." *Journal of Canadian Studies*, 12, no. 4 (November 1974), 3-16.

Cullis, Tara. "Science and Literature in the Twentieth Century." *Canadian Literature*, 96 (Spring 1983), 86-101.

Dällenbach, Lucien. "Intertexte et autotexte." *Poétique*, 27 (1976), pp. 282-96.

Davey, Frank. "Surviving the Paraphrase." *Canadian Literature*, 70 (Autumn 1976), 5-13.

————— . *Surviving the Paraphrase*. Winnipeg: Turnstone Press, 1984.

Davies, Robertson. *Tempest-Tost*. Toronto: Clarke Irwin, 1950.

————— . *Leaven of Malice*. Toronto: Clarke Irwin, 1954.

_____ . *A Mixture of Frailties*. Toronto: Macmillan, 1958.

_____ . *Fifth Business*. New York: New American Library, 1971 [1970].

_____ . *The Manticore*. Toronto: Macmillan, 1972.

_____ . *World of Wonders*. Toronto: Macmillan, 1975.

Dawson, Anthony B. "Davies: His Critics and the Canadian Canon." *Canadian Literature*, 92 (Spring 1982), 154-59.

Daymond, Douglas, and Leslie Monkman, eds. *Canadian Novelists and The Novel*. Ottawa: Borealis Press, 1981.

Dimić, Milan. "Towards a Methodology of Comparative Canadian Studies." *Canadian Review of Comparative Literature*, 6, no. 2 (Spring 1979), 115-17.

Dooley, D. J. *Moral Vision in the Canadian Novel*. Toronto: Clarke Irwin, 1979.

Dorsinville, Max. *Caliban Without Prospero: Essays on Quebec and Black Literature*. Victoria, B.C.: Press Porcépic, 1974.

Ducharme, Réjean. *L'Avalée des avalés*. Paris: Gallimard, 1966.

_____ . *L'Hiver de force*. Paris: Gallimard, 1973.

_____ . *Les Enfantômes*, Paris: Gallimard, 1976.

Duffy, Dennis. "Beautiful Beginners." In *Leonard Cohen: The Artist and His Critics*. Edited by Michael Gnarowski. Toronto: McGraw-Hill Ryerson, 1976, pp. 29-32.

Dumont, Fernand. *Le Lieu de l'homme: La Culture comme distance et mémoire*. Montréal: Éditions HMH, 1969.

Eco, Umberto. *Opera aperta*. Milano: Casa Ed. Valentino Bompiani, 1962.

_____ . *The Role of the Reader*. Bloomington, Ind.: Indiana University Press, 1979.

Edel, Leon. "Marginal *Keri* and Textual *Chetiv*: The Mystic Novel of A. M. Klein." In *The A. M. Klein Symposium*. Edited by Seymour Mayne. Ottawa: The University of Ottawa Press, 1975.

Elffers, J., und F. Leeman. *Anamorphosen: Ein Spiel mit der Wahrnehmung, dem Schein und der Wirklichkeit*. Cologne: Dumont, 1981.

Falardeau, Jean-Charles. *Notre Société et son roman*. Montreal: HMH, 1967.

_____ . "Le héros chez Langevin." In *L'Évolution du héros dans le roman québécois*. Montréal: Presses Universitaires, Conférences J. A. de Sève, 1968, pp. 20-33.

Fanon, Frantz. *Les Damnés de la terre*. Paris: F. Maspero, 1961.

Farley, T. E. *Exiles and Pioneers, 1825-1975*. Ottawa: Borealis Press, 1976.

Favreau, Michèle. "Hubert Aquin: propos recueillis sans magnétophone." *La Presse*, 30 avril 1966, p. 11.

Findley, Timothy. *The Wars*. New York: Delacorte Press, 1972.

_____ . *Famous Last Words*. Toronto: Clarke Irwin, 1981.

Fischer, Gretl K. *In Search of Jerusalem*. Montreal: McGill-Queen's University Press, 1975.

Fish, Stanley. *Self-Consuming Artifacts: The Experience of Seventeenth-Century Literature*. Berkeley: University of California Press, 1972.

_____ . *Is There a Text in This Class? The Authority of Interpretive Communities*. Cambridge, Mass.: Harvard University Press, 1980.

Fogel, Stan. "Lost in the Canadian Funhouse." *Queen's Quarterly*, 88 (Winter 1981), 690-707.

Fokkema, D. W. "Comparative Literature and the New Paradigm." *Canadian Review of Comparative Literature*, 9, no. 1 (March 1982), 1-18.

Foley, James, ed. *The Search for Identity*. Toronto: Macmillan of Canada, 1976.

de la Fontaine, Gilles. *Hubert Aquin et le Québec*. Montréal: Parti Pris, 1978.

Fowler, Alistair. "Genre and the Literary Canon." *New Literary History*, 2, no. 1 (Autumn 1979), 97-119.

Fowles, John. *The French Lieutenant's Woman*. New York: New American Library, 1970.

Friedman, Norman. "Point of View in Fiction: The Development of a Critical Concept." *PMLA*, 70 (1955), pp. 1160-84.

Frye, Northrop. "Conclusion," in *The Literary History of Canada*, vol. 3. Toronto: University of Toronto Press, 1965, pp. 318-32.

_____ . *The Bush Garden: Essays on the Canadian Imagination*. Toronto: Anansi, 1971.

_____ . "Haunted by Lack of Ghosts." In *The Canadian Imagination*. Edited by David Staines. Cambridge, Mass.: Harvard University Press, 1977, pp. 29-45.

Gadamer, Hans. *Wahrheit und Methode: Grundzüge einer philosophischen Hermeneutik*. Tübingen: Mohr, 1960.

García Márquez, Gabriel. *One Hundred Years of Solitude*. Trans. from the Spanish by Gregory Rabassa. Picador, 1978. Originally published as *Cien Años de Soledad*. Buenos Aires: Editorial Sudamericana SA, 1967.

Gaulin, André. "La vision du monde d'André Langevin." *Etudes littéraires*, 6, no. 1 (août 1973), 153-67.

Gelfant, Blanche. "The Hidden Mines in Ethel Wilson's Landscape (or, An American Cat among Canadian Falcons)." *Canadian Literature*, 93 (Summer 1982), 4-23.

Genette, Gérard. *Palimpsestes: La littérature au second degré*. Paris: Seuil, 1982.

Gibson, Graeme. *Five Legs*. Toronto: Anansi, 1979.

Gilbert, Stuart. *James Joyce's Ulysses*. New York: Vintage Books, 1955.

Girouard, Laurent. "En lisant *Le Cassé*." *Parti Pris*, 2, no. 4 (décembre 1964), 62-64.

Gnarowski, Michael, ed. *Leonard Cohen: The Artist and His Critics*. Toronto: McGraw-Hill Ryerson, 1976.

Godard, Barbara. "The Avant-garde in Canada." *Ellipse*, 23-24 (1979), 98-113.

_____ . "The Oral Tradition and National Literatures." *Comparison*, 12, (Spring 1981), 15-31.

Godbout, Jacques. *Salut Galarneau!* Paris: Seuil, 1967.

Godbout, Roger. "Le Milieu, personnage symbolique dans l'oeuvre d'André Langevin." *Livres et auteurs canadiens* (Montréal: Jumonville, 1966), pp. 198-203.

Goethe, Johann Wolfgang von. *Faust*. Stuttgart: J. G. Cotta'sche Buchhandlung, 1888.

Goldmann, Lucien. "Note sur deux romans de Marie-Claire Blais." *La Revue de l'Institut de sociologie de Bruxelles*, fascicule 3 (1969), 515-23.

Gombrich, E. H. *Art and Illlusion: A Study on the Psychology of Pictorial Representation*. London: Phaidon, 1972.

Gotlieb, Phyllis. "Klein's Sources." *Canadian Literature*, no. 26 (Autumn 1965), 82-84.

_____ . "Hassidic Influences in the Work of A. M. Klein." *The A. M. Klein Symposium*. Edited by Seymour Mayne. Ottawa: The University of Ottawa Press, 1975, pp. 47-64.

Grace, Sherrill E. "Wastelands and Badlands: The Legacies of Pynchon and Kroetsch." *Mosaic*, 14, no. 2 (Spring 1981), 21-34.

_____ and Lorraine Weir, eds. *Margaret Atwood: Language, Text and System*. Vancouver: University of British Columbia Press, 1983.

Grant, Judith Skelton. *Robertson Davies*. Toronto: McClelland and Stewart, 1978.

Greene, Graham. *Our Man in Havana*. Harmondsworth: Penguin, 1962.

Greenstein, Michael. "History in *The Second Scroll*." *Canadian Literature*, 76 (Spring 1978), 37-46.

Greffard, Madeleine. "*Une Saison dans le vie d'Emmanuel*. Kaléidoscope de la réalité québécoise." *Les Cahiers de Sainte-Marie*, no. 1, Montréal (mai 1966), pp. 19-24.

Grimm, G., ed. *Literatur und Leser: Theorien und Modelle Zur Rezeption literarischer Werke*. Stuttgart: Reclam, 1975.

Groulx, Lionel. *L'Appel de la race*. Montréal: Fides, 1965 [1922].

Grove, Frederick Philip. *The Master of the Mill*. Toronto: New Canadian Library, 1961 [1941].

Hallyn, Fernand. "Anamorphose et allégorie." *Revue de Littérature Comparée*, 56, no. 3 (juillet-septembre 1982), 319-30.

Harrison, Dick. *Unnamed Country: The Struggle for a Prairie Fiction*. Edmonton: University of Alberta Press, 1977.

Harvey, Jean-Charles. *Les Demi-Civilisés*. Montréal: Les Editions de l'homme, 1962 [1934].

Hayman, David. "Double Distancing: An Attribute of the 'Post-Modern' Avant-Garde." *Novel*, 12, no. 1 (Fall 1978), 33-47.

Hayne, David M. "Les Grandes Options de la littérature canadienne-française." *Études françaises*, 1, no. 1 (février 1965), 68-89.

_____ . "Literary Movements in Canada." *Canadian Review of Comparative Literature*, 6, no. 2 (Spring 1979), pp. 121-23.

Hébert, Anne. "Le Torrent," in the volume of *nouvelles* entitled *Le Torrent*. Montréal: Beauchemin, 1950.

Hébert, Pierre. "Forme et signification du temps et du discours immédiat dans *Poussière sur la ville* : le récit d'une victoire." *Voix et Images*, 2, no. 2 (décembre 1976), 209-30.

_____ . "Le Discours immédiat : essai de modèle et lecture de *Poussière sur la ville* d'André Langevin." *Présence francophone*, no. 14 (printemps 1977), 105-20.

Herlan, James. "Quebec Criticism in Translation: The Ideology of Aesthetics." *Essays in Canadian Writing*, no. 26 (Summer 1983), 150-68.

Hesse, M. G., ed. *Women in Canadian Literature*. Ottawa: Borealis Press, 1976.

Hoffman, Gerhard, Alfred Hornung, and Rüdiger Kunow. "'Modern', 'Postmodern' and 'Contemporary' as Criteria for the Analysis of Twentieth-Century Literature." *Amerikastudien*, 22, 1 (1977), 19-46.

Hutcheon, Linda. "Parody Without Ridicule: Observations on Modern Literary Parody." *Canadian Review of Comparative Literature*, 5, no. 2 (Spring 1978), 201-11.

_____ . *Narcissistic Narrative: The Metafictional Paradox*. Waterloo, Ont.: Wilfrid Laurier University Press, 1980.

_____ . "A Poetics of Postmodernism?" *Diacritics*, 13, no. 4 (Winter 1983), 33-42.

_____ . *A Theory of Parody: The Teachings of Twentieth Century Art Forms*. New York and London: Methuen, 1985.

Imbert, Patrick. *Roman Québécois Contemporain et clichés*. Ottawa: Les Presses de l'Université d'Ottawa, 1982.

Ingarden, Roman. *Das literarische Kunstwerk*. Tübingen: Niemayer, 1960.

Iqbal, Françoise Maccabée. *Hubert Aquin, romancier*. Quebec City: Les Presses de l'Université Laval, 1978.

Iser, Wolfgang. *Die Appellstruktur der Texte: Unbestimmtheit als Wirkungsbedingung literarischer Prosa*. Konstanz: Universitätsverlag Konstanz, 1970.

————. *The Implied Reader*. Baltimore: Johns Hopkins University Press, 1974; originally published in Germany under the title *Der implizierte Leser*. Munich: Wilhelm Fink Verlag, 1972.

————. *The Act of Reading*. Baltimore: Johns Hopkins University Press, 1974; originally published in Germany under the title *Der Akt des Lesens*. Munich: Wilhelm Fink Verlag, 1976.

Jauss, Hans Robert. "Levels of Identification of Hero and Audience." *New Literary History*, 5, no. 2 (1973), 283-317.

————. "Negativität und Identifikation: Versuch zur Theorie der ästhetishchen Erfahrung." *Poetik und Hermeneutik VI*. Munich: Wilhelm Fink Verlag, 1975.

————. *Toward an Aesthetic of Reception*. Trans. by Timothy Bahti. Minneapolis: University of Minnesota Press, 1982.

Joyce, James. *Ulysses*. London: The Bodley Head, 1960.

————. *Finnegans Wake*. London: Faber and Faber, 1957.

Kafka, Franz. *Die Verwandlung* in *Sämtliche Erzählungen*. Frankfurt: Fischer, 1970.

Kattan, Naim. "Montreal and French-Canadian Culture." *Tamarack Review*, 40 (1966), 40-43.

————. *Écrivains des Amériques*. Montréal: HMH, 1972.

Kayser, Wolfgang. "Wer erzählt den Roman?" *Die Vortragsreise*. Bern: Francke Verlag, 1950, pp. 82-101.

Kertzer, J. M. "The Past Recaptured" [re Ernest Buckler's *The Mountain and the Valley*]. *Canadian Literature*, 65 (Summer 1975), 74-85.

Klein, A. M. *The Second Scroll*. Intro. by M. W. Steinberg. Toronto: New Canadian Library, 1958 [1951].

Kline, Marcia. *Beyond the Land Itself*. Cambridge, Mass.: Harvard University Press, 1970.

Kristeva, Julia. *Sèméiôtikè: Recherches pour une sémanalyse*. Paris: Seuil, 1969.

Kroetsch, Robert. *The Studhorse Man*. New York: Pocket Books, 1971 [1970].

————. "A Canadian Issue." *Boundary 2*, 3, no. 1 (Fall 1974), 1-2.

————. *Alibi*. Toronto: Stoddart, 1983.

————. "Contemporary Standards in the Canadian Novel." *Open Letter*, 5, no. 4 (Spring 1983), 37-45.

————. "Beyond Nationalism: A Prologue." *Open Letter*, 5, no. 4 (Spring 1983), 83-89.

————, and Reingard Nischik, eds. *Gaining Ground: European Critics on Canadian Literature*. Edmonton: NeWest Press, 1985.

Kröller, Eva-Marie. "Comparative Canadian Literature: Notes on Its Definition and Method." *Canadian Review of Comparative Literature*, 6, no. 2 (Spring 1979), 139-50.

Langevin, André. *Poussière sur la ville*. Montréal: Le Cercle du Livre de France, 1953.

_____ . *L'Élan d'Amérique*. Montréal: Le Cercle du Livre de France, 1972.

Lapierre, René. *Hubert Aquin: l'imaginaire captif*. Montreal: Quinze, 1981.

Laurence, Margaret. *The Diviners*. Toronto: McClelland and Stewart, 1974.

Lawrence, R. G., and S. L. Macey, eds. *Studies in Robertson Davies' Deptford Trilogy*. English Literary Studies No. 20. Victoria, 1980.

Lecker, Robert, Jack David, and Ellen Quigley, eds. *Canadian Writers and Their Work: Essays on Form, Context and Development*. Toronto: Essays on Canadian Writing, 1982.

Leduc-Park, Renée. *Réjean Ducharme, Nietzsche et Dionysos*. Quebec City: Les Presses de l'Université Laval, 1983.

Lemelin, Roger. *Au Pied de la pente douce*. Montréal: Éditions de l'Arbre, 1944.

Leney, Jane. "'In the Fifth City': An Integral Chapter of *The New Ancestors*." *Canadian Literature*, 96 (Spring 1983), 72-80.

Lernout, Geert. "Twenty-Five Years of Solitude." *Canadian Literature*, 104 (Spring 1985), 52-64.

Lewis, Gertrude Jaron. "Vitzliputzli Revisited." *Canadian Literature*, 76 (Spring 1978), 132-34.

Link, Hannelore. *Rezeptionsforschung: Eine Einführung in Methoden und Probleme*. Stuttgart: Kohlhammer, 1976.

Lower, J. A. *Canada: An Outline History*. Toronto: Ryerson, 1966.

Lowry, Malcolm. *Under the Volcano*. London: Penguin, 1963 [1941].

Lukács, Georg. *The Theory of the Novel*. Boston: MIT Press, 1971.

Lyotard, Jean-François. *La Condition postmoderne: rapport sur le savoir*. Paris: Minuit, 1979.

MacLennan, Hugh. *Two Solitudes*. Toronto: Laurentian Library, Macmillan of Canada, n.d. [1945].

McCullough, Elizabeth, ed. *The Role of Women in Canadian Literature*. Toronto: Macmillan, 1975.

McLuhan, Marshall. "Magic That Changes Moods." *The Mechanical Bride: Folklore of Industrial Man*. Boston: Beacon Press, 1967 [1951].

MacLulich, T. D. "Our Place on the Map: The Canadian Tradition in Fiction." *University of Toronto Quarterly*, 52, no. 2 (Winter 1982-83), 191-208.

Marcotte, Gilles. "Réjean Ducharme contre Blasey Blasey." *Études françaises*, 2, nos. 3-4 (octobre 1975), 247-84.

Margeson, Robert. "A Preliminary Interpretation of *The New Ancestors*." *Journal of Canadian Fiction*, 4, no. 1 (1978), 96-110.

Margolin, Jean-Claude. "Aspects du surréalisme au XVIᵉ siècle: Fonction allégorique et vision anamorphotique." *Bibliothèque d'Humanisme et Renaissance*, 39 (1977), 503-30.

Marshall, Tom. "Theorems Made Flesh: Klein's Poetic Universe." *Canadian Literature*, 25 (Summer 1965), 43-52.

Marta, Jan. "Portrait of the Artist as a Fiction: Modernism through the Looking-Glass." *Canadian Review of Comparative Literature*, 9, no. 2 (June 1982), 208-22.

Massey, Irving. *The Gaping Pig: Literature and Metamorphosis*. Berkeley: University of California Press, 1976.

Mathews, John. "Abraham Klein and the Problem of Synthesis." *Journal of Commonwealth Literature*, 1 (Summer 1965), 49-63.

Mathews, Robin. *Canadian Literature: Surrender or Revolution*. Toronto: Steel Rail Publishing, 1978.

Mayne, Seymour, ed. *The A. M. Klein Symposium*. Ottawa: The University of Ottawa Press, 1975.

Memmi, Albert. *Portrait du colonisé*. Paris: Jean-Jacques Pauvert, 1966.

Merivale, Patricia. "Neo-Modernism in the Canadian Artist-Parable: Hubert Aquin and Brian Moore." *Canadian Review of Comparative Literature*, 6, no. 2 (Spring 1979), 195-205.

Merleau-Ponty, Maurice. *Phénoménologie de la perception*. Paris: Gallimard, 1945.

Middlebro, Tom. "Yet Another Gloss on A. M. Klein's *The Second Scroll*." *Journal of Canadian Fiction*, 4, no. 3 (1975), 117-22.

Mitchell, W. O. *The Vanishing Point*. Toronto: Macmillan, 1973.

Moisan, Clément. *L'Age de la littérature canadienne*. Montreal: Collections Constantes, Editions HMH, 1969.

_____ . "Quelques Propositions." *Canadian Review of Comparative Literature*, 6, no. 2 (Spring 1979), 117-19.

Monk, Patricia. "Confessions of a Sorcerer's Apprentice: *World of Wonders* and the Deptford Trilogy of Robertson Davies." *Dalhousie Review*, 56 (1976-77), 366-72.

_____ . *The Smaller Infinity: The Jungian Self in the Novels of Robertson Davies*. Toronto: University of Toronto Press, 1982.

Moss, John. *Patterns of Isolation in English-Canadian Fiction*. Toronto: McClelland and Stewart, 1974.

_____ . *Sex and Violence in the Canadian Novel: The Ancestral Present*. Toronto: McClelland and Stewart, 1979.

_____ . *A Reader's Guide to The Canadian Novel*. Toronto: McClelland and Stewart, 1981.

Nabokov, Vladimir. *Laughter in the Dark*. New York: New Directions, 1960.

_____ . *Pale Fire*. London: Weidenfeld and Nicholson, 1962.

Nadeau, Vincent. *Marie-Claire Blais : Le Noir et le tendre*. Montréal: Les Presses de l'Université de Montréal, Collection "Lignes québécoises," 1974.

Needler, Martin C. *Political Systems of Latin America*. Cincinnati: Van Nostrand Reinhold, 1970.

New, W. H. *Articulating West*. Toronto: New Press, 1972.

Northey, Margot. *The Haunted Wilderness: The Gothic and Grotesque in Canadian Fiction*. Toronto: The University of Toronto Press, 1976.

Onimus, Jean. "Les Jeux de l'humour et du roman." *La Table ronde*, no. 230 (mars 1967), 129-31.

Pacey, Desmond. "A. M. Klein." *Ten Canadian Poets*. Toronto: Ryerson, 1958, pp. 254-92.

_____ . "The Phenomenon of Leonard Cohen." *Leonard Cohen: The Artist and His Critics*. Edited by Michael Gnarowski. Toronto: McGraw-Hill Ryerson, 1976, pp. 74-93.

Paradis, Suzanne. "Marie-Claire Blais : Isabelle-Marie, Louise, Emilie, Yance. Grand-Mère. Madeleine. Femme fictive, femme réelle." *Le personnage féminin dans le roman féminin canadien-français de 1884-1966*. Montréal: Éditions Garneau, 1966, pp. 177-97.

Paterson, Janet N. "Le Roman postmoderne : Mise au point et perspectives." *Canadian Review of Comparative Literature*, 13, no. 2 (June 1986), 238-55.

Pivato, Joseph. "Eight Approaches to Canadian Literary Criticism." *Journal of Canadian Fiction*, 13, no. 3 (April 1979), 43-53.

Plottel, Jeanine Parisier. "Anamorphosis in Painting and Literature." *Yearbook of Comparative and General Literature*, 28 (1979), 100-09.

Powe, B. W. *A Climate Charged: Essays on Canadian Writers*. Oakville, Ontario: Mosaic Press, 1984.

Pütz, Manfred. "The Struggle of the Postmodern." *Kritikon Litterarum*, 2 (1973), pp. 225-37.

Quincey, Thomas De. *Confessions of an English Opium Eater*. London: Routledge, 1867.

_____ . *On Murder Considered As One of the Fine Arts*. In *The Collected Writings of Thomas De Quincey*, Vol. 13. Edited by David Masson. London: A. and C. Black, 1896-97.

Reiss, Timothy J. *The Discourse of Modernism*. Ithaca, N.Y.: Cornell University Press, 1982.

Renaud, Jacques. *Le Cassé*. Montreal: Parti Pris, 1964.

Ricardou, Jean, et Françoise Van Rossum-Guyon, eds. *Nouveau Roman : hier, aujourd'hui*, I. Paris: Union générale d'éditions, 1972, 2 vols.

Richler, Mordecai. *The Apprenticeship of Duddy Kravitz*. Toronto: McClelland and Stewart, 1969 [1959].

Ricoeur, Paul. "The Hermeneutical Function of Distanciation." *Philosophy Today*, 17, no. 2 (1973), pp. 129-41.

_____ . *Interpretation Theory: Discourse and the Surplus of Meaning*. Fort Worth: Texas Christian University, 1976.

Ringuet. *Trente Arpents*. Montréal: Fides, 1966 [1938].

Robidoux, Réjean, et André Renaud. *Le Roman Canadien-français du vingtième siècle*. Ottawa: Éditions de l'Université d'Ottawa, 1966.

Roper, Gordon. "Robertson Davies' *Fifth Business* and That Old Fantastical Duke of Dark Corners, C. G. Jung." *Journal of Canadian Fiction*, 1, no. 1 (Winter 1972), 33-39.

Ross, Brian L. "The Naked Narrator. *The Studhorse Man* and the Structuralist Imagination." *Canadian Literature*, 104 (Spring 1985), 65-73.

Rousseau, Jean-Jacques. *Rousseau juge de Jean-Jacques : Dialogues*. In *Jean-Jacques Rousseau : Oeuvres complètes*, vol. 1. Paris: Gallimard, 1959.

_____ . *Confessions*. In *Oeuvres complètes*, vol. 1. Paris: Gallimard, 1959.

_____ . *Du Contrat Social*. In *Oeuvres complètes*, vol. 3. Paris: Gallimard, 1959.

Roy, Gabrielle. *Bonheur d'occasion*. Montréal: Beauchemin, 1965 [1945].

Royer, Jean. *Écrivains contemporains : Entretien I 1976-1979*. Montréal: Éditions de l'Hexagone, 1982.

Sarraute, Nathalie. "De Dostoeivski à Kafka." *L'Ère du soupçon*. Paris: NRF, Gallimard, 1956.

Sartre, Jean-Paul. *La Nausée*. Paris: Gallimard, 1966.

_____ . *L'Imaginaire*. Paris: Gallimard, 1948.

Schmidt, Siegfried J. "The Empirical Science of Literature ESL: A New Paradigm." *Poetics*, 12 (1983), 19-34.

Scholes, Robert. "Metafiction." *Iowa Review*, 1, no. 4 (1970), 100-15.

Searle, John. *Speech Acts*. Cambridge: Cambridge University Press, 1969.

Servais-Maquoi, Mireille. *Le Roman de la terre au Québec*. Quebec City: Les Presses de l'Université de Laval, 1974.

Shek, Ben-Zion. *Social Realism in the French-Canadian Novel*. Montreal: Harvest House, 1977.

Shouldice, Larry. "Wide Latitudes: Comparing New World Literature." *Canadian Review of Comparative Literature*, 9, no. 1 (March 1982), 46-55.

Sirois, Antoine. "Littérature et Nationalisme." *Journal of Canadian Studies*, 11, no. 4 (November 1976), 54-56.

_____ . "La Périodisation dans les littératures du Canada." *Canadian Review of Comparative Literature*, 6, no. 2 (Spring 1979), 119-21.

Skura, Meredith Anne. *The Literary Use of the Psychoanalytic Process*. New Haven: Yale University Press, 1981.

Smart, Patricia. *Hubert Aquin : agent double*. Montréal: Les Presses de l'Université de Montréal, 1973.

Smith, A. J. M. *Towards a View of Canadian Letters: Selected Critical Essays 1928-1971*. Vancouver: University of British Columbia Press, 1975.

Sontag, Susan. "Against Interpretation." In the collection of essays entitled *Against Interpretation*. New York: Delta, 1979.

Staël, Mme de. "De la littérature." *Oeuvres complètes*. Geneva: Slatkine Reprints, 1967.

Staines, David, ed. *The Canadian Imagination*. Cambridge, Mass.: Harvard University Press, 1977.

Stanzel, Franz K. *Typische Formen des Romans*. Göttingen: Vandenhoek und Ruprecht, 1964.

Steele, Charles, ed. *Taking Stock: The Calgary Conference on the Canadian Novel*. Toronto: Essays on Canadian Writing Press, 1982.

Steinberg, M. W. "A Twentieth Century Pentateuch." *Canadian Literature*, 11 (Autumn 1959), 37-46.

Stevens, Donald B. *Writers of the Prairies*. Vancouver: University of British Columbia Press, 1973.

Stouck, David. "Ethel Wilson's Novels." *Canadian Literature*, 74 (Autumn 1977), 74-78.

Stratford, Philip. "Canada's Two Literatures: A Search for Emblems." *Canadian Review of Comparative Literature*, 6, no. 2 (Spring 1979), 131-38.

Suleiman, Susan, and Inge Crosman, eds. *The Reader in the Text: Essays on Audience and Interpretation*. Princeton: Princeton University Press, 1980.

Sutherland, Ronald. *Second Image: Comparative Studies in Quebec/Canadian Literature*. Toronto: New Press, 1971.

_____ . *The New Hero*. Toronto: Macmillan, 1977.

Tardif, Jean-Claude. "Les Relations humaines dans *Poussière sur la ville*." *Études littéraires*, 6, no 2 (août 1973), 241-55.

Thompson, Brent. "Ethel Wilson, Wary Mythologist." *Canadian Literature*, 102 (Autumn 1984), 20-32.

Todorov, Tzvetan. *Introduction à la littérature fantastique*. Paris: Seuil, 1970.

_____ . "Typologie du roman policier." *La Poétique de la prose*. Paris: Seuil, 1971, pp. 55-65.

Tompkins, Jane P., ed. *Reader-Response Criticism: From Formalism to Post-Structuralism*. Baltimore: Johns Hopkins University Press, 1981.

Tougas, Gérard. *Destin Littéraire du Québec*. Montréal: Québec/Amérique, 1983.

Tremblay, Michel. *La Grosse femme d'à côté est enceinte*. Paris: Robert Laffont, 1978.

Trofimenkoff, Susan Mann. "Nationalism, Feminism, and Canadian Intellectual History." *Canadian Literature*, 83 (Winter 1979), 7-20.

Vachon, G.-André. "Note sur Réjean Ducharme et Paul-Marie Lapointe (Fragment d'un traité du vide)." *Études françaises*, 2, nos. 3-4 (octobre 1975), 355-87.

Valdés, Mario, and Owen Miller, eds. *Interpretation of Narrative*. Toronto: University of Toronto Press, 1978.

————. *Identity of the Literary Text*. Toronto: University of Toronto Press, 1985.

Vanasse, André. "Analyse de textes—Réjean Ducharme et Victor-Lévy Beaulieu: les mots et les choses." *Voix et Images*, 3, no. 2 (décembre 1977), 230-43.

Van Rossum-Guyon, Françoise. "Point de vue ou perspective narrative." *Poétique*, 4 (1970), 476-97.

Van Schendel, Michel. *Ducharme l'inquiétant*, dans *Littérature canadienne-française*. Montréal: Les Presses de l'Université de Montréal, 1969. Conférence J. A. de Sève, 16 mars 1967.

Victorin, Marie. *La Flore laurentienne*. Montreal: Les Presses de l'Université de Montréal, 1964.

Waddington, Miriam. *A. M. Klein*. Toronto: Copp Clark, 1970.

————. "Signs on a White Field: Klein's *Second Scroll*." *Canadian Literature*, 25 (Summer 1965), 21-32.

Wain, John. "Making It New." In *Leonard Cohen: The Artist and His Critics*. Edited by Michael Gnarowski. Toronto: McGraw-Hill Ryerson, 1976, pp. 23-28.

Warning, Rainer, ed. *Rezeptionsästhetik: Theorie und Praxis*. München: Fink, 1975.

Warwick, Jack. "Un Cas typique de l'application de la méthode sociologique : les écrivains canadiens-français et leur situation minoritaire." *La Revue de l'Institut de sociologie de Bruxelles*, fascicule 3 (1969), pp. 485-502.

Watson, Sheila. *The Double Hook*. Toronto: McClelland and Stewart, 1959 [1954].

Weir, Lorraine. "Portrait of the Poet as Joyce Scholar: An Approach to A. M. Klein." *Canadian Literature*, 76 (Spring 1978), 47-55.

Weisgerber, Jean. "Les Avant-gardes littéraires : état présent des études." *Canadian Review of Comparative Literature* (Fall 1979), 389-404.

Westfall, William. "On the Concept of Region in Canadian History and Literature." *Journal of Canadian Studies*, 15, no. 2 (Summer 1980), 3-15.

Wiebe, Rudy. *Peace Shall Destroy Many*. Toronto: McClelland and Stewart, 1962.

————. *The Blue Mountains of China*. Toronto: McClelland and Stewart, 1970.

Wilson, Ethel. *Swamp Angel*. Toronto: New Canadian Library, 1962 [1954].

Wilson, Milton. "Klein's Drowned Poet." *Canadian Literature*, 4 (Autumn 1960), 5-17.

Wiseman, Adele. *The Sacrifice*. Toronto: Macmillan, 1956.

————. *Crackpot*. Toronto: McClelland and Stewart, 1974.

Woodcock, George. *Odysseus Ever Returning*. Toronto: McClelland and Stewart, 1970.

————, ed. *The Canadian Novel in the Twentieth Century*. Toronto: McClelland and Stewart, 1975.

————. "The Meeting of the Muses: Recent Canadian Fiction and the Historical Viewpoint." *Canadian Historical Review*, 15, no. 2 (June 1979), 141-53.

_____ . "The Song of the Sirens: Reflections on Leonard Cohen." In *Leonard Cohen: The Artist and His Critics*. Edited by Michael Gnarowski. Toronto: McGraw-Hill Ryerson, 1976, pp. 158-67.

Yale French Studies No. 65 [1983] [special issue on Quebec]. *The Language of Difference: Writing in Quebec(ois)*.

Zabus, Chantal. "A Calibanic Tempest in Anglophone and Francophone New World Writing." *Canadian Literature*, 104 (Spring 1985), 35-50.

Zima, Peter, ed. *Semiotics and Dialectics: Ideology and the Text*. Amsterdam: John Benjamin B.V., 1981.

Zubrugg, Nicolas. "Beyond Beckett: Wreckless Writing and the Concept of the Avant-Garde within Post-Modern Literature." *Yearbook of Comparative and General Literature*, 30 (1981), 37-56.

Index

Major discussion of a work or topic is indicated by italic page numbers.

The *Canadian Review of Comparative Literature/Revue Canadienne de Littérature Comparée*, a quarterly journal published by the Canadian Comparative Literature Association, provides a forum for scholars engaged in the study of literature from both international and interdisciplinary points of view. The journal publishes articles on the international history of literature, theory of literature, methods of literary scholarship, and the relation of literature to other spheres of human expression. The review encourages papers on the present state of research in certain areas of comparative literature, review articles, and studies on comparative Canadian literature; it publishes a yearly bibliography of comparative Canadian literature and a "Revue des revues" covering over 300 articles in some ninety major periodicals. Editorial inquiries should be directed to the Editor, M. V. Dimić, Department of Comparative Literature, The University of Alberta, Edmonton, Alberta T6G 2E6.

The Bibliothèque de la *Revue Canadienne de Littérature Comparée*/Library of the *Canadian Review of Comparative Literature* is published by Wilfrid Laurier University Press for the Canadian Comparative Literature Association. It is governed by the same basic editorial policies and the same editorial boards as the journal. Canadian comparatists and colleagues in other countries are encouraged to submit for consideration book-length manuscripts and topical collections of essays. Editorial inquiries should be directed to the Editor, M. V. Dimić, Department of Comparative Literature, The University of Alberta, Edmonton, Alberta T6G 2E6. Orders for the first four volumes (see the list on p. ii of the present volume) should be addressed to the respective publishers: 1 The University of Alberta Press, The University of Alberta, Edmonton, Alberta T6G 2E6. 2,3 Kunst und Wissen: Erich Bieber Verlag, D-7000 Stuttgart, West Germany. 4 University of Toronto Press, Toronto, Ontario M5S 1A6. Orders for volume 5 and subsequent volumes should be addressed to Wilfrid Laurier University Press, Waterloo, Ontario N2L 3C5.